SAMUEL BECKETT:
Debts and Legacies

Related titles from Methuen Drama

Beckett: A Guide for the Perplexed, Jonathan Boulter
Beckett and Death, edited by Steven Barfield, Matthew Feldman and Philip Tew
Beckett and Decay, Kathryn White
Samuel Beckett's Waiting for Godot, Mark Taylor-Batty and Juliette Taylor-Batty
Ten Ways of Thinking about Samuel Beckett: The Falsetto of Reason, Enoch Brater
The Plays of Samuel Beckett, Katherine Weiss

SAMUEL BECKETT:
Debts and Legacies
New Critical Essays

Edited by
Peter Fifield and
David Addyman

BLOOMSBURY
LONDON • NEW DELHI • NEW YORK • SYDNEY

Bloomsbury Methuen Drama

An imprint of Bloomsbury Publishing Plc

50 Bedford Square
London
WC1B 3DP
UK

175 Fifth Avenue
New York
NY 10010
USA

www.bloomsbury.com

First published 2013

© Peter Fifield and David Addyman, 2013

All rights reserved. No part of this publication may be reproduced or transmitted in any form or by any means, electronic or mechanical, including photocopying, recording, or any information storage or retrieval system, without prior permission in writing from the publishers.

The rights of the editors to be identified as the editors of these works have been asserted by them in accordance with the Copyright, Design and Patents Act, 1988

No responsibility for loss caused to any individual or organization acting on or refraining from action as a result of the material in this publication can be accepted by Bloomsbury or the author.

This book is sold subject to the condition that it shall not, by way of trade or otherwise, be lent, resold, hired out, or otherwise circulated in any form of binding or cover other than that in which it is published and without a similar condition, including this condition, being imposed on the subsequent purchaser.

British Library Cataloguing-in-Publication Data
A catalogue record for this book is available from the British Library.

ISBN: HB: 978-1-4081-8361-8
ePDF: 978-1-4081-8365-6
ePub: 978-1-4081-8452-3

Library of Congress Cataloging-in-Publication Data
A catalogue record for this book is available from the Library of Congress

Typeset by Newgen Imaging Systems Pvt Ltd, Chennai, India
Printed and bound in Great Britain

Contents

Acknowledgements   vii
Contributors   viii
Introduction   1
Peter Fifield

1. Franco-Irish Beckett: *Mercier et Camier* in 1945–6   19
   Andrew Gibson

2. 'Sweet thing theology': Beckett, E. M. Cioran and the Lives of the Saints   39
   David Wheatley

3. *En attendant Godot*: A New Philosophical Landscape   63
   David Addyman

4. Samuel Beckett: The Geometry of the Imagination   85
   Chris Ackerley

5. 'Stations of a Mourner's Cross': Beckett, Killiney, 1954   109
   Graley Herren

6. 'Close your eyes and listen to it': *Embers* and the Difficulties of Listening   133
   Julie Campbell

7. Somnambulism, Amnesia and Fugue: Beckett and (Male) Hysteria   153
   Ulrika Maude

8. Samuel Beckett, Video Artist   177
   Mark Nixon

| 9 | Sounds Worthy of the Name: Tone and Historical Feeling in Beckett's Drama
Iain Bailey | 191 |
| 10 | Wyndham Lewis's Pseudocouple: *The Childermass* as a Precursor of *Waiting for Godot*
Yoshiki Tajiri | 215 |

Index 239

Acknowledgements

The editors would like to thank all of the speakers in the series, and particularly those who have contributed work to this volume. Their participation in the seminars – in several cases, for its lifespan thus far – helps to make the study of Samuel Beckett's work so rewarding, and gives substance to the idea of a critical conversation in academic research. This genesis also allows us to thank one audience in advance of the work reaching a wider one. The seminars are attended with particular diligence by undergraduate and postgraduate students, and by academic staff both current and emeritus, from the universities in Oxford, Reading, Southampton, Cambridge, London, and Northampton. For all its regular realization it is no less an ideal that the newest research be subject to scrutiny by a group that ranges from students in the first flush of love with Beckett's work through to those who were the author's own friends and the earliest commentators on his work. This work is dedicated to all those who have attended the seminar as speakers and audience members.

Thanks must be extended to our editor at Bloomsbury, Mark Dudgeon, who recognized the seminar's value as a cauldron for new research, and was keen to see it disseminated. His interest and assistance have been exemplary. We would also like to acknowledge Dr Matthew Feldman (Teesside University) and Dr Erik Tonning (University of Bergen) who set up and ran the seminar from 2005 to 2010, and Dr John Bolin (University of Wollongong) who co-convened it in 2011. In its time the seminar has been supported by Regent's Park College, and it is currently funded by the Faculty of English and St John's College, all parts of the University of Oxford, support for which we are grateful.

We would like to thank the BBC for permission to quote material in Julie Campbell's essay from the Written Archives Centre. Our particular thanks go to Trish Hayes.

Contributors

Chris Ackerley is Professor of English at the University of Otago, New Zealand

David Addyman is a Research Associate in English at the University of Bergen, Norway

Iain Bailey is a Lecturer (Teaching Focused) at the University of Manchester, UK

Julie Campbell is Lecturer in English at the University of Southampton, UK

Peter Fifield is Junior Research Fellow in English at St John's College, University of Oxford, UK

Andrew Gibson is Research Professor of Modern Literature and Theory at Royal Holloway, University of London, UK

Graley Herren is Professor of English at Xavier University, USA

Ulrika Maude is Senior Lecturer in Beckett Studies and Modernism at the University of Reading, UK

Mark Nixon is Reader in Modern Literature at the University of Reading, UK, where he is also Director of the Beckett International Foundation

Yoshiki Tajiri is Associate Professor of English at the University of Tokyo, Japan

David Wheatley is Senior Lecturer in English at the University of Aberdeen, UK

Introduction

Peter Fifield
St John's College, University of Oxford

Beckett's work is in an enviable position. Obligatory reading for undergraduates in at least two languages, he is also the choice of experimental theatre companies and conceptual writers, as well as a touchstone for the great actors of our time. He has sufficient academic cachet to sustain a steady round of international conferences, seminars and summer schools, attracting lively and innovative research, but also attracts publications oriented to a wider audience of theatre-goers and cultural enthusiasts. Marrying difficulty and popularity is a special skill, and on first glance Beckett's work does not seem made for the job. Nowhere does it match the scholarly challenge posed by the crossword-puzzle trickiness of *Finnegans Wake*. And while Joyce's *Ulysses* provides the instructions for its own celebration in time and place, Beckett's work cannot – and does not – hope to reproduce the annual hoopla of Dublin's 'Bloomsday'. Would one memorialize *Waiting for Godot* by gnawing on a discarded bone, perhaps while loitering on any old road, on just another day? And how often ought the devout Beckett pilgrim repeat this strange ritual?

What, then, is the source of this varied cultural esteem? For all its apparent restraint in making specific cultural, historical, national, and aesthetic references, these categories can be seen, on closer inspection, to remain extensive and active in Beckett's writings. The works may have the air – perhaps the pretensions – of universality, but this does not come with the elimination of specificity. *Endgame*, for instance, depicts a post-apocalyptic world that, in the first decade of its performance in the 1950s and 1960s, would have resembled that threatened by the policies of nuclear proliferation and brinkmanship adopted by the United States and the Soviet Union.[1] But the relevance of Beckett's work has not, of course, abated since Perestroika and the end of the Cold War, especially since the play makes no explicit reference to any of this nuclear drama. Indeed, in the play's most famous readings Stanley Cavell shows the play gains much power from its use of the Noah myth while, conversely, Theodor Adorno stresses the play's use of 'forlorn particulars that mock the conceptual.'[2] The plot of *Endgame* is thus at once played out across the mythical and the banal, while touching little in between these two narrative registers. This space appears to adopt the shape of its audience's concerns. Thus a history of performance by and for the suffering and oppressed – prisoners in Germany and the United States, the besieged in Sarajevo, the victims of Hurricane Katrina – has amply demonstrated a facility for meaningful performance in a range of situations. But this meaning*ful*ness contrasts sharply with a popular perception of Beckett's work as a depiction of meaning*less*ness. Rather than a dry exposition of nihilism on the stage, Beckett's desolate scenes appear to make an eloquent and well-developed response to events personal, political, historical and, perhaps most important for their continuing value, recurrent.

While a certain restraint undoubtedly leaves this vital interpretative space, those specific references that are made also intimate something of Beckett's power and appeal. Here scholarly digging can lead us back to the texts' broader considerations. For example, the 'Spratt's medium' that Clov gives to Nagg in *Endgame* is a now-defunct dog biscuit.[3] Its use represents a significant change from the '*biscuit classique*' of the French *Fin de partie* by switching from human to animal food, emphasizing the inhumane and dehumanizing condition of the protagonists. What, then, do we gain from knowing more about Spratt's, who were the world's first large-scale manufacturer of dog biscuits? In the first instance their extensive marketing campaigns – they had the first billboard in London – would once have ensured a degree of ubiquity that would prevent any confusion as to the grimness of Clov's offering. But, equally important, following takeovers in 1950 and 1960, Spratt's were, by the play's premiere in 1957, in their own endgame as a brand. From one-time market dominance, the biscuit had, by the US debut of the play in 1958, actually disappeared from the American market.[4] And within only a few years of the play's appearance in the United Kingdom, stocks of Spratt's would also be dropping towards zero there.[5] So while the brand was likely chosen for its ease of recognition – something largely lost on modern audiences – the historical coincidence of the company's buy-outs affirms our modern experience of the play, returning us to Beckett's central theme: the decline towards exhaustion shared by biscuits and bicycles, painkillers, pap and, indeed, people.

Academic research, if this thumbnail can momentarily stand for such, thus stands to add to our understanding of the play as an historical artefact but also as something that remains current. This two-fold richness, with Beckett's literary golden ratio of particular and general, explains in part the prominence given to Beckett in successive waves of literary and philosophical criticism. He has been the subject of humanist, Marxist, post-structuralist, biographical and historicist studies.[6] He was cited in Michel Foucault's seminal essay 'What is an Author', and more recently his manuscripts have been at the forefront of genetic criticism and Digital Humanities.[7] But if it seems that Beckett's work is too much the laboratory for determined critics, it must be made clear that this is not simply something being done *to* his work by commentators. For no less of a paradox than the combination of sustaining meaning and dramatizing its loss, Beckett's work itself shows a tremendous capacity for renewal, which, while it remains fixated on processes of running down and reduction, testifies to the creative potency of the oeuvre. The 'nohow' of Beckett's aesthetic is not merely matched but exceeded by an 'on' that is demonstrated by a writing career of more than 60 years, and a list of posthumous publications that have given him a substantial afterlife.[8] The flurries of *How It Is*, a strange, beautiful novel that emerges from the creative exhaustion following *Molloy*, *Malone Dies*, *The Unnamable*, and the *Texts for Nothing*, does not quite, I suggest, demonstrate the positive adherence to the categories of love and truth that Alain Badiou has suggested, but it does show a marked capacity – indeed a compulsion – to do something more, and to write something new.[9]

In various places we can see Beckett force something new from a space of exhausted possibilities. We might consider, for instance, Beckett's subtitle for *Waiting for Godot*: 'A tragi-comedy in two acts' (*CDW* 7). Only this play – and only in English – in Beckett's whole oeuvre receives this sort of detailed description. Those plays that receive a subtitle at all are simply labelled plays, mimes, pieces or, in the case of the short *Come and Go*, the rarer term, dramaticule.[10] But Beckett's first serious work for the stage refers more clearly to established genres and a literary tradition than any of its successors. Is this a tragicomedy in the model of Shakespeare's late plays, sharing elements of tragedy and comedy? Indeed, we might discern there a gesture towards equilibrium that we find repeated in the play's two acts, two pseudocouples, two pieces of scenery, and the story of the two thieves crucified alongside Christ. There is an elegance to this arrangement, as if it reflects the metaphysical order that Vladimir notes, 'One of the thieves was saved. [*Pause.*] It's a reasonable percentage' (*CDW* 13).

But Vladimir's great sum of salvation is, of course, more than a little shaky, as in turn is the idea of *Godot*'s sense of balance. As Vladimir admits, only one of the four gospels (St Luke) mentions Christ saving one of the thieves crucified with him (*CDW* 14/Lk 23.39–43). More than this acknowledged discrepancy, though, Vladimir is bluffing his Bible when he suggests to Estragon that 'Of the other three two don't mention any thieves at all and the third says that both of them abused him' (*CDW* 14). All four mention two others crucified alongside

Christ. St Matthew (27.44) and St Mark (15.32) both relate the abuse of Christ by his fellow victims, and only St John gives no hint as to their behaviour (Jn. 19.18). If abuse earns the same treatment as the thief who asks for release in St Luke's account, the odds would seem to be not even but 5 to 1 against salvation.

But what does this wonky Christian metaphysics have to do with that subtitle? As Giorgio Agamben has recently reminded us, the question of genre was one of particular concern to Dante Alighieri and his first readers, the *Commedia* seeming to have been written against the poet's own better judgement. How could Dante have written a comedy when he so esteemed tragedy – Virgil's *Aeneid* is, *Inferno* states, a 'high tragedy' (XX.113) – a form that he states in *De vulgari eloquentia* to be 'the highest of all styles and the only one appropriate to the ultimate objects of poetry'?[11] Beckett's life-long love for Dante's writing – he had his 'schoolboy copy' with him at his death – has been extensively documented, but his marked preference for *Inferno* and *Purgatorio* does not encourage reflection on the *Commedia* as a comment on genre and structure.[12] This is particularly surprising considering the recurrence of three-fold structures in Beckett's work, most prominently the so-called trilogy of novels *Molloy*, *Malone Dies* and *The Unnamable*, which share with the *Commedia* a structural unity that is as compelling as it is difficult to account for properly.

The Dantean principle of comedy is understood by Boccaccio as the work's obedience to 'a turbulent principle, [that] is full of noise and discord, and ends finally in peace and tranquillity'.[13] In its ultimate concern for the fate of souls and its demonstration of divine justice the *Commedia* affirms the ultimate subjection of mankind to God's will. Agamben's own formula goes further and teases out the relation between the individual and the natural, post-lapserian guilt, which runs: '*tragedy appears as the guilt of the just and comedy as the justification of the guilty*'.[14] This eschatology is played out in the *Commedia* between the fates of those 'good' individuals who preceded the incarnation but were denied salvation, and those sinners who could witness it and achieve salvation by repentance. Thus Virgil, the just man, is condemned by the broader guilt of original sin, while Dante's personal failings are forgiven by Christ's death and resurrection. The *Commedia*'s genre makes clear that this tidiness is underpinned by salvation so that, as admirable a classical form as tragedy may be, comedy displaces it as Christ opens the possibility of redemption and affirms the inevitability of divine justice.

A great deal of this metaphysics remains extant and on show in *Waiting for Godot*, albeit with the marrow of belief sucked from its bones. Thus, the nature of sin and its personal and structural constituents is debated with keen interest but with a scepticism born of ignorance rather than of enlightenment-style rigour. Although familiar with the rudiments of prayer 'vague supplication' is now misdirected to Godot and has turned into a request for 'nothing very definite' (*CDW* 19). When Vladimir suggests repentance it is a bloodless variety where personal transgression slides into natural sin by means of imprecision and indecision, rather than theological discernment:

Vladimir	Suppose we repented?
Estragon	Repented what?
Vladimir	Oh ... [*He reflects.*] We wouldn't have to go into the details.
Estragon	Our being born?
(*CDW* 13)	

What is more, Vladimir laughs the entire suggestion down when Estragon makes him think better of himself, before recoiling with a pain in his groin. The same half-baked, or rather half-broken, system remains when Estragon cannot remember having read the Bible but maintains he has always compared himself to Christ; and when the prone Pozzo cries for help, he responds equally desperately to both of Estragon's guesses: 'Cain' and 'Abel'. Estragon concludes that 'He's all humanity' (*CDW* 78). The nature of original and personal sin; the mechanics of redemption; the stories of the Bible; the method and function of prayer: this whole Christian metaphysics is misunderstood, misremembered and disbelieved by Vladimir and Estragon. The structure that demands Dante's comedic form has here become subject to a deflationary laughter, where Godot appears to have delivered precisely what was requested: 'nothing very definite' (*CDW* 19).

What can be said, then, of *Godot*'s genre? It does not simply slide back into tragedy, where the great are brought definitively and unjustly low, for here there are neither great men nor great falls but only a mundane sense of stagnation. More austere than a happy balance of forces that would shelter the audience from the dramatic extremes of decline and resolution, the subtitle intimates, I suggest, the inaccessibility of such absolutes in the modern era. Where for Dante, 'Christ's death thus liberates man from tragedy and makes comedy possible', *Waiting for Godot* is paralyzed by the impossibility of attaining either mode.[15] There is neither divine rescue nor disinheritance, but a perpetually deferred judgement as to what should be done with these characters; to what sort of drama this could be, playing in the ruins of broken genres. The tragi-comedy subtitle is, then, an indication of decay, pointing to two roads that cannot be taken while stalled in between. This is reflected in the famous setting of the play on a 'country road' (*CDW* 11) that is never travelled. This figure, moreover, stands at the head of Beckett's whole oeuvre as an evocative and creative expression of impasse that is drawn from a seeming dead-end.

That better sense can be drawn from Beckett's work when put in touch with the literary canon, Christian theology, and the history of pet food manufacture, ought to suggest the reach of Beckett's work. For all its talk of impossibility and failure, it remains remarkably responsive to interpretative approaches, and appears to grow ever more fertile as shown by the research and performance it attracts. This rich appeal is reflected in the seminar series at the heart of this collection. *Samuel Beckett: Debts and Legacies* has been held at the University of Oxford for almost ten years. The annual talks have seen an international roster of speakers delivering new research on Beckett's life and work, his influences and his impact. Responding to the wealth of new archival material that became available in the 1990s, the speakers have often made use of empirical methods and materials to ground interpretation in a framework derived from historical sources. But just as the very viability of an historicist reading of recent events seems startling, that novelty itself recedes, so that the urgency of this task has begun to relent and the seminars have integrated new material with 50 years' worth of reception, performance and scholarship. As preferred research methods change, Beckett's value continues to accumulate. Indeed, with the proliferation of interpretations that focus on the compositional process, their historico-cultural context, and their interface with modern science and technology, what is galvanized and extended is Beckett's broader currency, rather than his historical or parochial standing. The present volume of ten essays includes work from four continents, and demonstrates the cumulative, recursive quality to the scholarship in this field, whereby new interpretations seek to integrate and interrogate their predecessors, rather than simply dismiss or displace them.

The essays in this volume make use of a range of resources that is larger than at any point in the study of Beckett's work. More important than this, however, is that so many of these resources are easy to access, published in widely available editions and online. Having put aside many notebooks, manuscripts and typescripts into a trunk during his life, Beckett left a potential glut of documents, which has been turned into a steady flow negotiated between publishers, academics, archives, collectors, and the author's literary estate.[16] We have seen two of the four projected volumes of selected letters published, as well as a far more extensive *Collected Poems* than has heretofore been available. Faber and Faber and Grove will soon issue the previously unpublished short story 'Echo's Bones', which was squeezed out of Beckett for inclusion in the 1934 collection *More Pricks than Kicks* by Chatto and Windus's Charles Prentice, who changed his mind when he saw the dubious fruits of his request. Still to emerge into the light, but given extensive introduction by scholarly texts, Beckett's 'Philosophy Notes' and 'German Diaries' are both due to be published in the next few years.[17] On a longer timescale, the *Samuel Beckett Digital Manuscript Project* continues to make available scans, transcriptions and interpretations of the drafts of Beckett's published works, aiming to cover the entire oeuvre.

All of this industriousness is not without its discontents, however. Most dangerous is that the wealth of published material is too readily taken to be the sum of material per se. Or, worse still, that the material traces are mistaken for the totality of the author: as if, to quote the document-wielding Morven of *Rough for Theatre II*, '[*Vexed, slapping his papers.*] [. . .] the client is here and nowhere else' (*CDW* 246). The implications of this controlled flow of material are most clearly apparent in the interpretation of Beckett's request that only letters bearing on his writings be included in posthumous publications of correspondence. This produces an 'authorized' Beckett in two senses of the term. First, it hopes to seal the figure of the author from that of the man, as if to enforce a privacy that withers, perhaps properly, with death. As critics ranging from Philip Hensher in *The Guardian* to John Pilling in the *Journal of Beckett Studies* have complained, the second volume of letters omits a series of particular importance between Beckett and his young American lover, Pamela Mitchell, that documents the deep trauma of Beckett's brother's long death, which the author attended in Ireland. As Graley Herren's essay in this volume explores, this period is understood to have been central to the development of *Endgame*, and so its poor coverage in the published correspondence does not simply leave Beckett a purer author, spared blushes, but a colder, less human figure, perhaps one incapable of any such embarrassment.

Second, this phenomenon verifies, denies or otherwise provides an official verdict on a range of texts and documents as if to fortify the integrity of the corpus. Behind the publication of 'new' letters, poems, translations and stories there lie innumerable questions of Beckett's unattributed involvement, his changing intentions for particular pieces, and the grubby matters of business, which are as important a facet of modernism as any notions of anomie, intellectual elitism or technological development.[18] Affirming or declining the status of particular texts for publication – particularly outside of any scholarly forum – remakes an author, in the public's view, into a figure who appears inseparable from his literary estate and publishers. In turn, this encourages a degree of suspicion towards this composite body that, as Stephen Dilks's *Samuel Beckett in the Literary Marketplace* shows, is perhaps ultimately more damaging than protective.[19] A further twist is discernable in that the return to prominence of the author, his intentions, and the compositional process in literary scholarship is now a direct cause for the return of the same complex, institutional, procedural idea of author that, under Barthes and Foucault, eroded the potency of author- and biography-based approaches in the 1960s. As Beckett oversaw the death of the author in the company of the theorists, he now ushers in its return. Quite apart from his continuing importance to literary theory, there is a recursive quality to this that is itself deeply Beckettian.

This process, then, reshapes the contours of the author and the oeuvre alike. It is a paradox worth noting that the admiration and sheer commercial punch afforded to Beckett's name – its supposed guarantee of literary merit – has seen some of his weakest works published posthumously; works that do not so much stand in the shadow of, say, *Endgame* and *Molloy*, but belong to a different version of the writer; one who is technically and imaginatively poorer. The evident weaknesses of texts such as *Eleutheria* and 'Echo's Bones' give to the reader a Beckett whose iconic statements about failure are not passed through a purifying aesthetic of 'failing better', but are raw and true. As this reformation continues, however, we are also repeatedly shown – if sometimes in relief – the magnitude of Beckett's achievement. The essays in this volume explore the richness of Beckett's plays, prose and poetry from a variety of approaches, considering the most popular works to some of the least read, seen and heard. Quite apart from the literary debts and legacies that the research seminar's name cites, the essays demonstrate the ongoing academic legacy of Beckett's works, as a summary will indicate.

Andrew Gibson examines *Mercier et Camier* and its English-language version *Mercier and Camier* against the background of the Irish and French cultural contexts within which the novel was written. While the Irish elements of the novel have received substantial critical attention, their French counterparts have been largely overlooked. Gibson redresses this imbalance, showing how references to both cultures 'flicker in and out' of the French and English versions of the novel. Beckett denounces the illiberalism and inequality that affected both Irish and French societies at the time, as the novels show. For these 'translations', as he suggests, are profoundly different novels. And this fundamental and irreconcilable difference, Gibson argues, is part of Beckett's refusal to accept the self-deceiving narratives of unified humanity that had begun to resurface in the immediate post-war years.

David Wheatley develops a reading of Beckett that juxtaposes his work with that of the Romanian-born francophone writer, E. M. Cioran. Still only partially translated into English, Cioran's work allows us better to understand Beckett's relationship with religious thought, practice and dogma. Ranging over a wide variety of texts, Wheatley shows how for both Parisian émigrés, religion does not foster a sober logical dismissal, but an opportunity to revel in the delights of blasphemy and heresy.

David Addyman engages directly with an issue that has been a long-running concern in discussions of Beckett's theatre: presence. Addyman approaches the subject through the discussions that Beckett had on space in his correspondence with Georges Duthuit around the time of the composition of *En attendant Godot*, arguing that these and Beckett's translations of two of Duthuit's works, 'Byzantine Space' and *The Fauvist Painters*, provide the clearest indication of Beckett's understanding of presence.

Chris Ackerley develops an intricate and ambitious thesis reaching across several of Beckett's prose works, suggesting that Schopenhauer's distinction between arithmetic (unfolding in time) and geometry (extending in space) informs the aesthetic structure (the 'involuntary unity') of Beckett's early novel *Dream of Fair to middling Women*. He passes to that novel's successor, *Murphy*, whose protagonist inherits the mental structure of the earlier novel's main character, supplemented by that of Carl Jung. In turn, this is interwoven with Beckett's reading of Windelband's *History of Philosophy* on Leibniz's *Monadology*. Pursuing this trajectory to *The Unnamable* and beyond, he argues that the final novel of Beckett's so-called trilogy is a compelling instance of involuntary unity, and he glances forward to the use of this structure in Beckett's later writing.

Graley Herren traces the dynamic but delicate interplay of the personal and the creative in the composition of Beckett's *Fin de partie/Endgame*. Considering the impact that the death of Beckett's brother Frank had on the writer's literary imagination Herren makes a nuanced case that this enforced death-watch restored rather than depleted Beckett's imagination. Making use of letters and drafts from the period he demonstrates the greater importance of the personal than has been possible before now.

Julie Campbell's essay treads interesting methodological ground by turning to the reception of one of Beckett's most difficult radio plays. Comparing the classroom reception that is now the usual one for *Embers* with that of the first radio audiences, she thus combines observations of contemporary student engagement with the records held at the BBC's Written Archives to unpack the precise nature of the challenges that the play presents. Radio is, as Campbell observes, a very particular medium, and one that makes particular demands of its listeners. These are developed further by Beckett's use of the medium, which deviates from the conservative forms that are habitually broadcast, and into experiment, fragmentation and anti-realism.

Ulrika Maude considers the challenge posed by some of Beckett's works to the habitual view of hysteria as a female malady. Drawing on the performative, quasi-artistic neurology of Jean-Martin Charcot, she suggests that male hysteria, and particularly its manifestations in somnambulism and ambulatory automatism, is evoked in *Molloy*, the four novellas, and also in *Film*. Recovering the manner and methods of silent film, Beckett's 1964 work – his only one in that genre – exploits the long-running intimacy between male hysteria and cinema. Quite apart from the impact on his own work in several forms, she notes Beckett's connection to the language of hysteria via his reading and translating of surrealist texts in the 1930s, settling Beckett's development in a cultural field suffused with representations, appropriations and re-imaginings of this illness.

Mark Nixon considers Beckett's use of video in the abandoned enterprise called 'Film Vidéo-Cassette projet'. Written in 1972, between *Film* and his later drama for television, it echoes the concerns of the earlier text and anticipates those of the later technology. Responding to the medium itself, it adds, as Nixon shows, a crucial degree of reflexivity whereby the recording and playback structure is domesticated: the viewer is able to record and watch earlier versions of herself as viewer. Rather like the use of the reel-to-reel tape machine in *Krapp's Last Tape*, this use of new technology shows not only Beckett's interest in novel gadgets, but the capacity of these machines and their operations to inscribe themselves within the human.

Addressing the idea of tone, Iain Bailey considers the demands of the 'sounded' media of the radio drama, *All That Fall*, drawing a connection with the silent sounds of Beckett's prose texts *The Lost Ones* and *Company*. Following the resurgence of academic interest in affect, Bailey argues that the emotional realm of the play is one intimately and inextricably bound to its particulars, rather than belonging to a broad humanitarian compassion for suffering. It forms, therefore, a counterpoint to the swelling discussions of negation that mark commentary on Beckett's work.

Rather than tracing a structural principle, Yoshiki Tajiri addresses a single term with wide usage and insufficient examination, pursuing further Fredric Jameson's comparison of Beckett's 'pseudocouples' to those of Wyndham Lewis. Now under-read, Lewis's 1928 novel *The Childermass* allows us to see afresh the contours of this staple of Beckett's work and critical work on it. The flattened nature of these characters – their being not quite full enough to stand alone nor sufficiently identical to be one – leads Tajiri to associate their comic qualities with the mechanical comedy of Henri Bergson – a long-term touchstone for accounts of Beckett's sense of humour – and Michael North.

Notes

1 *Fin de partie*'s premiere took place at the Royal Court Theatre in London on 3 April 1957 before transferring to the Studio des Champs-Élysées in Paris on 26 April. The first performance of *Endgame* was on 28 January 1958 in the Cherry Lane Theatre, New York, and the first performance in London of the English play was at the Royal Court on 28 October 1958.
2 Stanley Cavell, 'Ending the Waiting Game: A Reading of Beckett's *Endgame*', *Must We Mean What We Say?* (Cambridge: Cambridge University Press, 1976). Theodor W. Adorno, 'Trying to Understand

Endgame', in *Notes to Literature*, vol. 1, translated by Shierry Weber Nicholson (New York: Columbia University Press, 1991), 252.
3   Samuel Beckett, *The Complete Dramatic Works* (London: Faber and Faber, 1990), 97. Subsequent references are made parenthetically as *CDW*.
4   'The History of the Pet Food Industry' http://files.meetup.com/360837/The%20History%20of%20The%20Pet%20Food%20Industry.pdf (Accessed 9 August 2012).
5   They were taken over by General Mills in 1950 and by Spillers in 1960. The latter now make Bonio, which has the same bone-shape as Spratt's biscuits.
6   So extensive is the criticism available that one can make a bibliography of bibliographies. Working towards the most recent, see James T. F. Tanner, *Samuel Beckett; a Checklist of Criticism* (Kent, OH: Kent State University Press, 1969); Raymond Federman and John Fletcher, *Samuel Beckett: His Works and His Critics: An Essay in Bibliography* (Berkeley: University of California Press, 1970); Cathleen Culotta Andonian, *Samuel Beckett: A Reference Guide* (Boston: G K Hall, 1989); Charles A. Carpenter, *The Dramatic Works of Samuel Beckett: A Selective Bibliography of Publications about his Plays and their Conceptual Foundations* (London: Continuum, 2011). For a broad narrative of the development of criticism on Beckett's writings, see David Pattie, *The Complete Critical Guide to Samuel Beckett* (London: Routledge, 2000).
7   See in particular the Samuel Beckett Digital Manuscript Project, accessible at www.beckettarchive.org.
8   'Nohow on' was the name that Beckett gave to the collected issue of his three late novels *Company, Ill Seen Ill Said* and *Worstward Ho*. For reflections on Beckett's afterlife as a writer see Peter Fifield, 'Samuel Beckett: Out of the Archive: An Introduction', *Modernism/modernity* 18.4 (2011), 673–9.
9   Alain Badiou, *On Beckett*, edited by Alberto Toscano and Nina Power (Manchester: Clinamen, 2003).
10 We are also given the number of acts in the subtitles for *Endgame, Happy Days* and *Play*.

11 Giorgio Agamben, *The End of the Poem: Studies in Poetics*, translated by Daniel Heller-Roazen (Stanford: Stanford University Press, 1999), 3.
12 The essential work on Beckett's relationship to Dante is Daniela Caselli, *Beckett's Dantes: Intertextuality in the Fiction and Criticism* (Manchester: Manchester University Press, 2006).
13 Agamben, *The End of the Poem*, 2.
14 Ibid., 8.
15 Ibid., 13.
16 Reference to the trunk of documents is made in several places in the critical literature, one of which is Everett C. Frost, '"Notes Diverse, Holo[graph]" Preface', *Samuel Beckett Today/Aujourd'hui* 16, Notes diverse holo: Catalogues of Beckett's reading notes and other manuscripts at Trinity College Dublin, with supporting essays, edited by Matthijs Engelberts and Everett Frost with Jane Maxwell (2006), 19.
17 The exemplary texts on these resources are Matthew Feldman, *Beckett's Books: A Cultural History of the Interwar Notes* (London: Continuum, 2006) and Mark Nixon, *Samuel Beckett's German Diaries: 1936–1937* (London: Continuum, 2011).
18 See Lawrence Rainey, *Institutions of Modernism: Literary Elites and Public Culture* (New Haven: Yale University Press, 1998) for one of the founding historicist interpretations of modernism on these grounds.
19 Dilks's book develops a thesis with a whiff of the conspiracy theory, where Beckett is seen to have carefully manipulated all of his acquaintances in a self-aggrandizing ruse of immense magnitude. Efforts to protect the privacy and reputation of the writer are thus transformed into a strategy of reverse publicity, selling Beckett as a sage but enigmatic figure apparently superior to the shallow razzmatazz of promotional work.

Works cited

Adorno, Theodor W. 'Trying to Understand *Endgame*' *Notes to Literature*, vol. 1, translated by Shierry Weber Nicholson (New York: Columbia University Press, 1991).

Agamben, Giorgio. *The End of the Poem: Studies in Poetics*, translated by Daniel Heller-Roazen (Stanford: Stanford University Press, 1999).

Andonian, Cathleen Culotta. *Samuel Beckett: A Reference Guide* (Boston: G K Hall, 1989).

Badiou, Alain. *On Beckett*, edited by Alberto Toscano and Nina Power (Manchester: Clinamen, 2003).

Beckett, Samuel. *The Complete Dramatic Works* (London: Faber and Faber, 1990).

Carpenter, Charles A. *The Dramatic Works of Samuel Beckett: A Selective Bibliography of Publications about his Plays and their Conceptual Foundations* (London: Continuum, 2011).

Caselli, Daniela. *Beckett's Dantes: Intertextuality in the Fiction and Criticism* (Manchester: Manchester University Press, 2006).

Cavell, Stanley. 'Ending the Waiting Game: A Reading of Beckett's *Endgame*'. *Must We Mean What We Say?* (Cambridge: Cambridge University Press, 1976).

Dilks, Stephen John. *Samuel Beckett in the Literary Marketplace* (Syracuse, NY: Syracuse University Press, 2011).

Federman, Raymond and John Fletcher. *Samuel Beckett: His Works and His Critics: An Essay in Bibliography* (Berkeley: University of California Press, 1970).

Feldman, Matthew. *Beckett's Books: A Cultural History of the Interwar Notes* (London: Continuum, 2006).

Fifield, Peter. 'Samuel Beckett: Out of the Archive: An Introduction', *Modernism/modernity* 18.4 (2011): 673–9.

Frost, Everett C. '"Notes Diverse, Holo[graph]" Preface', *Samuel Beckett Today/Aujourd'hui* 16. Notes diverse holo: Catalogues of Beckett's reading notes and other manuscripts at Trinity College Dublin, with supporting essays, edited by Matthijs Engelberts and Everett Frost with Jane Maxwell (2006): 19–27.

'The History of the Pet Food Industry' http://files.meetup.com/360837/ The%20History%20of%20The%20Pet%20Food%20Industry.pdf (Accessed 9 August 2012).

Nixon, Mark. *Samuel Beckett's German Diaries: 1936–1937* (London: Continuum, 2011).

Pattie, David. *The Complete Critical Guide to Samuel Beckett* (London: Routledge, 2000).
Rainey, Lawrence. *Institutions of Modernism: Literary Elites and Public Culture* (New Haven: Yale University Press, 1998).
Tanner, James T. F. *Samuel Beckett; A Checklist of Criticism* (Kent, OH: Kent State University Press, 1969).

1

Franco-Irish Beckett: *Mercier et Camier* in 1945–6[1]

Andrew Gibson
Royal Holloway, University of London

This essay aims to build on the growing number of serious scholarly accounts of *Mercier et Camier* (and *Mercier and Camier*) from Steven Connor to Séan Kennedy to Elizabeth Barry.[2] It is an attempt to think of *Mercier et Camier* as a text that is linked to two contexts, Irish and French, about the relationship between its French and Irish dimensions, and about the meaning of that relationship, taking a rather different direction to Barry's excellent essay 'Translating Nationalism', but also coinciding with it at certain points.[3] The Franco-Irish theme is not unimportant. *Mercier et Camier* is the first text of any length that Beckett writes in French. He did this at a time when he had been going back and forth between Paris and Dublin, and at a time when he had been thinking about Franco-Irish relations. It is worth recalling the exact if by now familiar detail of Beckett's movements and involvements during the immediate period of the gestation and composition of the novel.[4] He was awarded the Croix de Guerre on 30 March 1945 for his resistance work. With the war still going on he left a Paris he described as 'grim',[5] profoundly disturbed and spiritually if not literally shell-shocked, for Dublin, on 8 April. He left Dublin with the Irish Red Cross Hospital team, bound for a St-Lô bombed virtually out of existence in a single night by the Allies, on 7 August. He stayed there, working with the team, until 25 December, when he returned to Paris. He was back in Ireland from 21 April to 29 June 1946.

His poem 'Saint-Lô' was published on the 24 June 1946. According to Knowlson, he wrote the haunting *The Capital of the Ruins* for Radio Éireann in the same month (*Damned*, 350). *The Capital of the Ruins* is of course about St-Lô, and also about Franco-Irish relations. Beckett began writing *Mercier et Camier* almost immediately afterwards, on 5 July. He finished a draft of it by 26 September, and was revising it up to 13 October. He sent it to Bordas on 15 December. *Mercier et Camier*, then, is a text of 1946. The English translation of course followed very late, being published in 1974. According to Knowlson, Beckett did not fish the French text 'out of ... his "trunk" in the cellar' until early in 1970,[6] because others were asking him for new texts to publish. As Steven Connor showed some time ago, the translation is sufficiently different from *Mercier et Camier* as effectively to require separate treatment as a distinct work.[7] I will add a little to that particular argument. The later English text and the changes in it nonetheless shed an interesting light on the French one.

We should also be precise about the two historical contexts. There is much work to be done here, but my recent *Samuel Beckett: A Critical Life* has supplied an adequate account of the French context for the purposes of this chapter, the detail being much indebted to Paxtonian and post-Paxtonian histories of 1940s France.[8] Here are just a few of the more salient points. The Liberation of Paris took place 19–25 August 1944. 1944 was the year of the extra-judicial purge in France, of widespread vigilante action. The public maltreatment of women alleged to have consorted with the Germans was the most notorious instance. Terrible in itself, however, it was merely a synecdoche. Some of the most appalling features of Vichy France – internments, denunciations, arbitrary arrests, atrocities by paramilitaries, even torture – were duly maintained in the hands of those seeking revenge on Vichy. The traditional French court system was simplified, and justice frequently rushed. Improvised court martials took place. Extra-judicial murder was common. The victims of the widespread practice of 'popular justice' might meet execution without trial. Those it condemned died on the street, in their houses or at the hands of lynch mobs. The sense of a barbaric reversion loomed large. Sartre thought that France was in danger of collapsing into 'mediaeval sadism'.[9] Beckett must have known about all this, not least because, as the second volume of the letters shows, he was a reader of *Les Temps modernes*, *Nouvelle revue française*, and the two originally clandestine Resistance newspapers, *Franc-tireur* and *Combat*, where much of the most relevant material appeared (including the Sartre quote).

But 1944 was not 1945–6. With de Gaulle's provisional government of France increasingly exerting its hold, 1945 saw the launch of the official purge. Even before it produced a new constitution or elected a new parliament, the provisional government instituted new courts of justice. The new juridical formulations were exceptionally harsh. The systems and processes of the pre-war French judiciary, again, were drastically simplified on the principle that clear and straightforward questions of good and evil were at issue, and clear and straightforward judgements had to be the order of the day. Alas, flagrant travesties of justice resulted. Local people and press frequently influenced courtroom proceedings. Juries were blatantly packed. Judges passed sentences that were harsh, undiscriminating and dismayingly unjust. While certain categories of persons suffered much, others frequently escaped scot-free. De Gaulle saw collaborationist writers, publishers and literary figures as major enemies and declared that they deserved no mercy. Hence the writer Robert Brasillach, for example, who had been Beckett's contemporary at the École Normale, was executed as early as 6 February 1945. Meanwhile, collaborationist lawyers, businessmen and newspaper magnates frequently escaped notice and began quietly to re-establish themselves in post-Liberation France.

The Ireland which Beckett discovered in 1945, and then again in 1946, had had a very different experience of the war years, as Robert Fisk, Eric Girvin and above all Clair Wills tell us.[10] The country had been officially neutral for the duration of the war, declaring a state of emergency which lasted from 3 September 1939 to 2 September 1946. Neutrality had mixed effects. For obvious reasons, life in Ireland tended to feel more relaxed and secure than life in, say, England or France. But the government also gave itself sweeping new powers that continued throughout the so-called Emergency: internment and censorship of the media, press and correspondence, for example. The economic effects of the Emergency were similarly ambivalent. The general quality of life in a poor country became even poorer, with food and petrol shortages and rationing.[11] Yet neutral Dublin with its blaze of lights (no wartime blackout) could also offer the visitor steak, cream cakes, knickerbocker glories, cosmetics, jewellery and leather goods, to a degree that startled and entranced visitors from outside, not least, London.[12] Ireland became a plentiful source of items, like butter, that war had made rare in Britain. So, too, the new aircraft manufacturing industry in Belfast provided work for southern Irishmen and women. Equally, the wealthy from Ulster fled to Dublin hotels. In these respects, the economic contrast between life in Dublin and life in London and, above all, grimly impoverished Paris was peculiarly marked.

The obvious difficulty with Irish neutrality was that it led to a policy of impartiality or even-handedness in a war founded for so many on a categorical morality. Thus, for example, secretary for the Irish Department of External Affairs Joseph Walshe wrote approvingly of the Vichy government of whose moral derelictions Beckett had vivid, first-hand experience. Most notoriously, on 2 May 1945, Taoiseach Éamon de Valera visited the German Ambassador to Ireland to express sympathy with the German people over Hitler's death. At the same time, neutrality also went hand in hand with an effort at high-mindedess, especially in 1945–6. On 18 May 1945, for example, de Valera announced a £12 million Irish aid programme for Europe, proclaiming that 'we shall endeavour to render thanks to God by playing a Christian part in helping, so far as a small nation can, to bind up the wounds of suffering humanity'.[13] Beckett indirectly benefited from this programme, at least insofar as it enabled him to get back from Ireland to France. But he was also deeply sceptical about the new Irish humanitarianism. At the same time, 1946 saw a previously sequestered Ireland getting dragged into a relationship with a larger world, conspicuously on 17 June, when, as Beckett noted, Aer Lingus inaugurated the first direct Dublin-Paris air service.[14]

The second volume of Beckett's *Letters* makes clear that he was as unenamoured of Eire in 1945-6 as in previous decades, if now in different ways. It is not clear, however, that he shared a Churchillian contempt for Irish neutrality in itself. After all, there had been good reasons for neutrality, notably the country's insignificant and hopelessly under-equipped armed forces. Beckett, rather, is caustic about Eire in 1945-6 on four main points. First, it had become at best more illiberal and repressive and, at worst, something of a police state. Secondly, in pointed contrast to the France in which he had suffered for five years, it seemed well-appointed, well-fed, and unreally safe in a wartorn world. 'My friends', he remarked, pointedly meaning Frenchmen and women, 'eat sawdust and turnips while all of Ireland safely gorges'.[15] Eire is a 'buffet-sanctuaire', an eating place-cum-haven from a nasty world, 'lousy with guzzling tourists'.[16] Compare St-Lô, 'just a heap of rubble'.[17] Thirdly, as Wills says, Beckett shared the disquiet among intellectuals that neutrality had allowed Ireland to insulate itself from the suffering of the contemporary world, that it had become in that sense a futile culture.[18] This is surely why *The Capital of the Ruins* tells us that, while the Irish of 1945-6 may receive 'a vision and sense of a time-honoured conception of humanity in ruins' in St-Lô, at the moment, they can 'hardly give' one.[19] Beckett told Simone de Beauvoir that 'il existe simplement une misère qu'il s'agit de défendre jusqu'au bout, dans le travail et au dehors du travail'.[20] If so, a newly independent Ireland had forgotten that wretchedness. Fourthly, the Irish self-insulation of

1939–45 gave the lie to de Valera's attempt to claim the moral high ground. The French in St-Lô did not even appear to want the Irish there, which Beckett declares to be a 'very reasonable attitude'.[21] His hostility to a philosophy of good works carried out on the basis of a well-protected immunity from harm certainly in part fuels – if it does not determine – his ferocious onslaught on the emergence of post-war humanism and humanitarianism in general. By 15 December 1946, for example, he is beginning the strain of sceptical commentary on UNESCO, 'that inexhaustible cheese'[22] – note the image of plenty, again – that will continue in the letters for some time thereafter.

If Beckett is scathing about the Ireland of 1945–6, however, he is at least equally excoriating about immediately post-war France. 'All the wrong things, all the wrong way', he writes, to Thomas McGreevy.[23] First, the deprivations were chronic, and made worse by the survival and consolidation of the élites: life in post-war Paris, writes Beckett, 'is pretty well impossible, except for millionaires'.[24] But, being Beckett, it is not 'material conditions' that principally concern him, as he says.[25] What matters is the way in which the French were dealing or failing to deal with their recent history and its implications. There were people at St-Lô who were still furtively attached to 'the poor old misled man and hero of Verdun' (Pétain).[26] Eminences of the Vichy years were quietly reinstalling themselves in the upper echelons, and De Gaulle and the new dispensation were conniving in it. Hence Beckett's bitter irony at the expense of ex-collaborationists: 'Flourishing, especially the military representatives, they are happily engaged in reorganizing the salvation of the country. They are prepared to forget and forgive – the so rude interruption.'[27] Several things are at stake in this statement. First, Beckett singles out the military. We should recall, here, that, after defeat in 1940, large parts of the French army actually joined the *Wehrmacht*, and that far more of the officer class did so than joined de Gaulle, the Resistance or the maquis. Equally, in popular ascription at least, the French military defeat had been due to cowardice and the failure of military leadership. It is the very individuals responsible for France's demise who are now turning into the engineers of the new France. And not only that: secondly, Beckett also jibes ironically at those who, yet again, happily reassert the modern will to a social salvation made as painless as possible by a brusque cancellation of a past both murky and morally catastrophic. Thirdly, if it is the military 'representatives' and their like who lead the way in forgetting and, most ironically of all, forgiving, this was actually just the tip of the iceberg. In the context of the Purge and the early years of the Fourth Republic, the lines Beckett extracts from Racine's *Andromaque* take on a quite extraordinary power: 'Je ne sais de tout temps quelle injuste Puissance /Laisse le crime en paix et poursuit l'innocence. /De quelque part sur moi que je tourne les yeux,/ Je ne vois que malheurs qui condamnent les Dieux'; 'Voire', adds Beckett:[28] 'too right'. All the wrong things, all the wrong way: Beckett is surely thinking of the monstrous injustices of 1944 and after.

At the very least, as Barry says,[29] that an Irish world of reference in some sense flickers here and there throughout *Mercier et Camier* seems ungainsayable. Barmen are called barmen throughout, and a trench-coat is 'un trench-coat',[30] although admittedly both are possible in French. The currency is half-crowns, shillings and pence (*MeC* 25, 27, 121). Camier apparently has porridge for breakfast (*MeC* 201). John Jameson is 'J.J.' in French (*MeC* 85) although just 'malt' in the translation.[31] The 'gardien' (interestingly translated as 'ranger') regrets not having learnt 'la langue gaélique' (*MeC* 18–19, *MaC* 15). When Camier refers to himself and Mercier as on an island (*MaC* 109), there seems no reason to doubt which. Certainly the blurb of the 2006 Minuit edition does not doubt it: 'C'est l'Irlande, merveilleusement décrit ici, avec ses landes de bruyères, les jetées de ses ports lancées vers la large pour enlacer la mer, ses sentiers parmi les tourbières, les écluses du canal de Dublin'.[32] '[W]hat a gazetteer I am', as Beckett might have said, following the Unnamable.[33] Clearly what he thought was at stake in *Mercier et Camier* bore little resemblance to the blurb-writer's conception of it. Yet the novel nonetheless contains a fitful, non-evocative evocation of a spectral Ireland. This is matched by a range of historical references. As Séan Kennedy says, 'Patrick Sarsfield, nationalist hero of the Battle of Aughrim in 1691, the Old Military Road built after the 1798 Rising, Anglo-Irish support for the Boer War, Ireland's participation in World War One, and the events leading to Independence', are all referenced, and referenced for some reason, however obscure.[34] Kennedy's case for a similarly significant reference to the death of and memorial to IRA captain and Easter Rising hero Noel Lemass in section x of the French text is hardly disputable, whatever the meaning we give it.

The trouble is that one can adduce a countervailing set of French specifications, although they are not exactly of the same kinds as the Irish ones or symmetrical with them. It is remarkable how many of these Beckett leaves out or smudges in the translation, as though he wished the Frenchness of *Mercier et Camier* to fade from *Mercier and Camier*, while its Irishness remained, and even grew in proportion. This, again, is an index of the gulf between the text of 1946 and the text of 1974. Some of the French details are trivial. Beckett appears to have thought of the rum baba as French (as it seemed in the 1940s; it was indeed French-invented), because he discreetly changes it to a stoutly Anglo-Saxon cream horn in translation (*MeC* 47; *MaC* 32). The shelter in the form of the pagoda, although certainly open to an Irish identification, also summons up *belle époque Chinoiserie* in Paris, for example the pagoda Michel Morin had shipped whole from China to the Rue de Babylone in 1895 (by 1931 it had become a cinema; one can suppose that Beckett knew it as such). The references to Perpignan and Monaco also call up a French atmosphere and context (*MeC* 44, 79); Perpignan has disappeared in the 1974 text.

It would not be hard, on the basis of more extensive research, to fill in these bits and pieces with scraps of French geography and townscapes; Ruby Cohn even argued that the novel was set in France.[35] 'C'est la

France', we might for a moment be tempted to exclaim, 'merveilleusement décrite ici, avec ses landes de bruyères, les jetées de ses ports lancées...', and so on. Some of the Frenchness of the 1946 text is attributable to allusions, most of which, again, notably disappear in 1974. The references to Rimbaud's 'Les Corbeaux' (see *MeC* 121, 128–9, 187) can be reconstituted from the English translation.[36] But in 1946 there are also (admittedly casual and blatant) references to Chateaubriand and Baudelaire, both of which have disappeared in 1974 (*MeC* 189). Watt refers to Toussaint l'Ouverture (*MeC* 189); that too disappears.

But the Frenchness of *Mercier et Camier* is present above all in language and style; that is, not just the fact that it is written in French, but the ways in which Mercier, Camier, the narrator and other figures all use French, and the ways in which this 'lodges them in France', as it were. There are contexts for these usages that are as suggestive and potentially weighty (or weightless) as the contexts for the more substantial Irish references. Most obviously, perhaps, there are little plays with a Sartrean vocabulary of *engagement* (*MeC* 48, 155). But perhaps more interesting is Madden's 'je me mettais sur mon trente-et-un', 'I rose to [or dressed for] the occasion', literally 'I put on my 31' (*MeC* 60). One possible derivation of the (not uncommon) phrase is the distinctive numbering of French military officers' uniforms: 31 was for gala occasions. This would clearly link up to the series of military allusions in the novel. Or take the description of the 'gardien' as 'Invalide à quinze pour cent' (*MeC* 18), 'Invalided out at fifteen per cent' (the percentage marking the degree of physical capacity lost, as compared to the able-bodied). It Frenchifies the character, because it is frank and direct in the manner of the French First World War *pensions militaires d'invalidité*. The English of 1974 just has 'Invalided out with a grudging pension', fittingly for an English war pension, which put matters more reticently (*MaC* 14). Or take Camier after Mercier and he share a protracted giggle: 'Quelle franche gaieté.... On dirait du Vauvenargues' ('What frank gaiety... One would think it were from Vauvenargues'; *MeC*, 92). The allusion is to a minor French epigrammatist who might indeed have interested Beckett, because he came halfway between La Rochefoucauld and Chamfort, and again it does not appear in 1974. It is learnedly, almost obscurely, French; but the phrase 'franche gaieté' is more interesting. It had long been a critical cliché in accounts of Molière, Beaumarchais and the like, and there is a parodic edge to it here that is French-directed.

Or take two little quirks of Camier's: first, his pronunciation of 'expliquer' as 'espliquer':

> Je te dois des esplications, disait Camier. Camier disait toujours esplications. Presque toujours.
> Je ne te demande pas d'eSplications, disait Mercier. (*MeC* 62)

According to Ivan Fónagy, this slippage – thought of as the silencing of the [k] from the [ks], as also in escursion, esplosion, escuser, esprès, esprimer, estraordinaire, estrait, espedition – was a characteristic trait of French popular speech that, in the early twentieth century, like other such, was beginning to have a worrying effect on educated utterance.[37] In that respect, its social connotations were close to those of the glottal stop in the more recently emergent Estuary English. It was one of the examples of linguistic democratization that the great disciple of Saussure, Charles Bally, cited in his groundbreaking lectures on the sociological aspects of the French language between 1918 and 1936.[38] Fónagy also associates it with Queneau – recalling that the second volume of the letters show that Beckett was conscious of Queneau during this period – and particularly Zazie in *Zazie dans le métro*.[39] Camier, then, is effectively taking sides in a French sociolinguistic issue. So, too, less markedly, in his preference for the 'o' rather than then 'e' form of 's'asseoir', 'assoyait' rather than 'asseyait':

> Après un moment de silence Camier dit:
> Si on s'assoyait, cela m'a vidé.

Tu veux dire s'asseyait, dit Mercier.
Je veux dire s'assoyait, dit Camier. (*MeC* 15)

This, again, has certain connotations. In the late eighteenth century, for example, in his Languedocian-French dictionary, Pierre-Augustin Boissier-Sauvages reprehended the use of the 'o' form with the implication that it was backward and unsophisticated, treating the Languedocians' use of French rather as Swift and Sheridan treated Irish uses of English.[40]

Two things initially seem clear. First, the French text of *Mercier et Camier* of 1946 is not a translation into French of a pre-existing mental set of Irish references. The 1946 text has a French as well as an Irish content. Secondly, while the 1946 text certainly plays some clever and subtle games with and for the benefit of the French reader, it is not such a game in itself or as a whole, not least because no French reader could have conceivably got all the Irish references. *Mercier et Camier* is characterized by a 'strange hybridity', as Barry says,[41] and has both an Irish and a French dimension; but there is a tension between them, they do not coincide. However, I do not want to try to squeeze more life out of that old chestnut, the question of whether *Mercier and Camier* is a fundamentally abstract or a vestigially representational text, which limits the forms of possible understanding of it. If, as Beckett writes in the letters, *Watt* was a book 'written in dribs and drabs',[42] *Mercier et Camier* is a book of Irish dribs and French drabs. It marshals a set of Irish materials, however idiosyncratic, a set of French materials similarly curious, and disposes them in a certain manner. It is, quite clearly, a Franco-Irish text, and what it is really about has to do with that. Certain elements in it obviously balance on a Franco-Irish fulcrum. As we know, the names Mercier and Camier are clearly both French, and Irish via the Huguenots who sought refuge in Ireland. The station in the French text is referred to as both a 'gare' and a 'station', a square as both a 'place' and a 'square' (*MeC* 11, 43).

In the context of 1939–45, the 'pénurie de carburant' (*MeC* 52), the fuel shortage referred to can be equally Irish and French, but is certainly of the period. And so on. If the French *Mercier et Camier* in 1946 and the Irish *Mercier et Camier* in 1946 often do not coincide, there are moments when they also do come together. The question is what is at stake in this play of coincidence and non-coincidence. Three responses follow, by way of conclusion.

First, the French and Irish dimensions of *Mercier et Camier* sometimes seem to be pointing in the same direction or saying the same thing. Take for example the 'gardien' (*MeC* 19): on the one hand, he is an ex-First World War Irish officer, as his having fought in Flanders not France indicates. On the other hand, the references to him 'chiant dans ses bottes' ('shitting in his boots') in Flanders fields and to his 'plâtras de décorations', his 'rubble' or, as Beckett rather nicely translates it, his 'clatter of decorations' takes on a historically more immediate, more vivid and piquant set of connotations if one pushes it back instead into Paris, 1945 (*MeC* 23; *MaC* 16). The proud array of decorations on De Gaulle's chest had been prominently on display in photographs of him since the Liberation. So, too, there was a sudden clatter of decorations in the corridors of power as the General rewarded patriots, favourites and Resistance fighters, including Beckett, while military officers whom the *Blitzkrieg* had left shitting in their boots in 1940 and who had supported Vichy quietly crept back into the fold.

The anti-militarism of the passage, then, is not only marked but cuts two ways. Indeed, it fits in with a clutch of comic and/or disparaging anti-militarist and anti-heroic references in the novel. Kennedy has noted how far such references sabotage a masculinist Irish tradition. If one factors 1939–45 into the equation, as he does not, one can add to his case. *Mercier et Camier* makes quite a lot of a vocabulary with military implications: advance and retreat, expedition, marching, etc. The novel comically and ironically plays Mercier and Camier's hapless peregrinations off against it. In particular there is a comedy of Mercier and Camier failing to keep in step. 'Tu as ton rythme', as Camier says, 'moi j'ai le mien', 'You have your rhythm, I have mine' (*MeC* 34). But such moments also surely conceal barbed jokes at the expense of the Irish 'Step Together' movement between 1940–5. This was a State-run programme, incorporating displays of men and arms, sporting contests and pageantry, and issuing in mass marches and manifestations of uniformity, all in appropriate formation, designed as a show of strength. The irony was that Irish neutrality was founded on the opposite, weakness. Even more strikingly, Clair Wills shows that, in line with a notion of a pan-European, orthodox Catholic cause, the Step Together movement in some degree resembled and even leaned towards quasi-military and semi-fascist forms of organization in Vichy France, the important aspect of Vichy France being of course Catholicism, and the dream of 'a New [Catholic] Europe'.[43] But in Vichy, too, the movement was the more pathetic in that its assertiveness was specious, founded on a humiliating defeat.

Beckett clearly worked to overturn the structure of this deception, insisting on casting reality at the level precisely of the weakness, failure and defeat that Vichy and de Valera's Ireland wished to deny. Here again, then, the French and Irish dimensions of *Mercier et Camier* come together. But, as Barry nicely remarks, 'the fragile alliance between Ireland and France is under threat'.[44] Placing other elements in the novel in both French and Irish contexts starts to pull them in different directions. Perhaps the best example of this is the murder of the policeman. Kennedy thinks this is a 'sinister' instance of cultural amnesia, a forgetting of a history of violence from which Mercier and Camier themselves cannot be exculpated.[45] But it is not at all clear from what features of the text one would derive this moral perspective.[46] Beckett declared in 1937 that there was no animal he loathed 'more profoundly than a civic guard, a symbol of Ireland with his official, loutish Gaelic complacency'.[47] It is hard to reconcile this with Kennedy's reading. But it is equally impossible, in an Irish context, to think of Beckett as somehow fulfilling his loathing in the novel. It was the IRA who murdered Irish policemen during the war, during much of which they were actually collaborating with the German *Abwehr*. But in Vichy France the position was the other way round. Pétain's *milice* were not exactly a police force. But the Vichy police themselves had a special unit, the GMR, trained to fight the Resistance. Simon Kitson, for instance, has shown that the French police during the Second World War were used both as a tool of collaboration between the Vichy regime and the Nazi occupier and to enforce internal political reform.[48] The police responded enthusiastically, not least because the new regime's main opponents – communists, Jews, other 'foreigners' and misfits – were also traditional police targets. They handed communists over to the Nazis and played an important role in the deportations to the camps. The Resistance and the maquis not only engaged the police in pitched battles but also carried out selected assassinations of police. Can it be a coincidence not only that the 'gardien' twice refers to Mercier and Camier as 'assassins', but that there is no equivalent in the English text? (*MeC* 25, 29) True, later in the war, the French police abruptly converted to patriotism.[49] This was not to seem convincing, however, to a generation of intellectuals, writers, political radicals, Jews, *métèques* ('metics', Mediterranean immigrants), workers etc. for some of whom, at least, one great post-war idol would be that notorious foe of the French police, Jean Genet. Incidents like the murder of the policeman in Beckett's *Mercier et Camier* should not be set apart from this context.

Thus 'Irish' and 'French' readings of the murder of the policeman do not match up with one another. The Franco-Irish text does not add up or form a whole, as it seemed to do in its treatment of militarism. It both coheres and incoheres. In a letter to Duthuit of 27 July 1948, Beckett writes passionately of 'la duperie de l'humain et l'achevé ... la duperie où tous depuis toujours.... se sont rejoints' ('the fraudulence of the human and the achieved ... the fraudulence according to which all have always been at one').[50] The unity of the human: the war had brutally destroyed all illusion of it, quite beyond any power of serious thought. And yet there they were again, the old humanist discourses, springing up buoyantly within a few months of Hiroshima and Nagasaki, not least in Paris and Dublin, notably, in the first instance, around the UN, UNESCO, UNRRA, etc. Beckett is extremely scathing about them. He will not buy into the dupery of unity. Even in *The Capital of the Ruins*, he had been emphatic about this: 'their way of being we, was not our way', he writes, of the French and Irish, 'and our way of being they, was not their way' (*CSP* 277). Written directly after *The Capital of the Ruins*, *Mercier et Camier* produces the same kind of play between French and Irish similarities and French and Irish differences. In this respect, it is surely no accident that we get pointed references so early in the text to both St Ruth and Sarsfield, the major players in the greatest failure to achieve Franco-Irish unity in Irish history (in 1690). There is no one, no *un*, no UN. This is an important aspect, developing in 1946, of Beckett's attack on what, a few years later, with the London production of *Godot* that opened in 1955 in mind, he was to call the 'redemptive perversion'.[51] There are few concepts more key to understanding him. Barbara Halberstam and Colin Wright have recently described present cultural formations as disablingly in thrall to a 'toxic positivity'.[52] If they are right, as they themselves both recognize, Beckett is an excellent point from which to set out on the labour of destruction. Beckett's so-called pessimism is usually described as abstract, generalized. But it was not: it was precisely historical. It was a form of historical work, a work of negation, a response to what Kafka called the injunction to perform 'the negative ... laid down for us' in the knowledge that 'the positive is given us already' ('Das Negative zu tun, ist uns noch auferlegt, das Positive ist uns schon gegeben').[53] In 1946, Beckett was finding that, yet again, almost immediately after catastrophe, the positive was already ours, all over again. He set his face against that development, and one aspect of doing so was the refusal of slack, fallacious and self-deceiving concepts of unity.

Notes

1. All translations from French and German are my own except where otherwise indicated.
2. See Elizabeth Barry, 'Translating Nationalism: Ireland, France and Military History in Beckett's *Mercier et Camier*', *Irish Studies Review*, 13.4 (2005), 505–15; Steven Connor, '"Traduttore, Traditore": Samuel Beckett's Translation of *Mercier et Camier*', *Journal of Beckett Studies*, 11–12 (1989), 27–46; and Séan Kennedy, 'Cultural Memory in *Mercier and Camier*: The Fate of Noel Lemass', in Marius Buning, Matthijs Engelberts and Sjef Houppermans (eds), *Samuel Beckett Today/Aujourd'hui* 15 (2005), 117–31.
3. My thanks to Séan Kennedy for drawing my attention to this essay.
4. I take all details from Samuel Beckett, *The Letters of Samuel Beckett. Volume 2: 1941–1956*, edited by George Craig, Martha Dow Fehsenfeld, Dan Gunn and Lois More Overbeck (Cambridge: Cambridge University Press, 2011).
5. Interview with Lawrence Harvey, undated; quoted in James Knowlson, *Damned to Fame* (London: Bloomsbury, 1996), 340.
6. Ibid., 574.
7. See Connor, 'Traduttore', *passim*.
8. For a detailed, relevant account of the 'Paxtonian revolution' in the study of post-war French history, see Andrew Gibson, *Samuel Beckett: A Critical Life* (London: Reaktion, 2009), 95–127. The book can also be consulted for an appropriate range of historical sources not cited here.
9. In *Combat*, 2 September 1944.
10. Robert Fisk, *In Time of War: Ireland, Ulster, and the Price of Neutrality 1939–1945* (London: Gill & Macmillan, 1983); Brian Girvin, *The Emergency: Neutral Ireland 1939–45* (London: Pan Macmillan, 2007);

and Clair Wills, *That Neutral Island: A History of Ireland During the Second World War* (London: Faber and Faber, 2007).
11 Wills, *That Neutral Island*, 4.
12 Ibid., 6.
13 Quoted in Ronan Fanning, *Independent Ireland* (Dublin: Helicon, 1983), 128.
14 See SB to GR, 27 May 1946, in *Letters 2*, 32.
15 SB to FY, quoted in Anthony Cronin, *Samuel Beckett: The Last Modernist* (London: HarperCollins, 1996), 343.
16 See SB to GR, 25 April 1946, and to JVV, 15 May 1946, in *Letters 2*, 29–30.
17 SB to TM, 19 August 1945, in *Letters 2*, 18.
18 See Wills, *That Neutral Island*, 413–14.
19 Samuel Beckett, *The Capital of the Ruins*, in *Complete Short Prose 1929–1989*, edited with an introduction and notes S. E. Gontarski (New York: Grove Press, 1995), 275–8 at 278; hereafter cited in text as *CSP*.
20 'Simply, there exists a wretchedness that one must stand by to the end, in one's work and outside it'. SB to SdB, 25 September 1946, in *Letters 2*, 41.
21 SB to TM, 19 August 1945, in ibid., 18.
22 SB to GR, 11 December 1950, in ibid., 206.
23 SB to TM, 4 January 1948, in ibid., 72.
24 SB to GR, 31 October 1945, in ibid., 24.
25 SB to TM, 4 January 1948, in ibid., 72.
26 SB to TM, 19 August 1945, in ibid., 19.
27 SB to AU, 11 December 1946, in ibid., 47.
28 '"I know not what unjust Power, from time immemorial/leaves crime in peace and hunts down innocence./ Wherever I turn my eyes, I see only woes which condemn the Gods". Yes indeed'. Oreste, *Andromaque*, 3.1, 773–6; Jean Racine, *Œuvres complètes* (Paris: Seuil, 1962), 113. SB to GR, 8 July 1948, in *Letters 2*, 80–1.
29 Barry, 'Translating Nationalism', 508.
30 Samuel Beckett, *Mercier et Camier* (1970) (Paris: Minuit, 2006), 33, 68–71, 77; hereafter cited in text as *MeC*.
31 Samuel Beckett, *Mercier and Camier*, translated by the author (1974) (London: John Calder, 1999), 48, 55; hereafter cited in the text as *MaC*.

32 'It is Ireland, marvellously described here, with its misty landscapes, the jetties of its ports thrust out into the open sea to embrace it, the paths through its bogs, the locks on the Dublin canal' (*MeC*, blurb).
33 Samuel Beckett, *Molloy, Malone Dies, The Unnamable* (London, John Calder, 1997), 319.
34 Kennedy, 'Cultural Memory', 128.
35 Ruby Cohn, 'Joyce and Beckett, Irish Cosmopolitans', *James Joyce Quarterly* 8.4 (1971), 385–91. Barry points this out, 'Translating Nationalism', 508.
36 The references are fleeting but clear, not least because of the obvious relevance of Rimbaud's great vision of the blood-boltered fields of the Franco-Prussian war in context.
37 Ivan Fónagy, *Dynamique et changement* (Paris: Peeters, 2006), *passim*.
38 For a scholarly account of this, see Clair Forel, *La Linguistique sociologique de Charles Bally* (Geneva: Droz, 2007).
39 Fónagy links Bally, Queneau and Queneau's Zazie together, for instance, in 'Le français change de visage?' *Revue Romane*, 24.2 (1989), 226–54 at 246.
40 Pierre Augustin Boissier de Sauvages de la Croix, *Dictionnaire Languedocien-François, ou Choix des mots Languedociens les plus difficiles à rendre en François*, 2 vols (Paris: J. Martin, 1821), vol. 2, 271.
41 Barry, 'Translating Nationalism', 509.
42 SB to GR, 14 May 1947, in *Letters 2*, 55.
43 See Wills's valuable discussion in *That Neutral Island* at 352–6.
44 Barry, 'Translating Nationalism', 506.
45 Kennedy, 'Cultural Memory', 119.
46 This raises other problems, notably how difficult it may be for generations whose attitudes to the police have been much determined by 'the terrorist threat' to grasp or hear hostile attitudes that were by no means uncommon among older generations, not least amongst those whose experience of the police might have had much to do with their wartime roles. This was, certainly, repeatedly the case in France. There is also a serious question regarding how to respond to the elements of violence in Beckett's texts – a violence that criticism has so far tended to shirk.
47 SB to TM, 28 September 1937, quoted Cronin, *Samuel Beckett*, 262.

Franco-Irish Beckett 37

48 Various parts of Kitson's work are relevant here, but see, for example, 'From Enthusiasm to Disenchantment. The French Police and the Vichy Regime, 1940-1944', *Contemporary European History* 11.3 (2002), 371-90.
49 On which, see Kitson, 'From Enthusiasm to Disenchantment'.
50 SB to GD, 27 July 1948, in *Letters 2*, 83.
51 See SB to CL, 22 November 1955, in *Letters 2*, 573.
52 Barbara Halberstam, *The Queer Art of Failure* (Durham and London: Duke University Press, 2011), 3 and *passim*. I am grateful to Colin Wright for drawing my attention to what is a compellingly suggestive term, in an excellent paper on the theme to the New Lacanian School in London.
53 Franz Kafka, *Hochzeitsvorbereitungen auf dem Lande und Andere Prosa aus dem Nachlaß*, edited by Max Brod (New York: Schocken Books, 1953), 42.

Works cited

Barry, Elizabeth. 'Translating Nationalism: Ireland, France and Military History in Beckett's *Mercier et Camier*', *Irish Studies Review*, 13.4 (2005), 505-15.
Beckett, Samuel. *The Capital of the Ruins*, in *Complete Short Prose 1929-1989*, edited with an introduction and notes by S. E. Gontarski (New York: Grove Press, 1995), 275-8.
—. *Complete Short Prose 1929-1989*, edited with an introduction and notes by S. E. Gontarski (New York: Grove Press, 1995).
—. *Molloy , Malone Dies , The Unnamable*, translated by Patrick Bowles and the author (London, John Calder, 1997).
—. *Mercier and Camier*, translated by the author [1974] (London: John Calder, 1999).
—. *Mercier et Camier* [1970] (Paris: Minuit, 2006).
—. *The Letters of Samuel Beckett. Volume 2: 1941-1956*, edited by George Craig, Martha Dow Fehsenfeld, Dan Gunn and Lois More Overbeck (Cambridge: Cambridge University Press, 2011).

Boissier de Sauvages de la Croix, Pierre Augustin. *Dictionnaire Languedocien-François, ou choix des mots Languedociens les plus difficiles à rendre en François*, 2 vols (Paris: J. Martin, 1821).

Cohn, Ruby. 'Joyce and Beckett, Irish Cosmopolitans', *James Joyce Quarterly* 8.4 (1971), 385–91.

Connor, Steven. '"Traduttore, Traditore": Samuel Beckett's Translation of *Mercier et Camier*', *Journal of Beckett Studies*, 11–12 (1989), 27–46.

Cronin, Anthony. *Samuel Beckett: The Last Modernist* (London: HarperCollins, 1996).

Fanning, Ronan. *Independent Ireland* (Dublin: Helicon, 1983).

Fisk, Robert. *In Time of War: Ireland, Ulster, and the Price of Neutrality 1939–1945* (London: Gill & Macmillan, 1983).

Fónagy, Ivan. 'Le français change de visage?' *Revue Romane*, 24.2 (1989), 226–54.

—. *Dynamique et changement* (Paris: Peeters, 2006).

Forel, Clair. *La Linguistique sociologique de Charles Bally* (Geneva: Droz, 2007).

Gibson, Andrew. *Samuel Beckett: A Critical Life* (London: Reaktion, 2009).

Girvin, Brian. *The Emergency: Neutral Ireland 1939–45* (London: Pan Macmillan, 2007).

Gray, Tony. *The Lost Years: The Emergency in Ireland 1939–45* (New York: Little, Brown & Co., 1997).

Halberstam, Barbara. *The Queer Art of Failure* (Durham and London: Duke University Press, 2011).

Kafka, Franz. *Hochzeitsvorbereitungen auf dem Lande und Andere Prosa aus dem Nachlaß*, edited by Max Brod (New York: Schocken Books, 1953).

Kennedy, Séan. 'Cultural Memory in *Mercier and Camier*: The Fate of Noel Lemass', in Marius Buning, Matthijs Engelberts and Sjef Houppermans (eds), *Samuel Beckett Today/Aujourd'hui* 15 (2005), 117–31.

Kitson, Simon. 'From Enthusiasm to Disenchantment: The French Police and the Vichy Regime, 1940–1944', *Contemporary European History* 11.3 (2002), 371–90.

Knowlson, James. *Damned to Fame: The Life of Samuel Beckett* (London: Bloomsbury, 1996).

Racine, Jean. *Œuvres complètes* (Paris: Seuil, 1962).

Wills, Clair. *That Neutral Island: A History of Ireland During the Second World War* (London: Faber and Faber, 2007).

2

'Sweet thing theology': Beckett, E. M. Cioran and the Lives of the Saints

David Wheatley
University of Aberdeen

The careers of Samuel Beckett and his Romanian contemporary E. M. Cioran (1911–95) both take place on the contested threshold between tradition and modernity. Each man's career was marked by migrations across cultural and linguistic boundaries, and also by a life-long and profound engagement with questions of theology. With an indelicate allusion to the New Testament in its title, Beckett's *More Pricks Than Kicks* (1934) was banned by the Irish Free State, while as late as 1957 Beckett was still attracting unwelcome attention from the Lord Chamberlain for Hamm's blasphemous prayer in *Endgame*. Where the Irish tradition at least is concerned, however, Beckett's problems in reconciling religion and modernity are far from unprecedented. Paul Durcan's poem, 'Irish Hierarchy Bans Colour Photography', from his 1978 collection *Sam's Cross*, amusingly illustrates the same dilemma. Keen to deny the populace access to a technicolour world, the hierarchy of Irish Catholic bishops declare by ecclesiastical *fiat* that all photographs must remain in black and white. Though Durcan's poem is presented as a grotesque fantasy, the church has taken a keener interest in photography than he might imagine. Pope Leo XIII marked the birth of photography with a poem, '*Ars Photographica*', in 1867, as fondly recalled by Martin Cunningham in Joyce's short story 'Grace', the one ecclesiastical fact Joyce's amateur theologians manage to get right amid a farrago of errors.[1] Leo was succeeded by Pius X, whose response to technological and other innovations can be found in the 1907 encyclical *Lamentabili Sane Exitu*. Though chiefly concerned with doctrinal conformity Pius also notes that in the struggle between religion and science, the former can be reconciled to the latter only at the expense of religious dogma, or a fatal declension into Protestantism and all its heresies. It was this firm line in the face of passing fashion that won the caustic admiration of Guillaume Apollinaire in 'Zone', a poem that moved Beckett to one of his finest translations: 'You alone in Europe Christianity are not ancient / The most modern European is you Pope Pius X'.[2]

Samuel Beckett's career is full of difficult thresholds, between Ireland and France, English and French, tradition and modernity, and moving from one to the other is rarely achieved without some occasion of outrage and denunciation. While Pius X may have been 'alone in Europe' in his ironic modernity, however, Beckett's trajectory as a young man on the move in the 1930s left him with his own experience of this condition. Beckett forged many important friendships in Paris with other writers and artists, principally painters, including the van Velde brothers, Henri Hayden, Giacometti and Avigdor Arikha, but one friend whose links with Beckett have yet to receive much critical attention is Romanian-born E. M. Cioran (1911–95). Of the *émigré* figures who made Paris their home in mid-century, Cioran, with his cultural displacement, passionate pessimism, addiction to the fragment, unclassifiable *oeuvre* and entirely relaxed view of the obscurity in which he laboured for most of his life, would appear to have had more in common with Beckett than most. Beckett would acquire numerous connections with Eastern Europe in later life, including his friendships with Václav Havel and Antoni Libera, but as a young man did not venture east of the Danube, perhaps the closest he came being an unanswered letter to Sergei Eisenstein in 1936. Judging by his name, the syphilitic Monsieur Verolesco mentioned in *Eleutheria* is a Romanian, but in the 1930s this too lay in the future.

Cioran does not warrant an entry in the *Faber/Grove Companion to Samuel Beckett* and for Beckett's biographers is a marginal figure, not featuring at all in Deirdre Bair's 1979 biography, while Anthony Cronin in *The Last Modernist* merely recycles a story from Cioran's essay on Beckett in *Exercises d'admiration*. James Knowlson reports only that, in the late 1970s, Beckett found 'he had less in common with Cioran in terms of outlook than he had at first thought'.[3] Cioran's name is notably absent, too, from Shane Weller's study of Beckett and nihilism, *A Taste for the Negative*. Yet the second volume of Beckett's published letters shows an awareness of Cioran's work on Beckett's part as early as 1956, when he praises *La Tentation d'exister* to Kitty Black.[4] Also informative on the friendship are Cioran's vast *Cahiers 1957–1972*, their 999 pages as tantalizingly short of a thousand as the Lynch family's collected ages in *Watt*. Numerous encounters with, or glimpses of Beckett are described: Cioran sees Beckett reading a paper in the Jardin du Luxembourg but is reluctant to disturb him; Beckett praises Cioran's book *Le Mauvais démiurge* ('*Dans vos ruines je me sens à l'abri*'); Beckett is high-spirited ('*en verve*') in company.[5] Cioran was among the small number of Beckett's friends who were also friendly with Suzanne Beckett, and some of the allusions to Beckett occur in the context of meetings with Suzanne alone, as when she complains to Cioran on 21 August 1970 that Beckett wastes his time on '*des gens de second ordre*', a fact she attributes to May Beckett's career as a nurse (*Cahiers* 825). Beckett and Cioran's friendship can also be triangulated through the person of another Parisian refugee from the madness of war-time Romania, Paul Celan. Celan translated Cioran's *Précis de décomposition* into German, though as John Felstiner reports, whether or not he was aware of Cioran's tainted political past in Romania is unknown.[6]

One striking difference between the two men, despite their shared passion for music, was their attitude to Bach, a difference not without a theological dimension. Throughout Cioran's life, Bach was his byword for artistic perfection, a figure whom God himself can only envy, whereas Beckett found the 'inexorable purposefulness' of his art (as he described it to another Romanian, Marcel Mihalovici) intolerable.[7] Despite these differences, Beckett was not averse to enlisting Cioran's artistic advice. In his essay on Beckett, Cioran recalls the two men spending an evening attempting to translate the English title 'Lessness'. Cioran suggested Boehme's *Ungrund*, by analogy with *Urgrund*, and wrote to Beckett the next day with *sinéité*. Beckett replied, Cioran continues, that he had thought of it too, perhaps *'au même instant'*.[8] Two letters on this subject reproduced in Cioran's *Œuvres* do not quite bear out this version of events (*Œuvres* 1264–5). Another passion which Cioran was conscious of sharing with Beckett was theology. In the Romanian's case, this came with a marked ethnological slant. Cioran frequently expressed his preference for God-haunted races (the Spanish and the Russian being his usual reference-points), and in May 1969 contemplated writing a book on the Irish, having been struck by an Irishman *'qui n'avait que "Almighty God" à la bouche'* in conversation, while of Beckett's ethnicity he argues that *'Il est important et il n'est pas important du tout que Beckett soit Irlandais'* (*Cahiers* 724; *Exercises d'admiration*, in *Œuvres* 1579).

Like Beckett, Cioran had been drawn to Paris as a young man in the 1930s from a provincial culture, albeit one whose philistinism he was prone to exaggerate in later years, for reasons that might best be described as dissembling (the cosmopolitanism of nineteenth-century Bucharest having earned it the sobriquet *micul Paris*, or 'little Paris'). Also like Beckett, he had switched from writing in his native tongue to French, beginning with *Précis de décomposition* in 1949, though with Cioran there was no going back, to the point where in later life he would refuse to speak Romanian to visiting compatriots. Where Beckett is concerned, the savage indignation of his early writing on Ireland led many critics, initially at least, to assign to Ireland and elsewhere in his work the roles of tradition versus innovation, paralysis versus opportunity. One theme, however, that complicates this binary in an exemplary fashion, and forms an ideal point of entry for a comparative reading of Beckett and Cioran, is religion. As a non-believer keen to escape the influence of, first, his puritanical mother and, second, the Catholic triumphalism of Free State Ireland, Beckett had many disincentives to dwell on religion, yet, as Mary Bryden has shown in her *Samuel Beckett and the Idea of God*, there is scarcely a more ubiquitous obsession in his work, from the defenestrated Jesuits and Augustinian proof of God 'by exhaustion' in 'Whoroscope'[9] to the musing over whether 'God is love' half a century later in *Company* ('Yes or no? No').[10] Cioran too had a tangled personal relationship with religion. His father was a Romanian Orthodox priest, which made his 1937 book *Lacrimi și Sfinți* (*Tears and Saints*), with its psychosexual speculations and lurid blaspheming all the more shocking. Cioran's quickfire style as an aphorist plunges the reader into a bewildering range of subjects and tones, from high-minded ecstasy to frothing execration, while never straying far from an underlying monomania. 'In fact, there is only God and me', he writes of God; 'His silence invalidates us both.'[11]

If there is a well-adjusted shrugging off of religion, this is the response of neither Beckett nor Cioran. Though Beckett and Cioran are atheists, the transgressive force of blasphemy and heresy is too seductive to pass up for the more level-headed pleasures of a merely rationalist unbelief; between their unbelief and the Dawkinsite rationalism of our times, needless to say, there is little common ground. Their taste for religious transgression came with a well-established pedigree in modernist writing, from Lautréamont and Baudelaire to Joyce and Lawrence.[12] In *After Strange Gods*, which he subtitled *A Primer of Modern Heresy*, T. S. Eliot regretted the eclipse of blasphemy in the modern world, with all blasphemy's implied tributes to belief: 'first-rate blasphemy [...] requires both literary genius and profound faith',[13] and as such bespeaks an intellectual and spiritual engagement lacking under the humanist dispensation of Irving Babbitt and his followers. As Eliot observed of Baudelaire: 'it is better, in a paradoxical way, to do evil than to do nothing: at least, we exist. It is true to say that the glory of man is his capacity for salvation; it is also true to say that his glory is his capacity for damnation'.[14]

Blasphemy arises against a background of faith, but this background has a cultural as well as a strictly theological dimension for Beckett and Cioran, especially in that most formative of decades for each writer, the 1930s. Saints and their folklore have left an all-pervasive mark on the Irish landscape, references to which abound in early Beckett. A few years after the publication of *More Pricks Than Kicks*, Myles na gCopaleen involved *The Irish Times* in a costly libel action when he joked that Dublin's Institute for Advanced Studies had claimed that there were two St Patricks but no God, and for Belacqua too these cultural landmarks proliferate in a cultural economy not notably underwritten by any deity: 'What a Misfortune' alone contains references to St George (via *Gulliver's Travels*), the Church of St Nicolas [sic] in Galway, where Christopher Columbus is reputed to have prayed, 'St Augustine's ladder', St Paul, the fictional St Tamar, in whose church Belacqua marries Thelma and the almost-saint Julian of Norwich (beatified but never canonized).[15] Occasionally the spiritual manstuprations of Catholic Ireland would press Belacqua into self-identification as a Protestant, calling on his 'grand old family Huguenot guts' as a character witness,[16] but with the shift to London in *Murphy* this urge recedes, only for Catholicism to reappear in Beckett's work with his move to France. Jacques Moran is a flawlessly drawn bully of Catholic casuistry, with a soft spot for the Irish saints and their unusual habits, while the timetable for Malone's demise with which *Malone Dies* opens also has a distinctly Catholic feel, the secular feast of Bastille Day aside. In the poem '*Mort de A. D.*', Irish Catholicism follows Beckett to France in an elegy for his Saint-Lô colleague Arthur Darley, whose Catholic devotional reading often found him '*dévorant*

/la vie des saints une vie par jour de vie /revivant dans la nuit ses noirs péchés'. Where his Irish modernist poetic *confrères* are concerned, the devout Catholicism of all three is noteworthy, but it too was a far from parochial affair: Brian Coffey studied in Paris with Jacques Maritain and the grid-references of Thomas MacGreevy's faith, in his poems, are conspicuously more Hispanic and Mediterranean than they are stay-at-home Irish. In studying the young Beckett's religious contexts, however, the cultural *décor* of Ireland or France is only one dimension of the deeper questions they frame. His Protestantism heavily informs recent historicist readings of Beckett, Ireland and the 1930s, but there is more than matter enough in 'that sweet thing theology', as he will call it in a *Text for Nothing*,[17] to bring the distinctiveness of the young Beckett's position into focus, all local differences of sect aside.

To take a Catholic satirist by way of counter-example: in the work of Austin Clarke we find a relentless critique of the role of the Church in Irish life – its Puritanism, misogyny and brutal sadism. Clarke had suffered badly at the church's hands, to the point where his ceaseless complaining comes to seem a symptom too, but his satires are impeccably anti-clerical in their logic. He attacks the culpable institution and not its founding beliefs, whereas with Beckett the hostility against the church (a given) appears to extend irresistibly to its ideals and their originator too. As Moran puts it: 'It's a strange thing, I don't like men and I don't like animals. As for God, he is beginning to disgust me.'[18] In his 1938 poem 'Ooftish', Beckett launches a furious denunciation of the Christian doctrine of the atonement. Like a toad swallowing flies, God the father devours the sins and sufferings of his creations, relishing the agony of Christ on the cross. Indignant at the suggestion that suffering may be for the good of our souls, Beckett performs a desperate *reductio* of humanity to a state of irremediable misery:

> it is you it equals you any fool has to pity you
> so parcel up the whole issue and send it along

the whole misery diagnosed undiagnosed misdiagnosed
get your friends to do the same we'll make use of it
we'll make sense of it we'll put it in the pot with the rest
it all boils down to blood of lamb.[19]

In *Milton's God*, William Empson polemicizes against Christian (or 'neo-Christian') criticism, arguing for Blake's reading of *Paradise Lost*, that Milton was 'of the devil's party'. To Empson, as to the Beckett of 'Ooftish', the Christian doctrine of the atonement, whereby Christ makes reparation on the cross for the sins of humanity, is sadism pure and simple, and the real blasphemy is the endorsement by Christian critics of the torture-worship he sees in the crucifixion. Empson was particularly outraged by Hugh Kenner's Christian readings of James Joyce, and Kenner's belief that Joyce intended Bloom and Stephen's interior monologues as satires on the mental poverty of the post-Christian condition: 'Mr Kenner implies with complacent approval [. . .] that the happiness felt by the reader in watching this exposure is like that ascribed to the blessed in the *Summa Theologica* from the punishment of the damned'.[20] Empson did not have the opportunity to read the recently rediscovered Irish Victorian James Henry (1798–1876), an important subterranean precursor of Beckett's, who spent the twentieth century in the limbo of the unpublished, but in his poem 'Out of the Frying Pan Into the Fire' Henry excavates with cruel precision the sadism he suspects below the surface of Christian grace ('Wherefore /Wast thou as I made thee?' God asks the 'millions and millions' of sinners he condemns to 'fire and snakes and instruments of torture').[21] No less than orthodoxy, Irish heresy has its annals and canon too: in 1696 the Deist John Toland's book *Christianity Not Mysterious* was burned by the hangman in Dublin, and the mysterious Adam Duff O'Toole was burned at the stake also in Dublin in 1328, for denying the incarnation of Christ and the resurrection of the dead and asserting that the Virgin Mary was a prostitute. Therein, surely, lie any number of concerned letters to Dum Spiro from the readership of his Catholic monthly *Crux*. Ireland stayed neutral during the Second World War, but in Romania the itch to torture millions and millions of sinners found a ready outlet. For Beckett and Cioran, the poles of the sacred and secular, the exalted and the profane, exist in a mutually informing dialectic, with the extremes of 1930s politics forming a fertile template for the psychological extremes investigated in their writing on religion. For both men the war and its build-up were a defining moment, if in very different ways. While Beckett preferred France at war to Ireland at peace, Cioran's loyalties were altogether murkier. The hysterical pessimism of Cioran's youth did not confine itself to an interest in the eccentricities of the saints, and in 1935 he published *Schimbarea la față a României* (*The Transfiguration of Romania*), a fascist and anti-Semitic screed which caused him much embarrassment in later life (a bowdlerized edition appeared shortly before his death; it was omitted from the Gallimard *Œuvres*).[22] Ion Antonescu's Iron Guard seized power in 1940, and, until Antonescu's overthrow in 1944, made Romania a willing Axis partner in the elimination of European Jewry. Cioran's complex relationship with Romanian fascism, including a brief spell as cultural adviser with the Romanian legation in Vichy France in 1941, has been meticulously documented in Marta Petreu's *An Infamous Past*.[23] Beckett's membership of the Résistance during the war and acts of solidarity with persecuted writers such as Fernando Arrabal and Havel have marked him down as one of the politically righteous among the great writers, untainted by the far-right deviations that proved so nearly fatal to Ezra Pound, Céline and Knut Hamsun. Nevertheless, the extent of the young Beckett's apoliticism should not be underestimated, nor his occasional youthful flashes of insensitivity airbrushed from the record, as when he complains to MacGreevy in 1937 of George Furlong, the curator of the National Gallery in Dublin, 'talk[ing] all the stock sentimental bunk about the

Nazi persecutions' (a definitive verdict on this topic will have to wait until the publication of the 1936-7 German diary).[24] The point of this is not to sit in judgement on a young man's indiscretions, but to remain alive to how easily he might have found himself the prisoner of an immature political misjudgement, as happened to his compatriot Francis Stuart, whose adventures in Nazi Germany formed the basis for his 1971 novel of elective disgrace, *Black List Section H*.

Introducing her English translation of Cioran's *Tears and Saints*, Ilinca Zarifopol-Johnston makes concerted efforts to play the book off against *The Transfiguration of Romania*, arguing that its critique of saintly fanaticism 'reveals the shortcomings' of the political tract and 'thereby undermines it'.[25] This is to underestimate the degree to which saints themselves are political figures, and their strong appeal to the reactionary mind. Francis Stuart published a pamphlet on *Mystics and Mysticism* in 1929 and repeatedly returns to the saints in his novels, from *Women and God* to *Redemption* and *Pillar of Cloud*. The fraught connection between religion and politics is not something Cioran dwells on in *Tears and Saints*, but from the outset – 'Saints cannot be *known*' (*TAS* 3) – Cioran's book presents itself as an anti-epistemology, an act of higher ignorance. The book is delivered in the disconnected short paragraphs and shorter aphorisms that would become his life-long signature: one 'Black diamond of pessimism' after another, the 'little sparkle hid in ashes' fantasized by Belacqua.[26] Cioran's understanding of the saints is heavily indebted to Nietzsche's flushing out of the will to power behind Christian renunciation. It is not suffering but the '*voluptuousness*' of suffering that interests the saint, he insists (*TAS* 48). The encounter with God is an indulgence, a trap, a 'last temptation' (*TAS* 9). He notes the popularity in the Middle Ages of treatises on *The Art of Dying*, a late example of which, by Jeremy Taylor, features in Beckett's *Human Wishes*. Mystical experience represents a counterblast to evolution since 'history is the product of the vertical line, whereas nothingness comes from the horizontal line' ('better on your arse than on your feet', as Beckett's Chamfort can confirm[27]).

In their extremity, saints surpass standard definitions of humility, to the point where they know 'how to be sad *for* God' (*TAS* 22). In the struggle with God, the saint's identification with the divine hits on a surer strategy than the blasphemer's for besting their creator-antagonist: 'One must think of God day and night in order to wear him out' (*TAS* 61). The desire for self-extinction is the most self-dramatizing act of all, projecting itself to the very heart of the godhead: 'If I cannot live, let me at least die in God. Or better still, let me be buried *alive* in him!' (*TAS* 63) In the negative theological manoeuvre of apophasis, or paralypsis, to speak of nothing is to speak of God but to speak of God too is to speak of nothing. 'God is the *positive* expression of nothingness', Cioran writes, echoing Beckett's formulation for Dr Johnson, that 'he must have had a vision of *positive* annihilation' (*TAS* 61). The hysterical grief of the saints' separation from God issues in their unceasing tears, but here too the inversion practised by negative theology is at work: 'Show me a single tear swallowed up by the earth! No, by paths unknown to us, they all go upwards' (*TAS* 3). Tears are a seductive alternative to more straightforward acts of charity if, as Cioran claims, 'Only tears will be weighed at the last judgement' (*TAS* 6). Even when the weeping saint is Francis of Assisi (whose 'absolute perfection' Cioran finds 'unforgivable'), there is still an element of Nietzschean exhibitionism to be exposed: when 'at the end of [Francis'] life he was about to go blind, the doctors found the cause to be an excess of tears' (*TAS* 62).

Cioran's fountain of tears wells up repeatedly in Beckett too, often dramatically in excess of their immediate occasion. Remembering Tennyson, the narrator of *Dream* speaks of a 'tale told at twilight of tears idle tears' ('tears! tears! tears!' adds the Smeraldina);[28] Mercier stages a remarkably lachrymose display over his cream horn ('the tears flowed, overflowed, all down the furrowed cheeks');[29] Pozzo, in

Newtonian style, declares that 'The tears of the world are a constant quality. For each one who begins to weep, somewhere else another stops';[30] 'Tears and laughter, they are so much Gaelic to me', quips Molloy, a Buridan's ass between the tautologous poles of Heraclitus and Democritus;[31] 'the tears stream down my cheeks from my unblinking eyes', says the Unnamable;[32] the animator in *Rough for Radio II* recalls the falling of a tear in Lawrence Sterne, 'a tear an angel comes to catch as it falls';[33] while the narrator of *How It Is*, by contrast, wonders whether he is enduring 'sadism pure and simple' but corrects himself: 'no since I may not cry'.[34] Impassivity would appear to be the terminal point of all our grief: as Adorno suggested, 'the only face left' in Beckett is one 'whose tears have dried up'.[35] This applies to religion too, since just as Molloy fails to distinguish between laughter and tears the Beckett character tends to veer between, or has difficulty distinguishing, acts of worship from those of execration. The best-known of Beckett's blasphemies is probably Hamm's aborted prayer in *Endgame* ('The bastard! He doesn't exist!'), but the anathema hurled skyward in *Mercier and Camier* is if anything even more bitter: 'As for thee, fuck thee', protests Mercier, before Camier corrects him:

> Is it our little omniomni you are trying to abuse? [...] You should know better. It's he on the contrary fucks thee. Omniomni, the all-unfuckable.[36]

The Beckett work that comes closest to realizing the vision of *Tears and Saints*, however, is *How It Is*. Whether he works on a small or large canvas the fragment is always central to Beckett's aesthetic, with its fractious dialectic of part and whole, but having announced in *Dream* that the experience of his readers would be 'between the phrases, in the silence',[37] he waited until *How It Is* to physically admit the silence into his text, as that text so memorably does. The 1992 essay collection *The Ideal Core of the Onion* reproduces an elaborate doodle from the *Human Wishes* notebooks of multiple crucified figures,[38] and an abandoned fragment from the drafts to *Endgame* features the husband and wife pseudo-couple of Ernest and Alice, the former attached to a mechanical crucifix with a veronica-like sudarium on his face,[39] but in *How It Is* Beckett realizes the pun of a cruci-fiction, pinioning his prose to the page in gasping fragments or 'versets'. Cioran is inordinately fond of the desert fathers, and the narrator of *How It Is* hallucinates the existence of 'others' who 'seek refuge in a desert place', albeit a rather muddy one in this case.[40] The narrator's agony is the universal fate, but no less solitary for that. I have cited the novel's injunction on tears, but this is not quite consistently applied: we find 'fewer tears too that too they are failing too', another moment of confusion between hilarity and grief ('laughter even and tears to match soon dried'), and a suggestion that tears though scarce may still take the place of words ('lacking all lacking less tears for lack of words' [*HII* 13, 81, 90]). Whatever about the narrator, the other's urge to give voice to grief must be condemned, as in the 'vile tears of unbutcherable brother' we find in part two (*HII* 64). If the intention of these displays is to elicit sympathy or forge any manner of human connection, the novel's Sadean world has other ideas. Of Krim, we read 'he the first to have pity happily to no effect' (*HII* 71). Displays of strong emotion towards God remain permitted, perhaps in the knowledge that in his divine apathia, athambia, aphasia, he will not respond, but here too the laughter-and-tears principle of confused extremes applies: 'curse God', we read, 'curse God or bless him' (*HII* 33).

Though God is absent, the ubiquitous postures of martyred distress are often awarded the saving grace of saintly dignity. Saints' crosses are a frequent motif: the narrator's victim in part two is splayed in the figure of a St Andrew's cross, or *crux decussata* of Russian orthodox tradition, 'top V reduced aperture'. Tormenter and victim mesh together in further references to 'Saint Andrew of the Black Sea' and 'Andrew of the Volga' (*HII* 49, 76, 78), and the narrator spreads his arms 'LIKE A CROSS' before the final extinction of his voice. For Cioran 'tears are the only commentary on saints' (*HII* 28), but in the largely tear-free world of *How It Is* we have commentators instead, the diligent scribes enforcing the law of citation that frames the text. The splayed victims are citations of the crucified Christ, but in a world that has annulled Christ's original sacrifice and its passionate atonement. Catholic tradition abounds in splinters of the true cross preserved as relics, but the sufferings of *How It Is* are atomized fragments for which no pattern of unity stands guarantor. As with Lucky's insistence on God's universal love for us, 'with some exceptions',[41] we seem to have stumbled on one of the blind-spots in the doctrine of grace, a world of pointless crucifixions to satisfy an unknowable God with no end in sight to the punishment and no forgiveness possible. As Cioran might say, though, 'Only God has the privilege of abandoning us. Men can only drop us'.[42] When we read, towards the end of part three, of whether 'it is still possible at this late hour to conceive of other worlds' (*HII* 125), the strangeness shades into science fiction territory. William Empson wrote of the influence of astronomy, and the possible existence of alien worlds, on John Donne, and in his poem 'The Innumerable Christ', Hugh MacDiarmid too has pondered the implications for the Christian story of extraterrestrial worlds:

> I' mony an unco warl' the nicht
> The lift gaes black as pitch at noon,
> An' sideways on their chests the heids
> O' endless Christs roll doon.[43]

Did Christ come to save the Martians? If so, why does he never mention them? If not, how seriously can we take him as a lord of all creation? One can easily imagine a sci-fi *How It Is*, directed by Kubrick and with a Ligeti soundtrack, but the more worlds we imagine there are the lonelier the denizens of *How It Is* become. Formally too, the longer the book goes on the more fragmenting its form becomes, connecting to nothing and no one but its own pitiful screams of distress.

It is the fragment, then, that provides both Beckett and Cioran the perfect vehicle for holding the dyad of God and man in brief and impossible balance. Shortly after the writing of *How It Is*, Beckett produced the versions of Chamfort that bring him as close as anything in his *oeuvre* to the aphorism form as practised by Cioran, a fact not lost on the Romanian. 'Is it not significant that he versified Chamfort?' Cioran asks, struck by Beckett's ability to find poetry in the gloomy Frenchman, given the 'absence of lyric impulse that characterizes the moralist's skeletal prose'.[44] Cioran too is squarely in Chamfort's tradition, and it would be tempting to render some of Cioran's more piquant black diamonds of pessimism into verse.[45] Chamfort recommended that we begin each morning by swallowing a toad, to ensure that nothing more unpleasant befall us for the rest of the day and, like denim trousers, the Chamfort maxim frequently appears in a condition best described as 'pre-distressed'. The practised impassivity between cosmic extremes resurfaces in a rebuke to Dante: 'I strike from hell's to grave on heaven's door: /All hope abandon ye who enter in'.[46] Here we reconnect with the closing verdict of 'Dante...Bruno. Vico..Joyce' that paradise represents a 'static lifelessness of unrelieved immaculation'.[47] The alternative, once more, is purgatorial, the 'flood of movement and vitality released by the conjunction of [the hellish and heavenly] elements'.

Purgatory refuses finality, opting instead for a bruising exposure to the twin extremes on either side of it. In their preference for the unpurged form of the fragment, lapsed from silence but amounting to no unity, Beckett and Cioran are condemned to an utterance that falls forever short of the sanction of systemic thought. Attempts to turn Beckett into an actual philosopher, or better (better-worse) again, a saint, have not been wanting, but as John Calder's *The Philosophy of Samuel Beckett* shows, take place only by overruling his all-important 'neithering' principle of unknowing, the ludicrous inability to tell tears from laughter, heaven from hell, that goes to the heart of Beckett's work. As in Adorno's joke about Soviet critics who discussed the Marxist dialectic like town councillors, and who would conduct a town-hall meeting like a discussion of the Marxist dialectic, we are dealing with a category error when readers persuade themselves that the point of Beckett's radical uncertainty is to illuminate 'society's newly found dependence on short-term solutions and on the values that lie behind it, which are a recipe for catastrophe', to take a random Calderism.[48] Although the young Beckett describes Purgatory as a 'flood of movement and vitality', his ability to ricochet between heaven and hell without succumbing to either is also what gives his work its capacity for unearthly, one might almost say religious, moments of calm and release, from the 'leaden light' of *Malone Dies* which so pleased Cioran,[49] to the god-cursing but eerily beautiful prose of *For to End Yet Again* and other late works. Cioran's work too, though orchestrated more noisily than Beckett's, and with a more hyena-like quality in its mirthless laugh, has similar moments of unnerving, quasi-mystical calm, as when his thoughts turn to music at the close of *Tears and Saints*: 'Boredom is tuneless matter. Melancholy is the unconscious music of the soul. Tears are music in material form' (*TAS* 104).

His mystical metaphors helped him 'to hold in a single thought justice and reality', wrote Yeats,[50] and their God-haunted prose allows Beckett and Cioran to synthesize the language of belief and blasphemy in ways encountered in few if any other modern writers. The tendency to contextualize religious themes in Beckett as part of the Anglo-Irish experience, I have suggested, has sometimes masked this side of his work by diverting attention from its full transgressive force. Correspondingly, attempts to reclaim Beckett as a religious thinker are not without sanitizing risks of their own. To Declan Kiberd, Beckett is 'a supremely religious artist',[51] whose work renovates Protestant values of private conscience and distrust of art and the self. Should his blasphemous tendencies appear at odds with the scholastic piety of his 1930s poet friends, this is because 'secular liberals and Catholic conservatives conspired to prevent a sympathetic hearing for these artists'.[52] This is to recruit Beckett to a local row, with Sean O'Faolain on the one hand and Archbishop McQuaid on the other, and the strait gate of post-revisionist Irish literary historiography somewhere in between. The culpable moral equivalence of secularists and religious conservatives is a theme to which Kiberd returns in a discussion of the best-known of all modern blasphemies, Salman Rushdie's *The Satanic Verses*. Given the complicity of Enlightenment values in colonialism, Kiberd argues, Rushdie's appeal to Western concepts of free speech in defence of his right to offend religious believers makes him 'just as much a fundamentalist as the Ayatollah'.[53] No doubt this qualifies as blasphemy in its own right, against jaded post-Enlightenment orthodoxy, but Empson's thoughts on this equivalence, let alone Beckett or Cioran's, might make for interesting reading. Rushdie, like Beckett and Cioran before him, possesses no actual fires and snakes and instruments of torture, whereas the Ayatollah does. This seems a distinction worth insisting on.

To talk of Western-style 'free speech' in the context of the extorted groans and blasphemies of *How It Is* would be another category error, however: from Beckett's perspective, the opposition of Enlightenment and Christian standpoints is just another local row. Kiberd ends his discussion of Beckett as a religious writer by repeating the claim, from Beckett's review of MacGreevy, that 'All poetry [...] is prayer',[54] but the young Beckett's own attempt to translate this impulse into a critical vocabulary is far from consistent. He praises MacGreevy's poems for articulating a 'nucleus of endopsychic clarity', but reviewing Denis Devlin's *Intercessions* three years later announces that 'art has nothing to do with clarity, does not dabble in the clear and does not make clear'.[55] Here, then, is yet another of Beckett's cosmic-sized aporias, but even making allowances for the critical vagaries of youth, the scale of the *volte-face* suggests something fundamentally wrong in Kiberd's appropriation of Beckett for the party of divine illumination.

If Beckett must be a 'supremely religious artist', perhaps we can at least allow that he is simultaneously a supremely anti-religious artist too.

The Eliot of *After Strange Gods* found himself in the peculiar position of warming to blasphemy as a covert tribute to orthodoxy, but for readers deficient in ultramontanist nostalgia the benefits of heresy are necessarily of a different order. If Cioran was any kind of fanatic, it was a 'fanatic of indifference',[56] and to Beckett too it was the in-between, neither-one-thing-nor-the-other state of purgatory that appealed over heaven and hell; the key word in his plays, after all, was 'perhaps'. Revisiting Malone's self-characterization as a 'tepid' soul, the narrator of *How It Is* speaks of 'joy and sorrow those two their sum divided by two and luke like in outer hell' (*HII* 35). Here then is tepidity raised to a higher art, and granted the intensity, the fanaticism if need be, lacking among lesser devotees. As Yeats wrote in 'The Cold Heaven':

> Ah! when the ghost begins to quicken,
> Confusion of the death-bed over, is it sent
> Out naked on the roads, as the books say, and stricken
> By the injustice of the skies for punishment?[57]

Beckett and Cioran choose the coldness of a closed heaven and the road before them over the warmth of any fireside seat at journey's end. Long after heaven and hell have lost their power to compel, Beckett and Cioran's faithfully blasphemous texts will still supply the 'partially purgatorial agent' that we the 'partially purged' require,[58] the injustice of the skies they promise our fitting punishment but also the most bracing of rewards.

Notes

1 As noted by Terence Brown: 'Joyce's Magic Lantern', in *The Literature of Ireland: Culture and Criticism* (Cambridge: Cambridge University Press, 2010), 27.

2 Guillaume Apollinaire, 'Zone', translated by Samuel Beckett: see Samuel Beckett, *Selected Poems 1930-1989*, edited by David Wheatley (London: Faber and Faber, 2009), 145.
3 James Knowlson, *Damned to Fame: The Life of Samuel Beckett* (London: Bloomsbury, 1996), 654.
4 Samuel Beckett, *The Letters of Samuel Beckett. Volume 2: 1941-1956*, edited by George Craig, Martha Dow Fehsenfeld, Dan Gunn and Lois More Overbeck (Cambridge: Cambridge University Press, 2012), 678-9.
5 E. M. Cioran, *Cahiers* (Paris: Gallimard, 1997), 613, 715, 793; hereafter cited in the text as *Cahiers*.
6 John Felstiner, *Paul Celan: Poet, Survivor, Jew* (New Haven: Yale University Press, 1997), n. 6, 306.
7 Quoted in Miron Grindea, 'Beckett's Involvement with Music', in Mary Bryden (ed.), *Samuel Beckett and Music* (Oxford: Clarendon Press, 1998), 184.
8 E. M. Cioran, *Œuvres* (Paris: Gallimard, 1995), 1576; hereafter cited in the text as *Œuvres*.
9 Beckett, *Selected Poems*, 3-8.
10 Samuel Beckett, *Company, Ill Seen Ill Said, Worstward Ho, Stirrings Still*, edited by Dirk Van Hulle (London: Faber and Faber, 2010), 34.
11 E. M. Cioran, *Tears and Saints*, translated by Ilinca Zarifopol-Johnston (Chicago: University of Chicago Press, 1998), 73; hereafter cited in the text as *TAS*.
12 For an account of heresy and Anglophone modernist writing, see Damon Franke, *Modernist Heresies: British Literary History, 1883-1924* (Columbus: Ohio State University Press, 2008).
13 T. S. Eliot, *After Strange Gods* (London: Faber and Faber, 1934), 52.
14 T. S. Eliot, 'Baudelaire', in T. S. Eliot, *Selected Prose* (London: Penguin, 1953), 184.
15 Samuel Beckett, *More Pricks Than Kicks*, edited by Cassandra Nelson (London: Faber and Faber, 2010), 110, 114, 115, 118, 137.
16 Ibid., 152.
17 Samuel Beckett, *Texts for Nothing and Other Shorter Prose 1950-1976*, edited by Mark Nixon (London: Faber and Faber, 2010), 24.
18 Samuel Beckett, *Molloy*, edited by Shane Weller (London: Faber and Faber, 2009), 109.

19. Beckett, *Selected Poems*, 37.
20. William Empson, *Milton's God* (London: Chatto & Windus, 1961), 233–4.
21. James Henry, *Selected Poems of James Henry*, edited by Christopher Ricks (Dublin: Lilliput Press, 2002), 54–5.
22. For more on Cioran's early political (mis)adventures and attempts to atone for them in later life, see my 'E. M. Cioran and the Art of Disgrace', *Dublin Review* 27 (2007), 25–36.
23. Marta Petreu, *An Infamous Past: E.M. Cioran and the Rise of Fascism in Romania* (Chicago: Ivan R. Dee, 2005).
24. Beckett to Thomas MacGreevy, 14 May 1937, Samuel Beckett, *The Letters of Samuel Beckett. Volume 1: 1929–1940*, edited by Martha Dow Fehsenfeld and Lois More Overbeck (Cambridge: Cambridge University Press, 2009), 496.
25. Ilinca Zarifopol-Johnston, Introduction to *Tears and Saints*, xx.
26. Samuel Beckett, *Dream of Fair to Middling Women* (Monkstown: Black Cat Press, 1992), 47.
27. Beckett, *Selected Poems*, 165.
28. Beckett, *Dream*, 149; *More Pricks Than Kicks*, 143. See also John Pilling, *Samuel Beckett's More Pricks Than Kicks: In a Strait of Two Wills* (London: Continuum, 2011), 181.
29. Samuel Beckett, *Mercier and Camier*, edited by Seán Kennedy (London: Faber and Faber, 2010), 24.
30. Samuel Beckett, *Waiting for Godot*, edited by Mary Bryden (London: Faber and Faber, 2010), 29.
31. Beckett, *Molloy*, 35.
32. Samuel Beckett, *The Unnamable*, edited by Steven Connor (London: Faber and Faber, 2010), 3.
33. Samuel Beckett, 'Rough for Radio II', in Samuel Beckett, *All That Fall and Other Plays for Radio and Screen*, edited by Everett Frost (London: Faber and Faber, 2009), 64.
34. Samuel Beckett, *How It Is*, edited by Édouard Magessa O'Reilly (London: Faber and Faber, 2009), 54.
35. T. W. Adorno, 'Trying to Understand Endgame', in *Notes to Literature, Volume 1*, in Rolf Tiedemann (ed.), translated by

Shierry Weber Nicholson (New York: Columbia University Press, 1993), 290.
36 Beckett, *Mercier and Camier*, 19.
37 Beckett, *Dream*, 137.
38 Reproduced in Mary Bryden, 'Beckett's Pinioned People', in John Pilling and Mary Bryden (eds), *The Ideal Core of the Onion: Reading Beckett Archives* (Reading: Beckett International Foundation, 1992), 45–62 at 57.
39 RUL MS 1227/7/16/2. See also Mary Bryden, *Samuel Beckett and the Idea of God* (Basingstoke: Macmillan, 1998), 142.
40 Beckett, *How It Is*, 8; hereafter cited in the text as *HII*.
41 Beckett, *Waiting for Godot*, 40.
42 E. M. Cioran, *The Trouble with Being Born*, translated by Richard Howard (London: Quartet, 1993), 38.
43 Hugh MacDiarmid, 'The Innumerable Christ', in Hugh MacDiarmid *Complete Poems Volume I*, edited by Michael Grieve and W. R. Aitken (London: Penguin, 1985), 32.
44 E. M. Cioran, 'Beckett: Some Meetings', in *Anathemas and Admirations*, translated by Richard Howard (London: Quartet, 1992), 129–36 at 136.
45 The present author's attempts can be found in 'E. M. Cioran in Tatters', in David Wheatley, *A Nest on the Waves* (Loughcrew: The Gallery Press, 2010).
46 Beckett, *Selected Poems*, 171.
47 Samuel Beckett, *Disjecta: Miscellaneous Writings and a Dramatic Fragment*, edited by Ruby Cohn (London: John Calder, 1983), 33.
48 John Calder, *The Philosophy of Samuel Beckett* (London: John Calder, 2001), 94.
49 Cioran, *Anathemas and Admirations*, 134.
50 W. B. Yeats, *A Vision* (London: Macmillan, 1981), 25.
51 Declan Kiberd, *Inventing Ireland: The Literature of the Modern Nation* (London: Jonathan Cape, 1995), 454.
52 Ibid., 466.
53 Declan Kiberd, *The Irish Writer and the World* (Cambridge: Cambridge University Press, 2005), 153–6.

54 Beckett, *Disjecta*, 68.
55 Ibid., 94.
56 Cioran, *The Trouble with Being Born*, 40.
57 W. B. Yeats, *Collected Poems* (London: Macmillan, 1982), 140.
58 Beckett, *Disjecta*, 33.

Works cited

Adorno, T. W. 'Trying to Understand Endgame', in Rolf Tiedemann, *Notes to Literature, Volume 1*, translated by Shierry Weber Nicholson (New York: Columbia University Press, 1993), 241–75.
Beckett, Samuel. *Disjecta: Miscellaneous Writings and a Dramatic Fragment*, edited by Ruby Cohn (London: John Calder, 1983).
—. *Dream of Fair to Middling Women* (Monkstown: Black Cat Press, 1992).
—. *All That Fall and Other Plays for Radio and Screen*, edited by Everett Frost (London: Faber and Faber, 2009).
—. *How It Is*, edited by Édouard Magessa O'Reilly (London: Faber and Faber, 2009).
—. *The Letters of Samuel Beckett. Volume 1: 1929–1940*, edited by Martha Dow Fehsenfeld and Lois More Overbeck (Cambridge: Cambridge University Press, 2009).
—. *Molloy*, edited by Shane Weller (London: Faber and Faber, 2009).
—. *Selected Poems 1930–1989*, edited by David Wheatley (London: Faber and Faber, 2009).
—. *Company, Ill Seen Ill Said, Worstward Ho, Stirrings Still*, edited by Dirk Van Hulle (London: Faber and Faber, 2010).
—. *Mercier and Camier*, edited by Seán Kennedy (London: Faber and Faber, 2010).
—. *More Pricks Than Kicks*, edited by Cassandra Nelson (London: Faber and Faber, 2010).
—. *Texts for Nothing and Other Shorter Prose 1950–1976*, edited by Mark Nixon (London: Faber and Faber, 2010).
—. *The Unnamable*, edited by Steven Connor (London: Faber and Faber, 2010).

—. *Waiting for Godot*, edited by Mary Bryden (London: Faber and Faber, 2010).

—. *The Letters of Samuel Beckett. Volume 2: 1941–1956*, edited by George Craig, Martha Dow Fehsenfeld, Dan Gunn and Lois More Overbeck (Cambridge: Cambridge University Press, 2012).

Brown, Terence. 'Joyce's Magic Lantern', in Terence Brown, *The Literature of Ireland: Culture and Criticism* (Cambridge: Cambridge University Press, 2010), 27–35.

Bryden, Mary. 'Beckett's Pinioned People', in John Pilling and Mary Bryden (eds), *The Ideal Core of the Onion: Reading Beckett Archives* (Reading: Beckett International Foundation, 1992), 45–62.

—. *Samuel Beckett and the Idea of God* (Basingstoke: Macmillan, 1998).

Calder, John. *The Philosophy of Samuel Beckett* (London: John Calder, 2001).

Cioran, E. M. *Anathemas and Admirations*, translated by Richard Howard (London: Quartet, 1992).

—. *The Trouble with Being Born*, translated by Richard Howard (London: Quartet, 1993).

—. *Œuvres* (Paris: Gallimard, 1995).

—. *Cahiers* (Paris: Gallimard, 1997).

—. *Tears and Saints*, translated by Ilinca Zarifopol-Johnston (Chicago: University of Chicago Press, 1998).

Eliot, T. S. *After Strange Gods* (London: Faber and Faber, 1934).

—. *Selected Prose* (London: Penguin, 1953).

Empson, William. *Milton's God* (London: Chatto & Windus, 1961).

Felstiner, John. *Paul Celan: Poet, Survivor, Jew* (New Haven: Yale University Press, 1997).

Franke, Damon. *Modernist Heresies: British Literary History, 1883–1924* (Columbus: Ohio State University Press, 2008).

Grindea, Miron. 'Beckett's Involvement with Music', in Mary Bryden (ed.), *Samuel Beckett and Music* (Oxford: Clarendon Press, 1998), 183–5.

Henry, James. *Selected Poems of James Henry*, edited by Christopher Ricks (Dublin: Lilliput Press, 2002).

Kiberd, Declan. *Inventing Ireland: The Literature of the Modern Nation* (London: Jonathan Cape, 1995).

—. *The Irish Writer and the World* (Cambridge: Cambridge University Press, 2005).

Knowlson, James. *Damned to Fame: The Life of Samuel Beckett* (London: Bloomsbury, 1996).

MacDiarmid, Hugh. 'The Innumerable Christ', in Michael Grieve and W. R. Aitken (eds), *Complete Poems Volume I* (London: Penguin, 1985).

Petreu, Marta. *An Infamous Past: E. M. Cioran and the Rise of Fascism in Romania* (Chicago: Ivan R. Dee, 2005).

Pilling, John. *Samuel Beckett's More Pricks Than Kicks: In a Strait of Two Wills* (Continuum, 2011).

Wheatley, David. 'E. M. Cioran and the Art of Disgrace', *Dublin Review* 27 (2007), 25–36.

—. *A Nest on the Waves* (Loughcrew: The Gallery Press, 2010).

Yeats, W. B. *A Vision* (London: Macmillan, 1981).

—. *Collected Poems* (London: Macmillan, 1982).

3

En attendant Godot: A New Philosophical Landscape

David Addyman
University of Bergen

From the earliest accounts of his work, Beckett's turn to the theatre has been seen in terms of space, time and presence. Alain Robbe-Grillet, for example, famously wrote of *En attendant Godot* in 1953 that the characters' situation 'is summed up in this simple observation, beyond which it does not seem possible to advance: they are *there*, they are on the stage'.[1] A little later in the same essay, Robbe-Grillet writes that the characters are 'alone on stage, standing there, futile, without past or future, irremediably present'.[2] Richard N. Coe, writing in 1968, saw the shift in analogous terms:

> the spoken word approximates to the ever-renewed instantaneous present much more closely than does the written sentence; and if Beckett's novels are an attempt to 'discover a tense' in which past and future alike dissolve into the 'now', his plays resolve that problem by their very structure.[3]

In 1988 Steven Connor rejected Robbe-Grillet's understanding of presence, but claimed nevertheless that Beckett's drama was chiefly concerned with a deconstruction of presence. Most recently, David Pattie returned to these issues in 'Space, Time and the Self in Beckett's Late Theatre', writing, 'The characters are simply present. Vladimir and Estragon may not know precisely what happened yesterday, but they know that their present existence is confirmed, if only by the presence of each other'.[4] What none of these thinkers has examined, however, are the conceptions of space, time and presence with which Beckett was familiar at the time of composing *En attendant Godot* between October 1948 and January 1949. But with the publication of the second volume of letters, covering this period, a clearer sense of Beckett's thought on these matters can now be had. This essay aims to elaborate this thought, and to explore the extent to which it illuminates Beckett's shift to the theatre more generally, and *En attendant Godot* more specifically.

A few months either side of the composition of *En attendant Godot* Beckett expressed approval for a new understanding of space that had been developing in French intellectual circles throughout the 1930s and 1940s, and was to continue to do so through the 1950s and beyond. On 27 July 1948, just over two months before he started work on *Godot*, Beckett wrote to Duthuit, 'I feel so clearly what you say about space and the Italians'.[5] In *Three Dialogues*, on which Beckett was working in June 1949 (a few months after he informed MacGreevy that he was typing up *Godot*) he praised André Masson's 'so extremely intelligent comments on space'.[6] This is without doubt a reference to Masson's article, 'Divagations sur l'espace' [ramblings on space], published in the June 1949 edition of *Les temps modernes*, and quoted by Duthuit in the same (second) dialogue.[7] Duthuit is at the centre of this new notion of space, through his friendship with Masson and the philosophers Matthew Stewart Prichard and Maurice Merleau-Ponty, as well as through his family connections with Henri Matisse (his father-in-law). All of these were key figures in the 'turn to space'. The new understanding of space was radically at odds with the essentially geometric, Cartesian sense of space that Beckett would have found in any of what have come to be known as his 'canonical' sources – Leibniz, Kant and Schopenhauer, inter alia. Specifically, it is a conception of space which, unlike those just mentioned, includes time and presence, meaning that an examination of space will also elaborate the other two issues on which critics have focussed in their discussions of *Godot*, and will shed light on the treatment of these in the play.

An indication of what so interested Beckett in the summer of 1948 can be obtained from two works Duthuit published in 1949, with both of which Beckett had a close connection. The first of these is Duthuit's article 'Byzantine Space', which appeared in *Transition Forty-Nine* 5 (the same issue in which the *Three Dialogues* appeared), and which according to Beckett's biographer, James Knowlson, Beckett 'probably' translated.[8] The second is the much longer text, Duthuit's book-length study, *Les fauves*, on which Beckett certainly worked as translator, as Rémi Labrusse has shown.[9] *Les fauves* is informed by and explicitly refers to both the philosophy of Bergson, and to a lesser extent what was then cutting-edge work on space, Merleau-Ponty's chapter 'L'espace' in *Phenomenologie de la perception*, published just four years previously in 1945. Beckett is apparently comfortable enough with the concepts of these philosophers to translate them, though he did admit to Duthuit, 'Jamais vu un texte aussi difficile à traduire que le tien cette fois. Pour bien faire, il faudrait un an, en te consultant tous les deux jours'.[10] What is more, *Les fauves* is no short text: it totals approximately 60,000 words; 'Byzantine Space' adds another 9,000 words to that total. Just to put that in some kind of context, the much-discussed 'Philosophy Notes' amount to only a little more at 100,000 words.[11] At the very least, then, *Les fauves* is a significant addition to Beckett's library (after all, it can be stated with certainty that as translator he read every word of the text). But it is also significant for the light it sheds on the concerns of *Godot*.

One obvious objection is that Beckett did not begin work on the translation of *Les fauves* until autumn 1949, whereas *En attendant Godot* was written between 9 October 1948 and 29 January 1949 (but with typing up and revisions going on until at least March 1949 [see *Letters 2* 108 n.4 and 109]). But this objection does not stand up to closer examination. For one, Duthuit's thought was remarkably consistent, meaning that what he wrote in summer 1949 was a good reflection of what he had said to Beckett about space in summer 1948. Indeed, *Les fauves* was based on five articles that Duthuit had written for *Cahiers d'art* between 1929 and 1931, and although, as Labrusse points out, these were transformed 'de fond en comble' [from top to bottom] in the 1949 work, they also remained essentially true to Duthuit's earlier views.[12] In addition, *Les fauves* had probably been in gestation since spring 1948, when Robert Motherwell, editor at Wittenborn and Schultz (New York), invited Duthuit to contribute a volume on the fauves to 'The Documents of Modern Art' series, suggesting he base it on the five earlier pieces; a second request came in June 1948 from Wittenborn himself, a matter of weeks before Beckett's July letter.[13] So it might be expected that what Duthuit said to Beckett about space and the Italians at that time made its way into *Les fauves*. This is in fact the case: space and the Italians is precisely the subject of the work – and indeed of Duthuit's work as a whole. Yves Bonnefoy has pointed out that 'Georges Duthuit n'aura jamais eu des mots assez dure pour discréditer l'art italien' [for Georges Duthuit, there will never have been words harsh enough with which to discredit Italian art] (quoted in *Letters 2* 88 n.5). Duthuit's objection to Italian art is essentially an objection to its use of perspective to depict space (perspective being of course largely a Renaissance development), and his championing of the fauves stems from what he sees as their rejection of this mode of representing space.

Although the full title of the work – *Les fauves: Braque, Derain, van Dongen, Dufy, Friesz, Manguin, Marquet, Matisse, Puy, Vlaminck* – announces a concern with the whole fauvist movement, the book, like 'Byzantine Space', is chiefly interested in the work of Duthuit's father-in-law, Henri Matisse: he alone 'carried the ideas and intuitions of fauvism to their most extreme conclusions'; besides, Duthuit adds, 'it cannot be doubted that he was the initiator of the whole undertaking'.[14]

Duthuit writes of his earliest visits to Matisse's studio in the company of Prichard. Labrusse has shown that as a young man Duthuit became a follower of Prichard; indeed, he suggests that he was the Englishman's most faithful follower, and in *Les fauves* wrote the book that Prichard himself never could. Like Prichard, Duthuit made, as Labrusse puts it, 'de Byzance, de Bergson et de Matisse les pilliers intangibles à partir desquels s'est déployée sa vie' [of Byzantium, of Bergson and of Matisse the inviolable pillars from which he unfurled his life].[15] In Matisse's study the three – together with another philosopher of Prichard's circle, Camille Schuwer – developed a new conception of art, partly in response to 'the influence of the philosophy of time which had just been revealed to us – the universe has duration, that was a shock to us' (*FP* 9). There is a clear reference to Bergson here, made even more explicit in the French text, where the more easily recognizable term *durée* appears.[16] This is one of many occasions in *Les fauves* when the philosopher's terminology is employed; in addition, Bergson is also mentioned by name several times (the English index lists five instances, the French seven). Duthuit comments, 'on the whole, the two men [Matisse and Prichard] understood one another quite well, and [. . .] Matisse, like the English aesthetician [. . .] pursued in art directions more or less parallel to those which Bergson was then tracing in philosophy' (*FP* 2).

It is Bergsonian philosophy, then, that informs Duthuit's conception of space – the one that so excited Beckett in July 1948. And Duthuit is clear that this understanding of space is something new: 'we found ourselves, as far as space and painting were concerned, in a situation unprecedented since the sack of Constantinople by the Franks (1204)' (*FP* 1). The reference to the Byzantine capital indicates Duthuit's oft-repeated argument – found also in 'Byzantine Space' – that Western art had taken a wrong turn when the Byzantine empire was colonized and its aesthetic practice gradually subsumed under the Greco-Roman mimetic tradition. Duthuit sees Matisse's work as an attempt to recover the lost message of Byzantine art – more specifically, its conception of space – and a rejection of perspective is a key element this recovery.

Duthuit's charge against perspectival painting is that it makes painting 'static'; Matisse's work, by contrast, is like Byzantine architecture, 'dynamic'. At first sight, the argument seems ill-founded. *The Last Supper*, for example, by Leonardo, one of the artists Duthuit accuses of misrepresenting space, seems full of motion: many of the disciples are making agitated gestures and some have risen to their feet in response to Christ's announcement that one of them will soon betray him. But Duthuit's objection to Italian painting is explained with reference to the Bergsonian-Prichardian principles on which *Les fauves* rests.

Bergson holds that action or movement – and for him all life is movement – is indivisible. In order to illustrate this point he refers to what happens when we listen to a melody. He points out that we do not hear the individual notes of the tune one by one, but hear the melody as a whole, past, present and future, with the notes 'melting, so to speak, into one another'.[17] Bergson suggests that we hear the notes in one another – not simply as isolated, individual notes: 'their totality may be compared to a living being, whose parts, although distinct, permeate one another just because they are so closely connected' (*TFW* 100). As proof of this, Bergson offers the example of what happens when we hear a bum note: this affects a change in the whole experience of the tune. We realize that it has no relation to the tune as a whole: nothing to do with what has passed and nothing to do with what we expected to come next on the basis of what we have heard so far. Rather, the movements of a tune all flow into each other in 'mutual penetration' (*TFW* 101). And what is true for a tune is true for any other movement in life. Movement flows in a 'succession without distinction' (*TFW* 101); its moments are 'con-fused' – literally, fused together, fused with others. One could not get any sense of a tune simply by hearing one note; Bergson says that each note is *coloured* by its neighbours in the past and future (he uses the word 'tinged' [*teigner*]) – which will be significant in Duthuit's discussion of the operation of colour in Matisse's work.

Bergson's most famous example of pure indivisible fusion is of course *durée*: that is, action, movement, life experienced like a melody as a succession without distinction. When time is represented by clocks, this sense of pure fusion – and thus of things as they really are – is lost. Bergson called the attitude which views movement as succession rather than as mutual penetration 'spatialization', which he explains thus:

> we set our states of consciousness side by side in such a way as to perceive them simultaneously, no longer *in* one another, but *alongside* one another; in a word, we project time into space, we express duration in terms of extensity, and succession thus take the form of a continuous line or chain, the parts of which touch without penetrating each other. (*TFW* 101; emphasis added)

He explains further that 'we could not introduce *order* among terms without first distinguishing them and then comparing the places which they occupy; hence, we must perceive them as multiple, simultaneous and distinct' rather than as fused together. He goes on: 'in a word, we set them side by side', and we convert movement and interpenetration into simultaneity and separateness – which is to 'project them into space' (*TFW* 102).

Bergson's oeuvre-wide antipathy towards 'spatialization' – often reduced as in the last quotation simply to 'space' – has often been understood by commentators to be a hostility toward space per se. This does not seem to provide a firm basis on which Duthuit, Prichard and Schuwer – and indeed Beckett – might build a new understanding of space. In fact, though, Bergson's work demonstrates a keen sensitivity to real space and its difference from the geometrical conception of space which had dominated in philosophy from at least the time of Descartes – a difference analogous to that between real time or *durée* and clock time. Bergson did not simply see space as a metaphor to explain our conceptualization of time or movement as simultaneity; he was perhaps the first to see space itself as a movement, and to see that, like time or like a melody, space too could be 'spatialized' (i.e. misrepresented). Admittedly, this is not helped by his use of the same word 'space' to refer to both real space and spatialized space – that is, space conceived as interpenetrating movement, and space conceived as simultaneous, quantifiable succession. The confusion is apparent in the following passage:

> When, with our eyes shut, we run our hands along a surface, the rubbing of our fingers against the surface, and especially the varied play of our joints, provide a series of sensations, which differ only by their *qualities* and which exhibit a certain order in time. Moreover, experience teaches us that this series can be reversed, that we can, by effort of a different kind [. . .] obtain the same sensations over again in reverse order: relations of position in space might then be defined as reversible relations of succession in time. (*TFW* 100; emphasis in original)

Bergson immediately rejects this lesson of experience, saying it is a product of minds 'beset' (*TFW* 101) by a spatializing (i.e. conceptualizing, falsifying) attitude: by contrast, real space is experienced as an inseparable movement, like the notes of a tune. And like a melody, it cannot be reversed without creating a completely new movement. It is not clear if the word 'space' in the last sentence refers to real space, or its spatialized (and hence falsified) conception as simultaneity. Nevertheless, the hand clearly needs real space in which to move: a space in which the surface in question can exist and come into contact with the hand. Whether or not Bergson recognizes at the point of writing *Time and Free Will* how indebted his philosophy is to real space is moot. However, his next major work, *Matter and Memory*, as well as gradually settling on the terms 'concrete extension' or 'material extension' to refer to real space, is clear on the debt of action, movement and life to space, as the following passage shows:

> our present is the very materiality of our existence, that is to say, a system of sensations and movements and nothing else. And this system is determined, unique for each moment of duration, precisely because sensations and movements occupy places in space.[18]

The thesis here is astonishing: *duration is determined by places*. Duration needs somewhere to take place, and the distinctive character of each individual's *durée* – each individual's inner flux – is distinctive precisely because each individual is in a particular place, perceiving what only he can perceive.

For Bergson, then, places cannot be experienced in isolation; they must be experienced as part of the flow of life, part of *durée*, part of the 'melody' of life, *tinged* like notes in a melody, by other places. Duthuit calls this sense of space 'depth', blending it with Bergson's concept of 'material extension', as in the following passage: 'We live in material extension, it has *depth* and the masterpiece [i.e. a perspectival painting] has not, but represents an ideal world' (*FP* 7; emphasis added). Elsewhere he says that the problem for art, 'which is one of the oldest', is as follows: 'how to transfer three-dimensional space to a plane surface. And in so doing, to restore the requisite *depth*, which has been choked up and fragmented by the distinctions of analysis and everyday activity' (*FP* 4; emphasis added). Depth is best described as the sense of place that we get from living in it, not from any geometrical conception of it, such as that which is to be had from maps. Merleau-Ponty's *Phénoménologie de la perception*, whose chapter 'L'espace' begins with a discussion of the concept of depth, and is referred to in *Les fauves* (*FP* 84), speaks of geography as 'an abstract and derivative sign-language' in relation to 'the country-side in which we have learnt beforehand what a forest, a prairie or a river is'.[19] For him, we are not born with a sense of space already imprinted in our brains as Kant had held; there is no geometric grid pre-installed in our heads through which we experience the world. *Phenomenologie de la perception* argues that we gain a sense of space – up, down, beyond, near and far – as we move around in it, not *before* we do so; we know as we go, not before we go. Slowly, through a process that presumably involves much groping around and stumbling, and several false starts, we eventually 'graduate to a world' as Merleau-Ponty puts it.[20] Duthuit agrees, saying that it is in our coming to terms with real space that we carve out a sense of dimensions and geometry; real space comes first, geometry later (*FP* 7). Because of this necessity of experience to the constitution of depth, Merleau-Ponty refers to it as 'the most "existential" of all dimensions'. As such, it is an understanding of space that includes time. We do not simply experience the place that is in front of us, but hold on to past places as we make sense of our present situation, as we do in a melody. Past places 'colour' the present one, as notes colour adjacent notes in a melody, and the character of the place in which we find ourselves now is coloured by the places by which we came to it. Just as we hold the notes of a tune in mind, and have expectations of what is to come, we hold the 'melody' of a walk in mind. In our hometowns we have more 'depth' to our experience of places than when we are in other places: we 'see' around corners, behind buildings, over the rooftops (we might say that the 'tune' is more familiar). Sitting in Oxford, for example, I know that around the corner is another college, and not the Himalayas – but I know this only because I hold on to the past 'notes' in the 'melody' of space.

This brings me back to Duthuit's claim that classical, perspectival (to all intents and purposes, non-Matissian) painting is static: it assumes that a given place can be isolated from depth – that is, from the 'melody' of other places within which it appears. For him, classical painting assumes that movements in real space can be separated from one another without harm to the 'melody' of human experience – experience which is a 'succession without distinction', a 'mutual penetration'. This form of painting therefore 'spatializes' rather than evokes real space; it assumes that movement can be divided into movement and pauses, and each pause can be viewed on its own, isolated from the flow of action. Thus Duthuit describes the *Mona Lisa* as painted 'feature *after* feature' (*FP* 8), rather than as feature *fused with* feature. Viewed in terms of a melody, it is the same single note sounding for all time. The problem of painting then is to indicate the spatial melody within which each moment of life is situated – or emplaced. This is what is meant by 'the requisite *depth*', that 'most existential dimension', and without this, painting is lifeless. This is the key to Duthuit's antipathy towards Italian and other art.

Matisse achieves this sense of depth – to Duthuit's (initial) satisfaction – through the use of colour. This is where Bergson's word 'teigner' comes in. As the notes in a melody are 'tinged' by the notes which precede and follow them, and given a new tone, in Matisse's work colour tones tinge adjacent tones, a phenomenon known as 'simultaneous contrast' in the field of optics: the same pink square against a background now green, now violet, now orange will appear as a different tone every time. For Duthuit, awareness (and employment) of this effect allowed the early Matisse to 'leap the barbed wire' that had so long kept painters imprisoned in perspective. Rather than a lone, static 'note', the painting sounds a melody of tone in a 'succession without distinction', to use Bergson's phrase again. The canvas becomes a living entity in which the viewer must not look for the object represented, but experience the 'harmony' (Duthuit and Matisse use the word repeatedly) as colours 'tinge' one another as the viewer looks. Both the process of viewing and that of painting are thus active: Duthuit quotes Matisse speaking of having to repaint his canvas as he goes along, in response to the accumulated effect created by colours as they are added next to each other and affect each other in new ways, making the painting something in constant flow:

> This space is not limited – in the manner tacitly and more or less categorically admitted by the classics – by such and such an object placed in the foreground of a design. On the contrary, we cannot, without verging on the arbitrary, give a fixed beginning and ending to material scope. For it is pure continuity, above all continuity of colour [. . .] [Matisse's] work, apparently static, is, in reality, nothing but the embodiment of motion. [. . .] The reason being that depth is not feigned; that the picture really takes part in the play of solids and fluids, of colour and reflections. Each painted object has its own atmosphere, it is in the real depth.[21]

In this formulation, colour is not used in order to represent the object as it is in classical painting, but by analogy to suggest pure Bergsonian flow, or the 'melody' of depth.

However, a problem arises. If the character of each place is coloured by the places which led to it – by the route taken to it – then, as the anthropologist Tim Ingold points out, we must ask, 'where do these paths begin, and where do they end?'; likewise, 'if we see not at this moment in time, but over a certain period, how long is this period?'[22] Duthuit's answer would be that 'we cannot, without verging on the arbitrary, give a fixed beginning and ending to material scope': the period in question would seem to be the perceiver's entire life: when we encounter a place we are potentially in touch with all of our past life. From this point Matisse takes the *via positiva*, seeing awareness of this infinitely extended quality in place as leading to a truer, fuller sense of the self – a communion with a potentially infinite number of places from our past, and thus with ourselves. In 'Byzantine Space' Duthuit writes of Matisse that a 'direct, spontaneous fusion of the

I with the *NOT I* is sought – one so intimate that the painter ends by painting himself, by putting himself into the composition'.[23] In painting a scene – a place – he aims to paint the self. It is noteworthy that Duthuit goes no further than the phrase 'is sought'; indeed, in the closing pages of *Les fauves*, he worries that Matisse has become too spiritual, and talks too much about a union with the world through colour. Duthuit proclaims himself interested only in Matisse's early work, 'yesterday's stage, the humble stage of searching and doubt' and not in 'that of the zenith, of finding and certainty' (*FP* 87), adding on the penultimate page, 'At the outset my position with regard to Matisse was pretty well the reverse of what it has since become' (*FP* 99).

But if we backtrack to the descriptive part of Matisse's work, wherein space is endless and constantly in motion, and every object brings its own space with it, many parallels in Beckett's work become apparent. For one, this conception of space is echoed by Masson in 'Divagations sur l'espace' – the article of which Beckett approved; there, Masson speaks of 'a space become active, blossoming, ripening, disappearing. The opposite of "closed space"'.[24] But the idea of infinitely extended space also echoes Beckett's own description of a place in *Mercier and Camier* as 'unfinished, unfinishable'.[25] This is significant, for it demonstrates that Beckett did not acquire his sense of space from Duthuit, but that the latter perhaps helped him develop what was already there in embryonic form from his own reading of Bergson. Indeed, Beckett speaks of space and painting in similar terms to Duthuit as far back as the first of the so-called Cézanne letters, that of 8 September 1934. There, Beckett objected to what he called 'the *snapshot* puerilities of Manet and Cie'.[26] This is close to Duthuit's characterization of the depiction of moments divorced from depth in Renaissance painting as mere photography; that is, the instantaneous vision of a moment in isolation from duration, depth or melody.

Duthuit certainly considers Beckett's critical writings to be consistent with his own work. In the first few pages of *The Fauvist Painters*, he quotes 'the poet Samuel Beckett', specifically his article 'La peinture des van Velde ou le monde et le pantalon' (written in early 1945), saying, 'Beckett reminds us that creative time has nothing to do with the time of "that stop-watch painting"' (*FP* 6).[27] This reference to measuring time clearly evokes Bergson's distinction between clock (spatialized) time and lived time (*durée*), and suggests, as Duthuit does in *Les fauves*, that classical painting is static. Crucially, just as Bergson sees *durée* – the internal flux of consciousness – as deriving its unique character from places, Beckett explicitly related self to space in the letter to Duthuit of 11 August 1948, a few months before he began *Waiting for Godot*:

> One may just as well dare to be plain and say that not knowing is not only not knowing what one is, but also where one is, and what change to wait for, and how to get out of wherever one is, and how to know, when it seems as if something is moving, which apparently was not moving before, what it is that is moving, that was not moving before, and so on. (*Letters 2* 98)

Here the self and place are explicitly linked. But the self is also defined by the ability to go on (getting out of wherever one is) – that is, continuing to be oneself is predicated upon the sense that one has of one's current location. Given that such information could only come from the past – where one is is where one has come from – the letter suggests that a sense of self, as in Duthuit's work (and Bergson's and Merleau-Ponty's), is created when one can grasp the 'notes' in the melody of one's movements through space; in other words, self is predicated on depth. But it is here that the crucial difference between Beckett's and Matisse's, and to a lesser but still significant extent Duthuit's, work opens. We would expect Beckett to object even more strongly to Matisse's mysticism than does Duthuit.

And *The Fauvist Painters* seems to contain a suggestion of this. The closing pages contain a long dialogue with the non-existent 'Finnish impressionist' Folevilius, whose scepticism as to the possibility of achieving communion with space is what we would expect of Beckett. In these passages Duthuit plays a similar role to the one he plays in *Three Dialogues*, while 'Folevilius' argues the possibility of art out of existence – or at least the possibility of describing it, an objection that Beckett expressed in a letter to Duthuit: 'I have been reading too about painting, with your notes, but I have not been able to add anything. I think it is the descriptive side that paralysed me, or rather that did not unparalyse me' (*Letters 2* 123).

Beckett's *via negativa* sees the bound-up nature of space and self as leading to a situation in which it is impossible to ever actually be anywhere: how can we ever say where we are when every place exists joined in a 'melody' with an infinite number of other places? And if place is so central to self, how can we ever say who we are when we have lost our life in places that we have left behind, that we perhaps cannot even get back to? Beckett acknowledges depth – it is what makes existence a predicament, but also what makes art impossible – but as something ungraspable. Contrast this with Matisse, for whom depth is attainable and representable. For Beckett, depth is merely as a condition of being. For one, the *via positiva*: recovery of the self through a mystical communion with the totality of the universe; for the other, the *via negativa*, dissolution of the self through displacement.

This brings me to *En attendant Godot*. Estragon and Vladimir consistently fail to grasp the totality of the action in which they are situated, losing track of conversations (*CDW* 21, 24), while Pozzo likewise loses track of his possessions (*CDW* 34, 40, 45). But often this failure to grasp the 'melody' of action is explicitly linked to space – to what Duthuit would call depth – and to the inability to grasp it. Act Two, for example, sees Vladimir and Estragon trying to establish a link between the place in which they currently find themselves, and places they occupied at earlier stages in their lives. While Vladimir seems convinced that he is in the same place as the day before (i.e. in Act One) ('There I am again', *CDW*, 55), Estragon is less sure; Vladimir tries to convince him, leading to the following exchange:

Estragon	And all that was yesterday, you say?
Vladimir	Yes, of course it was yesterday.
Estragon	And here where we are now?
Vladimir	Where else do you think? Do you not recognize the place?
Estragon	(*Suddenly furious*) Recognize! What is there to recognize? All my lousy life I've crawled about in the mud! And you talk to me about scenery! (*Looking wildly about him.*) Look at this muckheap! I've never stirred from it! (*CDW* 57)

Estragon's troubles are compounded by the fact that he is unable to link his present place not just with the place of the day before, but with any other places from his past. He is, for example, unable to say if he was ever in the Macon country:

Vladimir	All the same, you can't tell me that this (*Gesture*) bears any resemblance to ... (*He hesitates*) ... to the Macon country, for example. You can't deny there's a big difference.
Estragon	The Macon country! Who's talking to you about the Macon country?
Vladimir	But you were there yourself, in the Macon country.
Estragon	No, I was never in the Macon country. I've puked my puke of a life away here, I tell you! Here! In the Cackon country! (*CDW* 57)

Estragon, if not Vladimir, is unable to bring places into a 'melody', and must experience them in isolation, punctually and locally. He is not up to the Matissian task of communing with the 'NOT I' in order to create the 'I'. The pair are emplaced – and Robbe-Grillet is right here – but displaced at the same time; however, the paradox is necessary: it is only in place that displacement can be experienced; otherwise, there would be no experience. The world which is so depth-ful is beyond the means of Estragon; he cannot 'graduate to a world'. All they can ever do in such conditions, as Estragon says, is give themselves 'the impression [they] really exist' (*CDW* 64). As in Beckett's letter of 11 August 1948, the sense of self is predicated on the sense of place. As in the letter, the emphasis in *Godot* is on *not* knowing, whether who one is or where one is.

But the play also simultaneously offers and withholds another type of depth, the imitation depth of perspectival painting. The set itself makes no attempt to represent the 'endroit' in which the action is supposed to take place. Robbe-Grillet described an early production thus:

> The set represents nothing, or just about. A road? Let's say, in a more general way: *outdoors*. The only notable detail consists of a tree, sickly, scarcely more than a bush, and without a single leaf; let's say, a skeleton of a bush.[28]

The fact that there is backdrop to speak of disallows the false depth of perspective. Indeed, Beckett complained about the set of the first London production, likening it – significantly – to the (perspectival) painting of Salvator Rosa.[29] But in a sensitive production of *Godot* the flatness and lack of realism in the backdrop is stressed. In such productions, the only suggestion of a backdrop is the large painted moon. *Godot* withholds imitation (perspectival) depth, in the same way that a painting by Cézanne or indeed by Matisse does. It is surely significant that in the letter of 28 October 1948, when he was three weeks into the composition of *Godot*, Beckett thanked Duthuit for helping him resolve a problem in the setting for the play – and specifically with the representation of the set:

> It did me good to talk to you about my play, in my stammering way. I have really taken in what you said about stage props. It will help me, it has already helped me. I see them as having a larger-then-life iniquity, in the derisory shade of a tree you could not even hang yourself on. (*Letters 2* 108)

Duthuit's ideas on depth and space in painting, then, seem to have fed into the action, dialogue and set of *Godot*. But Duthuit's writings function less as influence, more as an indication of what was at stake for Beckett in space, and as a way of expanding some of his earlier comments on this subject – all the time bearing in mind the manner in which Beckett's *via negativa* veers away from Matisse's and Duthuit's understanding of space. The insight into Beckett's thought on space provided by Duthuit's texts could also lead to new readings of the other works written during the 'frenzy in the room', when these issues were uppermost in Beckett's concerns, but it could also be read backwards into the fiction written around the time when Beckett began to see space and landscape painting apparently in Bergsonian terms – the works written from the time of the 'Cézanne letters', through 'La peinture des van Velde ou le monde et le pantalon', and beyond. This seems to suggest a new philosophical landscape: Bergson's concept of space positions itself explicitly against Kant's (and therefore implicitly against Schopenhauer), raising questions as to the suitability of the latter 'canonical' thinker's perspective to come to terms with Beckett's thought on space. But the helplessness that Vladimir and Estragon experience before space also suggests another dimension to Beckett's rejection of post-war French humanism analysed so brilliantly by Andrew Gibson.[30] After all, in a world which has just fought a bloody war over territory – that is, over space (is it significant that Pozzo, often likened to a concentration-camp guard, claims to command space?) – a little pessimism towards the possibility of gaining space might not go amiss.

Notes

1. Alain Robbe-Grillet, *For a New Novel*, translated by Richard Howard (Evanston, Illinois: Northwestern University Press, 1996), 115; italics in original.
2. Ibid., 121.
3. Richard N. Coe, *Beckett* (Edinburgh and London: Oliver and Boyd, 1968), 88.
4. David Pattie, 'Space, Time and the Self in Beckett's Late Theatre', *Modern Drama* 43 (Fall 2000), 393–403 at 394.
5. Samuel Beckett, *The Letters of Samuel Beckett. Volume 2: 1941–1956*, edited by George Craig, Martha Dow Fehsenfeld, Dan Gunn and Lois More Overbeck (Cambridge: Cambridge University Press, 2011), 86. Subsequent references made parenthetically as *Letters 2*.
6. SB to TM, 27 March 1949, in *Letters 2*, 146; see also 167–70; Samuel Beckett, *Proust and Three Dialogues with Georges Duthuit* (London: John Calder, 1999), 112.
7. I am grateful to Professor David Lomas (University of Manchester) for drawing my attention to the article by Masson. Duthuit cites, 'inner emptiness, the prime condition, according to Chinese esthetics, of the act of painting' (*Proust*, 109); see Masson, 961.
8. James Knowlson, *Damned to Fame: The Life of Samuel Beckett* (London: Bloomsbury, 1996), 369 and 775, n.58.
9. See Rémi Labrusse, 'Note sur l'histoire du texte et sur la présente édition', in Georges Duthuit, *Les fauves: Braque, Derain, van Dongen, Dufy, Friesz, Manguin, Marquet, Matisse, Puy, Vlaminck*, edited with an introduction and notes by Rémi Labrusse (Paris: Editions Michalon, 2006).
10. Quoted in ibid., xxxiii.
11. For an account of these see David Addyman and Matthew Feldman, 'Samuel Beckett, Wilhelm Windelband, and the Interwar "Philosophy Notes"', *Modernism/Modernity*, Samuel Beckett: Out of the Archive.

Edited by Peter Fifield, Bryan Radley and Lawrence Rainey 18.4 (November 2011), 755-71.
12 Ibid., vii. See also Georges Duthuit, 'Le fauvisme', *Cahiers d'art*, 1929, numéro 5, 177-92; numéro 6, 258-68; numéro 10, 429-34; 1930 numéro 3, 129-35; 1931, numéro 2, 78-82. These are reprinted in Georges Duthuit, *Représentation et présence. Premiers écrits et travaux 1923-1952*, edited by Yves Bonnefroy (Paris: Flammarion, 1974), 195-231.
13 Ibid., xxvii.
14 Georges Duthuit, *The Fauvist Painters*, translated by Ralph Manheim (New York: Wittenborn and Schultz,1950), 2. Subsequent references made parenthetically as *FP*.
15 Labrusse, 'Introduction', *Les fauves*, xi.
16 *Les fauves*, 26.
17 Henri Bergson. *Time and Free Will: An Essay on the Immediate Data of Consciousness*, translated by F. L. Pogson (Mineola: Dover Publications, 2001), 100. Subsequent references made parenthetically as *TFW*.
18 Henri Bergson, *Matter and Memory*, translated by N. M. Paul and W. S. Palmer (New York: Zone Books, 2005), 139.
19 Maurice Merleau-Ponty, *Phenomenology of Perception*, translated by Colin Smith (London: Routledge, 2002), x.
20 Ibid., 298.
21 Georges Duthuit, 'Byzantine Space', *Transition Forty-Nine* 5 (December 1949), 20-37 at 33-4.
22 Tim Ingold, *The Perception of the Environment: Essays in Livelihood, Dwelling and Skill* (London: Routledge, 2000), 227.
23 Duthuit, 'Byzantine Space', 34.
24 André Masson, 'Divagations sur l'espace', *Les Temps modernes* 44 (1949), 961-72 at 961; my translation (the original reads: 'Un espace devenu actif, fleurissant, mûrissant, s'évanouissant. Le contraire de «l'espace-limite»').
25 Samuel Beckett, *Mercier and Camier*, edited by Seán Kennedy (London: Faber and Faber, 2010), 62.
26 Samuel Beckett, *The Letters of Samuel Beckett. Volume 1: 1929-1940*, edited by Martha Dow Fehsenfeld and Lois More Overbeck (Cambridge: Cambridge University Press, 2009), 223.

27 The dating is Knowlson's. See Knowlson, 357 and 772 n.4.
28 Robbe Grillet, *For a New Novel*, 112.
29 See Knowlson, 417.
30 Andrew Gibson, *Samuel Beckett: A Critical Life* (London: Reaktion, 2009).

Works cited

Addyman, David and Matthew Feldman. 'Samuel Beckett, Wilhelm Windelband, and the Interwar "Philosophy Notes"', *Modernism/Modernity* Samuel Beckett: Out of the Archive. Edited by Peter Fifield, Bryan Radley and Lawrence Rainey 18.4 (November 2011), 755–71.

Beckett, Samuel. *The Complete Dramatic Works* (London: Faber and Faber, 1990).

—. *Proust and Three Dialogues with Georges Duthuit* (London: John Calder, 1999).

—. *The Letters of Samuel Beckett. Volume 1: 1929–1940*, edited by Martha Dow Fehsenfeld and Lois More Overbeck (Cambridge: Cambridge University Press, 2009).

—. *Mercier and Camier*, edited by Seán Kennedy (London: Faber and Faber, 2010), 62.

—. *The Letters of Samuel Beckett. Volume 2: 1941–1956*, edited by George Craig, Martha Dow Fehsenfeld, Dan Gunn and Lois More Overbeck (Cambridge: Cambridge University Press, 2011).

Bergson, Henri. *Time and Free Will: An Essay on the Immediate Data of Consciousness*, translated by F. L. Pogson (Mineola: Dover Publications, 2001).

—. *Matter and Memory*, translated by N. M. Paul and W. S. Palmer (New York: Zone Books, 2005).

Coe, Richard N. *Beckett* (Edinburgh and London: Oliver and Boyd, 1968).

Duthuit, Georges. 'Le fauvisme', *Cahiers d'art*, 1929, numéro 5, 177–92; numéro 6, 258–68; numéro 10, 429–34; 1930 numéro 3, 129–35; 1931, numéro 2, 78–82.

—. 'Byzantine Space', *Transition Forty-Nine* 5 (December 1949), 20–37.

—. *The Fauvist Painters*, translated by Ralph Manheim (New York: Wittenborn and Schultz,1950).

—. *Représentation et présence. Premiers écrits et travaux 1923–1952*, edited by Yves Bonnefroy (Paris: Flammarion, 1974), 195–231.

—. *Les fauves: Braque, Derain, van Dongen, Dufy, Friesz, Manguin, Marquet, Matisse, Puy, Vlaminck*, edited with an introduction and notes by Rémi Labrusse (Paris: Editions Michalon, 2006).

Gibson, Andrew. *Samuel Beckett: A Critical Life* (London: Reaktion, 2009).

Guerlac, Suzanne. *Thinking in Time: An Introduction to Henri Bergson* (Ithaca: Cornell University Press, 2006).

Ingold, Tim. *The Perception of the Environment: Essays in Livelihood, Dwelling and Skill* (London: Routledge, 2000).

Knowlson, James. *Damned to Fame: The Life of Samuel Beckett* (London: Bloomsbury, 1996).

Masson, André. 'Divagations sur l'espace', *Les Temps modernes* 44 (1949), 961–72.

Merleau-Ponty, Maurice. *Phenomenologie de la perception* (Paris: Gallimard, 1945).

—. *Phenomenology of Perception*, translated by Colin Smith (London: Routledge, 2002).

Robbe-Grillet, Alain. *For a New Novel*, translated by Richard Howard (Evanston, Illinois: Northwestern University Press, 1996).

Worth, Katherine. *Samuel Beckett's Theatre: Life Journeys* (Oxford: Clarendon Press, 2001).

4

Samuel Beckett: The Geometry of the Imagination

Chris Ackerley
University of Otago

'Du siehst, mein Sohn, zum Raum wird hier die Zeit'.
– Wagner, *Parsifal*, Act I.

Towards the end of Act I of Wagner's *Parsifal*, the faithful Gurnemanz invites the 'pure fool', Parsifal, to witness the ceremony of the Holy Grail. Here, the woods disappear, and a gateway opens through the rocky walls, revealing the mighty hall of the Grail Castle. There, Parsifal sees the Grail ceremony, but, failing to understand it, is thrust from the scene, to wander in the wilderness for many years, before returning to cure the wounded king. In one sense, the episode comprises a narrative frame enclosing a lengthy ritual; in another, it represents a single impression, a unified image, where time abates and narrative yields to spatial form: 'You see, my son, here time becomes place'. This Wagnerian moment lasts (by mundane count) some 40 minutes, but its aesthetic effect is that of a single stasis, duration translated into extension.

Beckett professed a profound dislike of Wagner's music, as antithetical to his impulse towards impotence and simplicity. In *Dream of Fair to middling Women*, a reluctant Belacqua accompanies the cultivated Liebert (whose original, Georges Pelorson, was a passionate Wagnerite) to *Die Walküre*, but Liebert is turned away because his fashionable plus fours are deemed unacceptable, whereas Belacqua's shabby attire (which he offers to exchange with the mortified aesthete) passes muster.[1] Earlier, returning from the *Schule Dunklebrau* outside Vienna (the *Hellerau* now redolent of dark beer), Belacqua gazes at the starfield, his head cocked up uncomfortably, 'like Mr Ruskin in the Sistine', looking for Vega. The Ruskin touch derives from that aesthete's description of Michelangelo's ceiling in 'Of Imaginative Penetration', in his *Modern Painters*;[2] Beckett added it to his manuscript later, perhaps to accentuate the mockery of Kant's celebrated praise of the starry heavens above. Compare, too, O'Casey's paycock, Jack Boyle, fixed in his fantasy to the wheel with a marlinspike: 'I often looked up at the sky an' assed meself the question – *what is the stars, what is the stars?*'

> The night firmament is abstract density of music, symphony without end, illumination without end, yet emptier, more sparsely lit, than the most succinct constellations of genius. Now seen merely, a depthless lining of hemisphere, its crazy stippling of stars, it is the passional movements of the mind charted in light and darkness. The tense passional intelligence, when arithmetic abates, tunnels, sky-mole, surely and blindly (if only we thought) through the interstellar coalsacks of its firmament in genesis, it twists through the stars of its creation in a network of loci that shall never be co-ordinate. The inviolable criterion of poetry and music, the non-principle of their punctuation, is figured in the demented performance of the night colander. The ecstatic mind, the mind achieving creation, take ours for example, rises to the shaftheads of its statement, its recondite relations of emergal, from a labour and a weariness of deep castings that brook no schema. The mind suddenly entombed, then active in an anger and a rhapsody of energy, in a scurrying and plunging towards exitus, such is the ultimate mode and factor of the creative integrity, its proton, incommunicable; but there, insistent, invisible rat, fidgeting behind the astral incoherence of the art surface. That was the circular movement of the mind flowering up and up through darkness to an apex, dear to Dionysius the Aeropagite, beside which all other modes, all the polite obliquities, are the clockwork of rond-de-cuirdom. (*Dream* 16–17)

This critiques Schopenhauer's sense of music as a direct manifestation of the Will. Beckett had already noted in *Proust* that for Schopenhauer music is the Idea itself, 'unaware of the world of phenomena, existing ideally outside the universe, apprehended not in Space but in Time only';[3] he concludes that for Proust music is 'the cataclytic element'.[4] Here, he indicates that music is not (as Schopenhauer contends) an escape from the suffering of willing, because the aesthetic pleasure that a spectator of the world experiences as representation, when consciousness is fully engaged, *is impossible for Belacqua*, who invokes the firmament as 'abstract density of music', but also the 'passional intelligence' of the perceiving subject. This phrase derives from Julien Benda's study of Bergson, referred to by Beckett in his Trinity College lectures.[5] Bergson's *durée* shares with Schopenhauer's Will a sense of the unbroken continuum; this is challenged by Proust's paradigm of involuntary memory, which isolates (and thus spatializes) a moment of time.

Pilling overlooks a key phrase in Belacqua's rhapsody: 'when arithmetic abates'. This may be crudely paraphrased as 'when time stops', as in Schopenhauer's *exercitium arithmeticae occultum nescientis se numerare animi*, his disagreement with Leibniz's view of music as 'an unconscious exercise in arithmetic in which the mind does not know it is counting.'[6] Beckett concludes that Schopenhauer 'rejects the Leibnitzian view of music as "occult arithmetic"';[7] the distinction, older than Plato, is between arithmetic as that which unfolds in time, and geometry, the ground of which is extension, or existence in space. In the medieval Quadrivium, arithmetic is associated with music and geometry with astronomy, the first pairing engaged with time and the second with space. Here, all four components of the Quadrivium are conspicuously present, to critique the kind of narrative with which Beckett is engaged and intimate why Belacqua is unsuited for the musical and/or narrative role he might have played. It is not (as Schopenhauer might assume) that the subject is an impure being who, unable to apprehend the *Ding-an-Sich*, incarnates his representations into inappropriate paradigms; but rather that the nature of Belacqua's mind disqualifies him as a Schopenhauerean subject, however much he, or Beckett, might agree with the philosopher's opening gambit, the principle of 'no object without a subject' that affirms the paradox of a phenomenal world, the existence of which is entirely dependent upon the individual's perceiving eye (*WWI* I §7 38).

Were Belacqua, to adopt the musical idiom of *Dream*, a *liù*, or *liù-liù* minded, he could be part of a little book that would be purely melodic: 'a lovely Pythagorean chain-chant solo of cause and effect' (*Dream* 10). Schopenhauer (*WWI* III §52 344) compares musical notes to actors, but the Pythagorean image derives from Burnet's *Greek Philosophy*,[8] on page 45 of which 'APMONIA' appears. Like the enigmatic Nemo, 'our principle boy' refuses to be condensed into a *liù*; he remains a 'regrettable simultaneity of notes' (*Dream* 11). Even 'when arithmetic abates', as in the night firmament above, the consequence is not (as in *Parsifal*) an aesthetic stasis of duration translated into extension but rather a turmoil that first seeks expression in geometry, in a conceit of 'astral incoherence': Bergson's passional intelligence as a *skymole*, tunnelling through interstellar coalsacks and stars in a 'network of loci that shall never be co-ordinate'. That is, the arithmetical, even when counting ceases, cannot find expression in such spatial form as the Cartesian analytical (co-ordinate) geometry, which might transform it into graphic form.

Before extension of this *topos*, a regrettable simultancity of metaphors must be quashed. These include the mind 'entombed', then active in anger and a 'rhapsody of energy' (a *rhapsody* is a musical cloak cut from other pieces), scurrying and plunging towards 'exitus'. This word derives from Thomas à Kempis, his *Laetus exitus tristus* theme, that a merry outgoing brings forth a sad homecoming,[9] intimating a narrative structure of coming and going that Beckett often used. The 'proton', that positive core of the atom around which the negative electron scurries, anticipates the nucleus of *The Unnamable*. As for Schopenhauer's argument that 'geometry must be translated into arithmetic if it is to be communicable' (*WWI* I §12 70): *incommunicable* might define the aesthetic stasis of time (arithmetic) translated into space (geometry), here unsuccessfully. Hence, the metaphysical image of the 'invisible rat', which is manifest in physical form later in *Dream* and in *Murphy*.[10]

The final image seeks to reconcile the others, by invoking St Bonaventura's *apex mentis*,[11] the doctrine of the spark within the mind consubstantial with the uncreated ground of the Deity. Dionysius the Areopagite was a follower of Paul,[12] of whom little is known, save that a Syrian monk attached his name in pious fraud, 400 years later, to theological tracts synthesizing Christian, Greek, Jewish and Oriental thought. His, Inge suggests,[13] is the sense of life ascending from its lower forms unto the divine by circular movement of the mind. Beckett 'clarifies' this mystical doctrine by another, also from Inge,[14] that of the 'Fünkelein', Meister Eckhart's 'little spark' at the *apex mentis*, the 'organ by which the personality communicates with God'. This synthesis is doomed, partly because that 'organ' must contend inside the physical body with the conarium of Descartes, but also because Belacqua, in defining the mysterious effect, misses 'our' point: that beauty, finally, is not subject to categories but must be 'transelemented' (Inge says *transelementated*)[15] into the one category furnished by those of the individual (*Dream* 35). Accordingly, the mystical Fünkelein offers no *exitus* to Schopenhauer's first premise concerning the dichotomy of subject and object: 'The world is my idea' (*WWI* I §1 3), or its restatement: 'All that in any way belongs or can belong to the world is inevitably thus conditioned through the subject, and exists only for the subject'.[16] This condition, tested and qualified, returns as the irrefragable doctrine of the self as 'sole elect'.[17]

Belacqua's mind does not comprise the traditional binary oppositions of Being and Not-Being, Body and Mind, but is tripartite.

In a 'distillation of Euclid' (*Dream* 120), it is 'trine': centripetal, centrifugal, and . . . not. Trine. The Grove *Companion* considers the consequences:

> His third being is the dark gulf, the glare of will and hammer strokes of the brain expunged; the wombtomb alive with the unanxious spirits of quiet cerebration; its center everywhere and periphery nowhere; an unsurveyed marsh of sloth. There is no authority for supposing this to be the real Belacqua, but emancipation from identity suits his complexion. He is sorry it does not happen more often. If he were free he would take up residence there. But in vain: it is impossible to switch off the inward glare. Which explains why his temper is bad and his complexion saturnine: 'He remembers the pleasant gracious bountiful tunnel, and cannot get back'. Here, in the embryo of *Dream*, is the larval stage of Murphy's mind.[18]

This anticipates much of Murphy's mind: his wish to descend into the dark centre; that dark centre as mystical experience, God an infinite sphere whose centre is everywhere and circumference nowhere (unlike Miss Counihan's bust; *Murphy* 19); a Kantian manifold (to drain the marsh of sloth); and a retreat to the womb. Belacqua's inability to switch off the inward glare prefigures Murphy's 'Cartesian catastrophe': Murphy discovers in his encounter with Mr Endon that he cannot achieve the dark centre and perceive himself so doing – tragedy arises because he cannot apperceive his own irrationality, so discovers, to his chagrin, that he is fundamentally sane. Belacqua's dark gulf lacks three essential qualities that structure Murphy's mind: the Geulincxian paradox of inner freedom from contingencies of the contingent world, though intimated, is not explicit, as soon it would be; Belacqua's mind lacks Murphy's geometrical zoning; and, crucially, it does not represent itself as Leibniz's monad. Instead, Belacqua is a 'cubic unknown', which implies, first, that the analytic geometry cannot depict him in graphic form until his roots are known; and, further, that he is only '*At his simplest trine*' not to be satisfied by three values, nor 50, nor any number. He may be a succession of terms, but these cannot be defined: 'They tail off vaguely at both ends and the intervals of their series are demented' (*Dream* 124); he may be described, but not circumscribed; his terms may be stated, but not summed (*Dream* 125). Murphy's dark centre, similarly, is a 'matrix of surds' (*Murphy* 70), a womb of irrationality; but that matrix is structured. *Murphy*'s narrative is rigorous, whereas the 'involuntary unity' of *Dream* (132) offers insufficient compensation for its lack of fixed centre and authorial will-lessness (whereas the involuntary memory of Proust's vast edifice is closely controlled). Beckett's embryonic impulses are quickened in *Dream*, but not until *Murphy* are they *emergal*, and only in *The Unnamable* are they fully formed.

I shall return to this, after clarifying some basic mathematical paradoxes that, reduced to fundamental sounds, or simple axioms, indicate Euclidean elements of Beckett's thought. First, a translation of arithmetic into geometry, or (as Schopenhauer prefers) geometry into arithmetic:

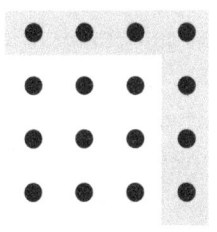

• • • •
• • • •
• • • •
• • • •

As Burnet notes, sums of the series of successive odd numbers {1, 3, 5, 7...} are called 'square numbers' and may be depicted thus.[19] Beginning at an *origin*, and begging for the moment the question of whether that point has dimension, successive odd numbers can be added as *gnomons* (shapes like a carpenter's square, as the shaded area above), the result always a square. Thus, a square of unit x in length has an area of unit x^2. This may be depicted geometrically, or as a graph, or translated into an arithmetical series {1, 4, 9, 16 ...}, or given algebraic expression: $x^2 = (x - 1)^2 + (x - 1) + x$. Thus time turns into space, space into time. Though a far cry from *Parsifal*, or the scholastic subtlety of Stephen Dedalus in 'Proteus', his 'ineluctable modality of the visible' (*nebeneinander*) and 'ineluctable modality of the audible' (*nacheinander*), the principles are not unrelated.

Burnet offers another sequence:[20]

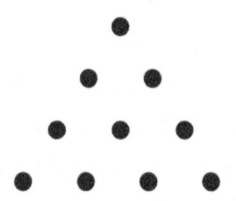

•

• •

• • •

• • • •

This is the *tetraktys*, considered by the Pythagoreans an emblem of perfection, an equilateral triangle containing the mystical numbers, in a series {1, 2, 3, 4} totalling 10. Again, this could be represented as the arithmetical sum of its successive stages: {1, 3, 6, 10, 15 ...}. Neary praises Miss Dwyer as a 'closed figure in the waste without form, and void! My tetrakyt!' (*Murphy* 5); his error intimates another closed figure, the kite, a Cartesian emblem of the mind strung precariously to its body.

Familiar to all is the geometrical proof of the Pythagorean theorem, whereby the universal algebra of $a^2 = b^2 + c^2$ is applied to a right-angled triangle with legs of unit 3 and 4 extending from an origin, and a hypotenuse of unit 5; if squares of 9 and 16 extend from two legs, the area they enclose equals the 25 of the hypotenuse. Such harmonic resolution encourages images of God or demiurges yielding what Beckett in *Proust* calls 'the sacred ruler and compass of literary geometry',[21] creating spatial order from chaos by geometrical extension. Yet consider the implications of the simplest of such figures, with legs of unit 1, these (perhaps) of no breadth extending from a point of no dimension. When a hypotenuse is drawn to connect their extremities, the outcome is (to use Beckett's phrase) the creation of 'closed place', a figure defined against the void. However, the length of that hypotenuse is √2, which is not rational (expressible as the ratio of two integers). To reveal this incommensurabilty of side and diagonal, as did Hippasos,[22] is to invite the wrath of the Pythagorean brotherhood, for rational numbers thus revealed are but an infinitesimal subset of all possible numbers, and the rational foundations of computation an entropic oasis in the vast waste of the 'incoherent continuum' (*Dream* 102). These terrifying matters find expression within the picture of Murphy's mind.

Murphy is a geometrical novel: it features kite-flying at the Round Pond; it notes the construction of the regular dodecahedron, traditionally the largest regular figure encompassed within a sphere (*Murphy* 32); Christ and the two thieves are defined as vertices of a triangle through which the perfect circle of God must pass; and Wylie insists that 'Our medians . . . meet in Murphy' (*Murphy* 127), that is, at the centre of an inscribed circle, which intimates that they (Neary, Wylie, Miss Counihan) want to enclose Murphy within the triangle of their lives.[23] Yet *Murphy* has arithmetical elements, such as the protagonist's irrational heart (*Murphy* 4), a condition of 'cardiac calculus'.[24] His consumption of biscuits in Hyde Park obeys the laws of permutation (or would, could he but overcome his infatuation with the ginger). The narrative observes the strictures of space and time in the Big World (London and Dublin, 1935), most dementedly in chapter 7 when Miss Counihan, avid to find Murphy, must delay her visit to the Great Wen to accommodate a 'fitting', less a new outfit than conformity to what Beckett later calls 'the frigid machinery of a time-space relationship'.[25]

Watt, conversely, is ostentatiously arithmetical, its narrative concerned with comings and goings, including those of a long line of servants who circle the still point of Mr Knott. The novel is dominated by seriality, or coincidence in time and place of independent systems that operate periodically in a given universe; and by permutations whose logical options enact an arithmetical comedy of exhaustion (in the manuscripts, often in greater detail). Yet *Watt* has its geometrical elements, as when Watt contemplates an 'object of note'[26] (the pun intentional), the picture in Erskine's room depicting a broken circle and point, each in ambiguous relationship to the other, 'in boundless space ... in endless time'. This phrasing derives from Schopenhauer, looking 'at once at objects which lie at unequal distances behind each other' (*WWI* I §4, 11, 15).

One intriguing sequence is the Frog Song,[27] which illustrates the machinery of transcendence (and of pre-established harmony). The structuring design is a Fibonacci sequence, with three frogs, Krek, Krick and Krock, croaking respectively at intervals of 3, 5 and 8. As they start in unison, there will be precisely 120 intervals (3 × 5 × 8) before the independent series again coincide. Musical notation renders this graphically, the final moment of coincidence constituting a chord, or instance of spatialization (a regrettable simultaneity of notes, as the narrator of *Dream* might say), insofar as the moment of synchronicity can be isolated by the perceiving mind from the musical (or arithmetical) sequence, suspended from time, and endowed with significance.

To clarify this point: long ago, in Toronto, I took my three-year old son to the zoo (on *exitus* he got excited because he saw a dog, but that is another story). In the wallow were three hippos: Daddy Hippo, who surfaced at intervals of (let us assume) 8; Mummy Hippo, who did so at intervals of 5; and Baby Hippo, who bobbed up at intervals of 3. Would there be a transcendent moment, when all three surfaced simultaneously? We waited partiently, but not in vain, for the aesthetic stasis finally occurred, all three ascending together. In that sunlit moment, I thought of the Frog Song, and of Eliot's 'The Hippopotamus'. The danger, of course, is to attribute significance to a synchronic moment that is the inevitable fulfilment of arithmetical periodicity. Yet that moment was isolated in my awareness from the continuum of time, and endowed with meaning. To return to the Frog Song: Beckett clearly acknowledges the *experience* of the transcendent moment, but (unlike Proust, or Joyce, or Virginia Woolf) refuses to endow it with value. Any other moment might equally have been chosen, but for reasons presumably relating to the neurological or psychological *conaria* of perception, some moments are more equal than others.

Ferdinand de Saussure differentiated the diachronic from the synchronic by means of chess (compare Murphy's encounter with Mr Endon). Chess may be considered *diachronically*, as beginning with White's first move (the primary cause of all his subsequent difficulties) and proceeding through time until the game is over. Alternatively, it may be considered *synchronically*, in that any given point (such as after White's forty-first move, a key moment in *Murphy*), may be considered as a pattern of spatial relationships and tensions independent of the moves that have created the position, or of what might ensue. For Saussure, the synchronic and the diachronic were separate systems; yet the aesthetic experience (frogs or hippos) requires the perceiving subject (if not immediately, at least on reflection, and, yes, the distinction is crucial) to be aware of the perception as occupying a point of coincidence structured by both. Compare Bergson's belief, articulated in *Mind and Memory,* that language by its very nature 'translates movement and duration in terms of space' (Gontarski, 66).

A final instance of interplay between *ars metric* (Beckett recorded the bawdy pun, from Chaucer's 'The Summoner's Tale', concerning the equitable division of a fart, in the 'Whoroscope Notebook') and geometry: *The Expelled* begins with its eponymous protagonist thrown down the steps, less concerned with the theological consequences of the Fall ('not serious') or the maieutic implications of expulsion than with the number of steps that constitute the *perron*. The true figure, he concludes, depends on whether the top and sidewalk should be included, but this leads to three answers (in a truth-table, four, as that including the top without the sidewalk is identical to that including the sidewalk without the top), with no certainty as to 'which of them was right'.[28] The dilemma recurs in the drama, when the blind Dan Rooney contends irritably that 'they' must change the number of steps in the night.[29] The debate is both pointless and of magnitude: does arithmetic (counting) begin with 0 or with 1? The Greek *monás* intimates 1, hence substantiality; but that was before zero entered Western thought. As Schopenhauer insists throughout *The World as Will and Representation* (the more usual title), our sense of self is poised between embodiment and pure subjectivity, which implies, in these terms, that it is located somewhere between 0 and 1, a transition that represents 'the analogue of creation'.[30] Burnet concludes: 'geometry cannot be reduced to arithmetic as long as the number one is regarded as the beginning of the numerical series. What really corresponds to the point is what we call zero'.[31] This, I contend, underlies the dilemma of when and where the Unnamable locates his being.

On the evening of 2 October 1935, having dined in Soho on sole, Beckett and his therapist, Wilfrid Bion, attended a lecture, the third of five, by Carl Jung at the Tavistock Clinic. Jung mentioned several things of lasting impact on Beckett, such as the little girl who had never really been born, and how complexes appear in visions and speak in voices, assuming identities of their own, so that unity of consciousness is largely illusory, as complexes emancipate themselves from conscious control, becoming visible or audible.[32] Jung showed a diagram from the previous lecture, featuring a series of concentric circles representing gradations of the mind from the outer light of ego consciousness to the dark centre. Beckett recalled: 'The closer you approach that centre, the more you experience what Janet calls an *abaisement du niveau mental*: your conscious autonomy begins to disappear and you get more and more under the fascination of unconscious contents'.[33] Jung's ten circles are grouped into four sets: the 'ectopsychic sphere', the 'endopsychic sphere', the 'personal unconscious' and the 'collective unconscious'.[34] His diagram became for Beckett a virtual archetype of awareness, and (a geometrical re-ordering of the chaos of Belacqua's inner being) was translated into the three zones of Murphy's mind: the light, the half-light and the dark. Rejecting the collective unconscious, Beckett was fascinated by the fascination; his inner zone is entirely that of the 'personal unconscious', attained as conscious autonomy abates.

In *The World as Will and Idea*, Schopenhauer insists that his reader be acquainted with the earlier *Fourfold Root of the Principle of Sufficient Reason*, part 3 of which discusses objects (and the knowledge thereof) in terms of geometry and arithmetic, position in space and succession in time. More mildly, I refer the gentle reader who seeks explicitation to my chapter 'Samuel Beckett and Science' in the Blackwell Beckett Companion (2010); or to its modal simulation, on my website.[35] I also note my subsequent article in the *Sofia Philosophical Review* (2011), on the nature and substance of the monad. Here, however, using the time-honoured principle of proof by assertion, I outline the complex argument that arises from these various attempts to interpret Murphy's mind in accordance with the principles of the Leibniz monad, beginning with its description as 'a large hollow sphere, hermetically closed to the universe without' (*Murphy* 67). To paraphrase the novel (chapter 6), we need not concern ourselves with the apparatus of Beckett's mind as it really was – that would be an extravagance and an impertinence – but as it pictured itself to be. Moreover, one should bear in mind (if only to ignore that stricture) Bergson's critique of Leibniz's monad, his insistence on the insufficiency of that model to derive the material world from consciousness.[36] And should the gentle skimmer choose to skip the next few paragraphs, as some do THAT chapter of *Murphy*, no neurological damage will be done.

With these reservations, an outline of Beckett's monad might begin with a translation of philosophical concerns into a 'network of loci'

(*Dream* 16). I draw an x-axis, extending from a mid-point of *physics* to *geology* (the inert) at one extremity and *mathematics* (the ideal) at the other. On this axis is placed the binary opposition of *genesis* (coming into being) and *ousis* (being). Surrounding it are complementary binaries, such as *Nominalism* and *Realism*, or *Phenomena* and *Noumena*. These categories are not exhaustive but represent crucial oppositions in Beckett's thought. They are placed in approximate relation to the inert and the ideal, and, once the vertical y-axis appears (a suggestion of the analytic geometry), in like approximation to the *mystical* as one polarity and the *psychological* as another. Following the 'upward movement of the mind', I image Leibniz's three categories of *petites perceptions* (below consciousness), *perception* and *apperception* (the mind's awareness of itself). The downward movement mirrors these in terms of Murphy's sense of the *light*, the *half-light* and the *dark*. Those tripartite paradigms qualify the binaries deployed elsewhere (consider Belacqua's sense of 'trine'), and an important distinction is implied between the 'voice within' of this descent (towards the dark) and the 'voice without' of the corresponding ascent (towards the light).

Two things more are required.[37] First, the diagram must be imagined, not in the two dimensions of the page but as assuming the qualities of a sphere, that it might be truly *monadic*. Secondly, a further axis passes through the mid-point (*physics*, or movement); this is that of *memory* (in Cartesian terms, the self extended into the past) and *time*, with the centre point reflecting Schopenhauer's sense of the *eternity of the present*. As Terence McQueeny perceives: 'As the ideal limit that separates the past from the future the present is as unreal for the senses as a point in mathematics. But if it is inaccessible to empirical consciousness it can be seen as the supreme reality for the metaphysical'.[38]

Leibniz considered monads to be metaphysical points, distinguishing them from the indivisible atoms of Democritus that had once 'charmed

The Geometry of the Imagination

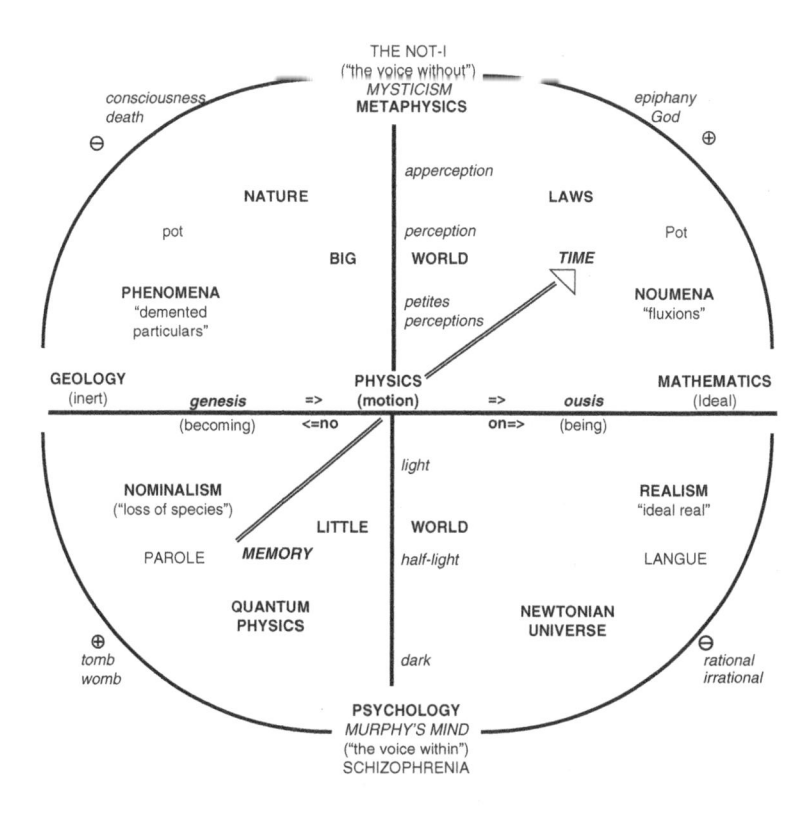

```
                        THE NOT-I
                     ("the voice without")
         consciousness   MYSTICISM           epiphany
         death           METAPHYSICS         God
           ⊖                                    ⊕
                          apperception
                 NATURE              LAWS
            pot            perception     Pot
                   BIG    WORLD    TIME
                           petites
              PHENOMENA   perceptions   NOUMENA
              "demented                 "fluxions"
              particulars"

     GEOLOGY              PHYSICS              MATHEMATICS
     (inert)              (motion)             (Ideal)
              genesis  =>          =>  ousis
              (becoming) <=no        on=> (being)
                           light
              NOMINALISM              REALISM
              ("loss of species")     "ideal real"
                    LITTLE   WORLD
              PAROLE MEMORY  half-light   LANGUE

              QUANTUM               NEWTONIAN
              PHYSICS               UNIVERSE
         ⊕                                    ⊖
         tomb            dark              rational
         womb                              irrational
                      PSYCHOLOGY
                      MURPHY'S MIND
                      ("the voice within")
                      SCHIZOPHRENIA
```

his imagination'.[39] He wished to avoid the 'idealist tar' (*Murphy* 67) of Cartesian dualism, but his insistence on the monads as units of substance, or simple self-active beings endowed with impulses of perception and appetition, led to the paradox of 'simple substance' that yet has no parts, and to the inevitable absurdity of the pre-established harmony that elicited Voltaire's ridicule. Beckett retained both his mockery of and respect for Leibniz by virtue of a crucial observation from Windelband, that monads be considered as not so much *physical* as *psychical* in their nature, since the *petites perceptions* (the infinitely small constitutive parts of their representative life) can be identified with '*unconscious mental states*'.[40] Beckett could thus identify the self as monadic, with every moment (of every perceiving subject) constituting a unique unit of identity. Further, he could align this sense of the Monad with Schopenhauer's fundamental principle of the perceiving subject as located between Will and Representation, the Is-Not and the Is (hence the 'Not I'), the unimaginable Zero and the atomistic One. This simple insight (his later word was 'neither'), underscores Beckett's most important prose, the *Three Novels*, with *The Unnamable* at the dark centre of these 'matters'.

Just as Jung's Tavistock diagram became a model for Murphy's mind, so Murphy's mind helped structure the *Three Novels*. That pattern is not entirely clear and distinct, for the opening of *Molloy* (in manuscript or the French text) suggests that the work began as binary rather than tripartite (Jungian Molloy against Freudian Moran). A third part, when conceived, was probably some form of *L'Innommable*, with *Malone Dies* an afterthought, a necessary interlude (like *Waiting for Godot*) to postpone the agony of parturition and give birth to the *monade nue*. Be this as it may (for much is speculative), the 'trilogy' exemplifies different levels of Murphy's mind, with *Molloy* refracting the outer zones of light, *Malone Dies* the half-light and *The Unnamable* the dark centre of personal consciousness, where Murphy felt 'the tumult of non-Newtonian motion', like a 'mote in the dark of absolute freedom', or a point in the ceaseless 'passing away of line' (*Murphy* 70).

In the 'Whoroscope Notebook', Beckett recorded from Henri Poincaré's *La Valeur de la science* (1905) the sentiment, 'Ces astres infinitements petits, ce sont les atomes', from a discussion of gravitation in which the French mathematician shows that Newtonian laws do not apply to the movement of electrons. *The Unnamable* responds in two ways. First, it offers the paradox of a *kosmos* both infinitely large and infinitesimally small, Malone and 'the others' wheeling about a fixed centre, like planets, yes, but electrons too. Here, macrocosm and microcosm, void and plenum even, are one. Secondly, it structures a universe that reflects recent advances in modern physics: relativity, uncertainty, Brownian motion, electromagnetic radiation, quantum physics, non-Euclidean geometry and, not least, splitting the atom (the etymology of which implies indivisibility). Indeed, Molloy's earlier sense, as identity fades, of waves and particles, nameless things, thingless names,[41] expresses in terms of Bohr's principle of complementarity his crisis of being. This anticipates the great mystery of *The Unnamable*, the Voice that can be located but not heard, or heard but not located, but not heard and located simultaneously.[42] The structure and intention of this novel may thus be seen as an (ultimately unsuccessful) attempt to crack the atom of Cartesian consciousness, this 'embodied' in the strange monadic figure of the narrator, who is aware of himself as placed in a universe where the categories (indeed, the ancient unities) of time and place and causation (action) are annihilated.

Is this 'being' substantial? Not with respect to time, for he is incapable of measuring time, 'which in itself is sufficient to vitiate all calculation in this connexion'.[43] Nor with respect to space, as the place may be vast or otherwise, 'it comes to the same thing'.[44] Nor, I venture, with respect to causation, as nothing is certain, and narrative fades to uncertainty, without 'issue' or conclusion. This is perfectly illustrated in the manuscripts, where the novel ends on precisely the last page of the second notebook:[45] had that notebook held ten more pages, the novel could have been ten pages longer. There are, to be sure (to be sure?), attempts to structure 'events', even after 'All these Murphies, Molloys and Malones'[46] are dismissed, for stories are told (or begun), and patterns appear (*B*asil, *M*ahood, *W*orm replicating *B*elacqua, *M*urphy, *W*att); but these are mere gestures to pass the time, or fill the void, where there is neither time nor extension. The theme, should one wish a theme (for the act of measurement distorts the object measured), is the search for the Voice, but in this quantum *kosmos* Newtonian laws of narrative do not apply.

The Unnamable, in terms of traditional categories and unities of time, space and causality, exemplifies, as *Dream* could not, a novel composed on principles of involuntary unity. Arithmetic (time) has abated, so narrative (virtually) disappears; geometry lacks dimension, so space becomes (almost) indefinite; logic is in abeyance, so relationship is (mostly) fraught. It unfolds in a gray world where these categories are in abeyance; its only unity is that of the monadic consciousness, enacting a process of perception, in the Schopenhauerean wilderness between Will and Representation. I began with a Wagnerian moment where/when time folds into space in a unit of apprehension; but that moment embraces a mere 40 minutes, whereas the Unnamable's last gasp (to adopt a spatial measure of time), is a paragraph that goes on for 120 pages and might easily be sempiternal, having beginning but no end.[47] Compared with *Dream*, which it emulates in so many ways, *The Unnamable* more truly meets the conditions of involuntary unity: no time, no place, no plot; and yet, paradoxically, a form that exemplifies obsessively the very unities that it rejects (*time* is that of actual experience, *place* is fixed and *action* is centred in one awareness). To compound the paradox, the novel's exploration of the dark centre of self, that realm of freedom, was possible only through the disciplined geometry of Jung's Tavistock diagram (without the collective unconscious), and the analytical absurdity of the Monad, a splendid little picture that is equally (as Beckett said of Leibniz) a great cod.[48]

This essay arose from a trivial (quadrivial) insight: that the elements of arithmetic and geometry in the night firmament passage of *Dream* create a stasis as unsatisfactory as the novel's 'involuntary unity' is unconvincing. Could there be a process, a unified field theory, perhaps, to bring these things together? *Murphy* suggests a way, given that Jung's diagram and Leibniz's monad structure both tripartite consciousness and narrative form – but in bringing these together the ideal of involuntary unity is lost. But not irrevocably: the three-fold structure of Murphy's mind applied to *The Unnamable* realizes a compelling involuntary unity that *Dream* can only dream about.

This was originally intended to be the preamble (exordium), to be followed by a weightier statement:[49] having briskly defined the ineluctable modalities of the arithmetical and geometrical up to and including the 'trilogy', I would apply these to Beckett's later works. *Waiting for Godot*, for instance, might be considered as arithmetical (*de capo* structure, vaudeville sequence), until Beckett, directing the play in the 1970s, chose to emphasize its iconic (spatial) qualities. *Endgame*, by contrast, flaunts its geometry, with its spherical setting within the skull, Clov's tangential cubical kitchen and Hamm's chair in the precise centre of the circle, where a Cartesian catastrophe is enacted. The narrator's love of arithmetic in *How It Is* might have critiqued the narrative structures of coming and going, even as these were changing, imperceptibly, into a geometrical sense of closed place, with time at bay. I might have explored the Beckett country of consciousness in the poem, 'bon bon il est un pays', or marvelled at time turning into space in 'La Falaise', or disputed the mathematical foundations of the *Three Dialogues* with Georges Duthuit (no ambiguity intended). I could have set the arithmetical sequences of the late prose (lives translated into two and a half billion seconds) against their geometrical settings (hexagon, cube and rotunda), and pondered the paradox of the late drama 're-presenting' an early Modernist aesthetic, the intellectual and emotional monad in an instant of time. And I might have ended with what Brett Stevens calls the 'purgatorial calculus' of *Quad*, where seriality (time) meets figure (space) in an enigmatic celebration of arithmetic and geometry, with its own dark centre and an asymptotic trajectory towards zero.[50] Because my preamble was so demanding, this could not be. Nor can I sign off with the *Quod erat demonstrandum* of the successful geometrical proof, premise as plenum; but by arguing that the scholasticism of *Dream* has entered the conceptual geometry of *The Unnamable* I hope to have shown that the 'involuntary unity' of the former was finally realized, through the mediation of *Murphy*, in the narrative structure of the latter; and then to have intimated how the little world of that novel, with its arithmetical and geometrical modalities, informs the works to come.

Notes

1. Samuel Beckett, *Dream of Fair to Middling Women*, edited by Eion O'Brien and Edith Fournier (Dublin: Black Cat Press, 1992), 37; hereafter cited in the text as *Dream*.
2. John Pilling, *A Companion to Dream of Fair to middling Women* (Tallahassee, FL: Journal of Beckett Studies Books, 2004), 31.
3. Samuel Beckett, *Proust*, in *Selected Works* IV, edited by Paul Auster (New York: Grove Press, 2010), 511–44 at 553.
4. Ibid., 554.
5. *A Companion to Dream*, 31; the source is Julien Benda, *Le Bergsonisme, ou, Une philosophie de la mobilité* (Paris: Mercure de France, 1912).
6. Arthur Schopenhauer, *The World as Will and Idea*, translated by R. B. Haldane and J. Kemp. 2 vols (Oxford: Oxford University Press, 1896), III §52 331; hereafter cited in the text as *WWI*.
7. *Proust*, 553.
8. John Burnet, *Greek Philosophy: Thales to Plato*. 1914; reprint (London: Macmillan, 1961), 45.
9. Thomas à Kempis. *The Earliest English Translation of De Imitatione Christi*, edited by John K. Ingram (London: Kegan Paul, Trench, Trubner & Co., 1893), 25.
10. *Dream*, 15; Samuel Beckett, *Murphy*, in *Selected Works* I, edited by Paul Auster (New York: Grove Press, 2010), 1–168 at 69; hereafter cited in the text as *Murphy*.
11. W. R. Inge, *Christian Mysticism*. 1899; 2nd edn (London: Methuen, 1912), 7, 360.
12. Acts 17.34.
13. Inge, 108.
14. Ibid., 156.
15. Ibid., 257.

16 Ibid., I §1 3-4
17 Samuel Beckett, *How It Is*, in *Selected Works* II, edited by Paul Auster (New York: Grove Press, 2010), 409–521 at 416.
18 C. J. Ackerley and S. E. Gontarski, *The Grove Companion to Samuel Beckett* (New York: Grove Press, 2004), 389; paraphrasing *Dream*, 120–5.
19 John Burnet, *Early Greek Philosophy*. [1892]; 3rd edn, revised (London: A. & C. Black, 1920), 103.
20 Ibid., 104.
21 *Proust*, 512.
22 *Murphy*, 32; from Burnet, *Greek Philosophy*, 55.
23 *Grove Companion*, 349.
24 Ibid., 278.
25 Samuel Beckett, 'Watt', in *Selected Works* I, edited by Paul Auster (New York: Grove Press, 2010), 169–379 at 184.
26 *Watt*, 272.
27 Ibid., 279–80.
28 Samuel Beckett, 'The Expelled', in *Selected Works* IV, edited by Paul Auster (New York: Grove Press, 2010), 247.
29 Samuel Beckett, *All that Fall*, in *Selected Works* III, edited by Paul Auster (New York: Grove Press, 2010), 175.
30 Brett Stevens, 'A Purgatorial Calculus: Beckett's Mathematics in "Quad"', in S. E. Gontarski (ed.), *The Blackwell Companion to Samuel Beckett*, (Oxford: Blackwell, 2010), 164–81 at 165.
31 *Greek Philosophy*, 84.
32 *Grove Companion*, 609.
33 Ibid., 290.
34 Carl Jung, 'The Tavistock Lectures' [1935], in *The Collected Works, XVIII: The Symbolic Life, Miscellaneous Writings*, translated by R. F. C. Hull (London & Henley: Routledge & Kegan Paul, 1977), 5–182 at 44.
35 www.otago.ac.nz/english/media/monadology.mov.
36 S. E. Gontarski, '"What it is to have been": Bergson and Beckett on Movement, Multiplicity and Representation', *Journal of Modern Literature* 34.2 (2011), 65–75 at 70.

37 The diagram of the monad in this chapter is heavily indebted to the one I developed in 'Samuel Beckett and Science', in *The Blackwell Companion to Samuel Beckett*, edited by S. E. Gontarski (Oxford: Blackwell, 2010), but this version includes a few minor changes.
38 Terence McQueeny, 'Beckett as a Critic of Proust and Joyce' (PhD thesis, University of North Carolina, 1977), 133.
39 Robert Latta, 'Introduction to Gottfried Leibniz', in *The Monadology and Other Philosophical Writings*, translated and edited by Robert Latta (London: Oxford University Press, 1898), 23.
40 Wilhelm Windelband, *A History of Philosophy*, translated by James H. Tufts. 2nd edn (New York & London: Macmillan, 1901), 424; his italics.
41 Samuel Beckett, 'Molloy', in *Selected Works* II, edited by Paul Auster (New York: Grove Press, 2010), 1–170 at 27.
42 *Grove Companion*, 435–6.
43 Samuel Beckett, *The Unnamable*, in *Selected Works* II, edited by Paul Auster (New York: Grove Press, 2010), 283–407 at 293.
44 Ibid., 289.
45 *Grove Companion*, 275.
46 *The Unnamable*, 297.
47 Ibid., 289–90.
48 *The Monadology*, 122.
49 *The Unnamable*, 296.
50 'A Purgatorial Calculus', 172.

Works cited

Ackerley, C. J. 'Samuel Beckett and Science', in *The Blackwell Companion to Samuel Beckett*, edited by S. E. Gontarski (Oxford: Blackwell, 2010), 143–64.
—. 'Monadology: Samuel Beckett and Gottfried Wilhelm Leibniz'. *Sofia Philosophical Review*, V.1 (2011), edited by Matthew Feldman and Karim Mandami: 122–45.
—. 'The Monad: build-up': www.otago.ac.nz/english/media/monadology.mov

Ackerley, C. J. and S. E. Gontarski. *The Grove Companion to Samuel Beckett* (New York: Grove Press, 2004).

Beckett, Samuel. *Dream of Fair to middling Women*, edited by Eion O'Brien and Edith Fournier (Dublin: Black Cat Press, 1992).

—. *Selected Works I–IV*, edited by Paul Auster (New York: Grove Press, 2010).

Benda, Julien. *Le Bergsonisme, ou, Une philosophie de la mobilité* (Paris: Mercure de France, 1912).

Burnet, John. *Early Greek Philosophy*. 1892; 3rd edn, revised (London: A. & C. Black, 1920).

—. *Greek Philosophy: Thales to Plato* [1914]; reprint (London: Macmillan, 1961).

Gontarski, S. E. '"What it is to have been": Bergson and Beckett on Movement, Multiplicity and Representation', *Journal of Modern Literature* 34.2 (2011): 65–75.

Inge, W. R. *Christian Mysticism* [1899]; 2nd edn (London: Methuen, 1912).

Jung, Carl. 'The Tavistock Lectures' [1935], in *The Collected Works, XVIII: The Symbolic Life, Miscellaneous Writings*, translated by R. F. C. Hull (London & Henley: Routledge & Kegan Paul, 1977), 5–182.

Leibniz, Gottfried. *The Monadology and Other Philosophical Writings*, translated and edited by Robert Latta (London: Oxford University Press, 1898).

McQueeny, Terence. 'Beckett as a Critic of Proust and Joyce' (PhD thesis, University of North Carolina, 1977).

Pilling, John. *A Companion to Dream of Fair to middling Women* (Tallahassee, FL: Journal of Beckett Studies Books, 2004).

Poincaré, Henri. *La Valeur de la science* (Paris: Flammarion, 1905).

Schopenhauer, Arthur. *The World as Will and Idea*, translated by R.B. Haldane and J. Kemp. 2 vols (Oxford: Oxford University Press, 1896).

Stevens, Brett. 'A Purgatorial Calculus: Beckett's Mathematics in "Quad"', in S. E. Gontarski (ed.), *The Blackwell Companion to Samuel Beckett* (Oxford: Blackwell, 2010), 164–81.

Thomas à Kempis. *The Earliest English Translation of De Imitatione Christi*, edited by John K. Ingram (London: Kegan Paul, Trench, Trubner & Co., 1893).

Windelband, Wilhelm. *A History of Philosophy*, translated by James H. Tufts. 2nd edn (New York and London: Macmillan, 1901).

5

'Stations of a Mourner's Cross': Beckett, Killiney, 1954

Graley Herren
Xavier University

The recent archival turn in Beckett studies has focused attention on the many diverse sources Beckett drew upon to produce his remarkable body of work. This return to Beckett's unpublished notes and manuscripts coincides fortuitously with the long-awaited publication of Beckett's selected letters. One thing that is becoming increasingly clear is that the sources for many of Beckett's works are deeply personal, despite his principled insistence that his life was not relevant to understanding his art, and despite his systematic efforts through the stages of revision to erase, de-emphasize, obscure or sublimate initial sources drawn from his life. When Deirdre Bair first proposed writing Beckett's biography, he dismissed the efficacy of such a project. She recalls, 'He told me his life was "dull and without interest" and "best left unchampioned". "The professors", he said, "know more about it than I do"'.[1] One of the first professors who championed his work, Lawrence Harvey, encountered similar resistance: 'Beckett said that in his view his life had nothing to do with his art. He didn't at least see any relation'. Ultimately, however, Harvey elicited a concession to the contrary: 'But later in speaking of the Irish place names that occur [...] he said, "Of course, I say my life has nothing to do with my work, but of course it does"'.[2] In his groundbreaking manuscript study,

The Intent of Undoing in Samuel Beckett's Dramatic Texts, Gontarski observes,

> the plays most often emerge from and rest on a realistic and traditional substructure, against which the final work develops dialectically. While Beckett labours to undo that traditional structure and realistic content, he never wholly does so. The final work retains those originary tracings and is virtually a palimpsest. What remains is the trace of an author struggling against his text, repenting his originary disclosure, effacing himself from the text.[3]

With the publication of the letters and increased accessibility to other archival material, there is greater critical capacity than ever before for retracing his tracks and restoring his self-effacements. These revelations open up new avenues into his works that were previously unknown or blocked off. Considered together, the correspondence, the manuscript drafts, and the final published works yield footprints that lead back to Beckett's intellectual, artistic and personal starting points.

The footprints I wish to follow in the present essay lead back to one of the most dreadful periods of Beckett's life, the four months he spent in Killiney in 1954 tending to his brother Frank who lay dying of lung cancer. Frank's dying stirred up other ghosts, most notably that of his mother May, who had died four years earlier. Beckett's morose state of mind was further exacerbated by his worries over Pamela Mitchell, an American woman 14 years his junior with whom he was having an affair, a relationship he was already regarding as impossible to continue much longer. On top of these difficulties, Beckett had also been mired for years in a crippling state of writer's block, which had only relented sporadically since his completion of *The Unnamable* in early 1950. Finally, add to all of this Beckett's acrimony towards Ireland and particularly Dublin, a forsaken homeland from which he felt increasingly alienated, and to which he always returned with reluctance and regret. These multiple overlapping circumstances all contributed to a remarkable series of letters, many of them to Pamela Mitchell. In his introduction to the second volume of *Letters*, Dan Gunn remarks upon this striking segment of the correspondence: 'It is in 1954, when he returns to Ireland again in order to be with his ailing brother, that Beckett writes letters which, taken as a sequence, are almost like stations of a mourner's cross.'[4] What is remarkable in retracing these stations is how familiar the terrain seems. That is because so many of the thoughts, lines, images and themes articulated in the letters were later put to artistic use in Beckett's creative work. These affinities are most apparent in the earlier drafts and final script for *Fin de partie* [*Endgame*], the play Beckett launched into immediately after Frank's death.[5] A comparative analysis between the letters, various gestations of *Endgame*, and other dramas produced after Frank's death provides a revealing case study of how Beckett drew upon personal experience and adapted it for creative use. The personal threnody may be muted by the time his works are published and performed, but faint strains and echoes remain clearly discernible.

'Die in Ireland'

Beckett came to view his home city of Dublin as a necropolis. From the Second World War onward, his life was in France. Following the liberation, he chiefly made trips back to Ireland to visit his mother May, ailing from Parkinson's disease. After her death in 1950, Beckett wrote more than once in his letters that he hoped never to return to Ireland again. But four years later he received a frantic call from his sister-in-law Jean, informing him that his brother had been diagnosed with advanced lung cancer. Beckett rushed to Dublin and would remain resident in Frank and Jean's house for the final four months of his brother's life. The house overlooked Killiney Bay south of the city.

The Becketts knew this area well. Frank and Jean had lived their entire married life there and raised their children, Caroline and Edward. Beckett's childhood home of Cooldrinagh was in nearby Foxrock and the family used to rent a holiday home in the adjacent seaside village of Greystones.[6] Young Samuel Beckett also went on excursions to Killiney with his lover Peggy Sinclair.[7] However, during the summer and fall of 1954, Killiney became the very epicentre of death and loss for him, and these morbid associations would leave a lasting impact on his life and work.

Paradoxically, Beckett's professional reputation as a writer was peaking when he arrived at Killiney in 1954. He had already completed the work that would earn him the Nobel Prize for Literature 15 years later. *En attendant Godot* had premiered in Paris the previous year to major critical acclaim, and preparations were under way for the London premiere. The huge success of *Godot* was also finally drawing attention to Beckett's neglected fiction, particularly his 'trilogy' of novels, *Molloy*, *Malone Dies* and *The Unnamable*. He had secured an indefatigable champion of his work in France with Jérôme Lindon of the publisher Éditions du Minuit and he had attracted the attention of maverick American publisher Barney Rosset, who signed a deal to publish and promote Beckett's work with Grove Press in America.[8] After years of toiling in obscurity, in his late forties Beckett was becoming a literary sensation – and he was thoroughly miserable. Even before Frank's illness, Beckett was in a hopeless state, no longer capable of producing any work he did not instantly hate. Aside from the piecemeal production of several short fictions (eventually published as *Texts for Nothing*), Beckett had failed to write anything new that he deemed publishable between the completion of *The Unnamable* in January 1950 and the multiple drafts of *Endgame* which he began working on extensively in 1955 but did not complete until 1957.

I propose that it is no coincidence that Beckett's intractable writer's block began just after the death of his mother in the fall of 1950 and finally began relenting after the death of his brother in the fall of 1954. In reviling everything he produced during this period, and in questioning his very decision to continue on as a writer, he took up the fallen standard of censure long carried by his mother, who had always hoped that her wayward son would return to his faith, his country and his family – in other words, that he would abandon his prodigal, dissolute, bohemian life and return home. Put another way, she wanted her youngest son to be a Trinity don, not a French *artiste*. She wanted him to embrace his responsibilities as a respectable member of the Irish middle class, following the examples of his father and brother, who had taken over the family surveying business after Bill's death. Alas, none of the correspondence between Beckett and his mother or his brother survives, but his letters to Irish confidante Tom MacGreevy make the family pressures abundantly clear. In 1932, for instance, Beckett frets to MacGreevy, 'Got a friendly letter from Mother, day after you left I think, written in Switzers: "Come home". [...] I wonder would my Father take me into his office. That is what Frank did. He went home after 3 years in India and went into the office. And now look at him. With a car and a bowler-hat'.[9] Furthermore, it appears that, at least at times, Frank may have shared their mother's disapproval. After returning home to Cooldrinagh from London upon conclusion of his psychotherapy, Beckett writes MacGreevy in 1936, 'Relations with M[other] as thorny as ever [...] The only plane on which I feel my defeat not proven is the literary. [...] Frank I feel censorious as not before. He is so successful' (*Letters 1* 299–300). Beckett clearly felt the burden of disappointing his family all the more keenly in comparison to his brother's more stable, conventional bourgeois life. His guilt was compounded by the knowledge that, in his absence, Frank was saddled with the lion's share of responsibility in looking after their mother during her declining years.

The published letters reveal very few intimate details about the brothers' relationship. But if Frank continued to harbour any disapproval of his younger sibling's life, the reverse was also true. Beckett worried over the toll the family business was taking on Frank's health. Even before the diagnosis of cancer, Beckett fretted to MacGreevy, 'Poor Frank is laid up, dizzy attacks, low blood pressure, heart tired. I don't like it at all [...] He takes that old office too much to heart, like Father' (*Letters 2* 435). Furthermore, Beckett regarded Dublin itself as conducive to illness, complaining again to MacGreevy, 'I think it is impossible to have health in Dublin. Of any kind' (*Letters 2* 145). Most revealingly, after he was installed in Killiney for his brother's death vigil, he reflected to Pamela Mitchell, 'The old Irish slogan "Die in Ireland." It's a dangerous place to come back to for any other purpose' (*Letters 2* 487n.3). One would think from this passage that Frank was not dying of cancer, he was dying of Ireland – and Beckett feared the disease was contagious, if not indeed congenital.

'Something is taking its course'

Beckett arrived in Killiney already in a state of creative stagnation that had persisted with little respite since his mother's death in 1950. He lamented to Mitchell, 'Never felt less like writing and I haven't felt like it for years, and never so revolted at the thought of the work done' (*Letters 2* 487n.3). Yet a glance at his chronology shows that the creative log-jam was just about to break free. Without knowing it, Beckett was accumulating experiences and rehearsing ideas that would soon replenish his depleted creative reservoir. *Endgame* is fundamentally born out of Frank Beckett's death; 'the gravedigger puts on the forceps' (*CDW* 84). Before his brother's illness, he had worked unsuccessfully on multiple scenarios involving invalids and attendants, but had aborted these manuscripts.[10] The play 'had a difficult birth', as Ackerley and Gontarski rightly note.[11] But Beckett's harrowing experiences in Killiney between May and September 1954 provided him with the necessary perspective, motivation and specific quickening agents to revivify previous efforts, add to them and reshape the lot into an eventually viable form. Frank's illness and death did not solve all of Beckett's creative problems by any means, but this personal experience did provide the impetus and direction to begin productive work again.

When Beckett was summoned to Killiney, he found himself cast in a servant's role – as if he had suddenly been plunged into a Beckett play. The experience clarified his identification with the character who would eventually become Clov, the exasperated factotum serving the irascible invalid eventually called Hamm. The play dramatises the life of Hamm, a blind tyrant who cannot stand, and Clov, his beleaguered servant and more-or-less adopted son who cannot sit, nor, it would appear, leave. They live in a shelter between the land and the sea, in a barren wasteland where nothing grows, where everything is either running out or breaking down, and yet the relief of a definitive end to the suffering remains elusive. Hamm also keeps his decrepit parents, Nagg and Nell, bottled up in ashbins on stage. They occasionally pop in to tell a story or share an anecdote, but for the most part, all the characters in *Endgame* are merely killing time, waiting to die or somehow otherwise to end. Knowlson briefly suggests in his biography that Beckett's experiences during this period anticipate the world of *Endgame*, and the publication of the second volume of letters substantiates this claim beyond doubt.[12]

The letters and play both capture the grinding tedium of waiting for death. 'Here things are taking their course' (*Letters 2* 492), Beckett writes in July 1954 to Jérôme Lindon, directly prefiguring Clov's assessment of the shared predicament in *Endgame*: 'Something is taking its course' (*CDW* 98, 107). There is also a shared sense of a brutal repetition from which none of the characters seem capable of escaping. Again, these lines from Beckett's letter to Mitchell might just as well be lifted from the script of *Endgame*: 'Here the damnable round continues. Complications are beginning and God knows for what atrociousness we are bound' (*Letters 2* 493). Beckett even characterizes himself to Mitchell in Clov-like terms as Frank's servant: 'Should have made quite a good butler, no, too much responsibility, but a superior kind of house-boy, a head house-boy, no, just an ordinary house-boy' (*Letters 2* 493n.1). By late August, there could be no doubt that Frank's condition was deteriorating, yet the end remained beyond reach. Clov crystallizes this condition in the opening lines of the play, which also echo Christ on the cross: 'Finished, it's finished, nearly finished, it must be nearly finished' (*CDW* 93). Finally, on 13 September 1954, Frank Edward Beckett died. Four days later, Beckett reported the sad news to Barney Rosset. This same letter, however, contains the first hint of new creative inspiration: 'Re future work, I feel very doubtful, though sometimes have premonitions of a brief & final haemorrhage prior to what condolers call the higher life' (*Letters 2* 502). This 'final haemorrhage' would become *Endgame*.

'... the only survivor of my family ...'

Let me be clear: I am not suggesting a simplistic equation whereby Clov equals Sam, Hamm equals Frank, Nagg equals Bill and Nell equals May. Although Beckett's early inspirations do include strikingly personal material, he complicates and obfuscates those sources through multiple drafts and effacements. With each successive revision, the material becomes decreasingly revealing on a personal level and increasingly complex on a formal level. Complexity often ensues in part from dialectical interaction with other source texts that wrestle with analogous problems. For present purposes his most relevant source text is the account of Noah given in Genesis.[13]

The play is replete with references to Noah, his sons and their lives after the flood. The post-apocalyptic environment and hermetically sealed shelter depicted in *Endgame* bear strong resemblances to the world Noah and his family occupied in the ark after God destroyed the rest of the world's human inhabitants. God charges his chosen survivors with repopulating the earth, a challenge that they accept. Conversely, procreation is a source of considerable anxiety in *Endgame*. Hamm alternately calls his father 'Accursed progenitor' and 'Accursed fornicator' (*CDW* 96), belligerently asking why he was born:

Hamm	Scoundrel! Why did you engender me?
Nagg	I didn't know.
Hamm	What? What didn't you know?
Nagg	That it would be you. (*CDW* 116)

At one point Clov is afflicted by a flea in his crotch, or perhaps it is a crab louse, prompting a slapstick routine of pouring insecticide powder down his trousers, out of the hysterical concern that 'humanity might start from there all over again!' (*CDW* 108). Furthermore, when Clov looks out of the window late in the play and discovers, to his horror, a boy on the horizon, his immediate reaction is to grab the gaff and prepare to bludgeon this 'potential procreator' (*CDW* 131) to death. The anxiety surrounding regeneration in the play is in part attributable to Beckett's retelling of the Genesis story from the perspective not of Noah but of Ham, Noah's son – that same son who viewed his father naked and was thus cursed to bear a race of servants – a prospect which accounts for Ham(m)'s reluctance to get on with the task of begetting heirs. Beckett editorializes upon the Noah story in a letter to Mitchell, written months after Frank's death while he was working on drafts of *Endgame*. 'I've been reading [...] in the Holy Bible the story of the Flood and wishing the Almighty had never had a soft spot for Noah' (*Letters 2* 522).

There is no question of choosing between Frank's death vigil and the Noah story as to which is the correct inspiration for *Endgame*.[14] Rather, Beckett latches on to the Noah story as an ideal conduit for dealing with the attendant anxieties of loss, sterility and regeneration raised by Frank's death, while simultaneously rechanneling the play's points of reference away from their personal origins. Beckett was acutely aware that, with Frank's death, he advanced to the head of the line as the last living member of his immediate family. He did not relish the promotion. In his first letter to Barney Rosset during the Killiney sojourn, he confronted the situation squarely: 'No there are no compensations for me in this country, on the contrary. And as so shortly to be the only survivor of my family I hope never to have to return' (*Letters 2* 486–7). Despite all Beckett's best efforts to renounce his Irish birthright, Frank's death threatened to confer upon him the burdens of legacy. These anxieties of lineage were potentially thrown into sharper relief by Beckett's own childlessness. By all accounts he and his long-time companion Suzanne Deschevaux-Dumesnil had quite consciously chosen not to have children.[15] Nevertheless, the frequency and intensity with which he turned to these themes reveal a preoccupation with barrenness, the various compulsions to propagate and the inevitable woe visited upon both parent and child once the call to reproduce is heeded.[16] Several of his plays from the late 1950s – *All That Fall* (1956), *Krapp's Last Tape* (1958), *Embers* (1959) – are animated by kindred tensions, but none treat these themes with greater urgency or ruthlessness than *Endgame*, where the personal roots of the dilemma lie deepest. Despite familial pressures, and against a besieged Irish Protestant backdrop that saw childlessness as tantamount to class betrayal, Beckett personally resisted the reproductive imperative.[17] Frank's death may have stirred up latent concerns about regeneration, but there is no indication from either Beckett's life or work that he fundamentally departed from his original position: God did Noah no favours by sparing him, and the mandate to repopulate the earth was a doomed proposition from the start. As Hamm sums it up, 'you're on earth, there's no cure for that!' (*CDW* 125).

'It was I was a father to you'

Nevertheless, Beckett was in effect bound by Frank's different opinions and choices. Unlike the prodigal younger son, Frank stayed in Ireland, held down a steady job, married, bought a house and had children. Even had Beckett been of a different mindset with respect to the reproduction question, one might have supposed the existence of Edward, son of the eldest son, would have relieved any burden to produce an heir.[18] However, quite apart from the issue of producing children, there is also a deep concern in *Endgame* with the rearing of children. We must remember that Hamm is not the biological father of Clov but rather a foster father. Hamm reprimands Clov for his ingratitude by reminding him of this fosterage arrangement:

Hamm	Do you remember when you came here?
Clov	No. Too small, you told me.
Hamm	Do you remember your father?
Clove	[*Wearily.*] Same answer. [....]
Hamm	It was I was a father to you.
Clov	Yes. [*He looks at* HAMM *fixedly.*] You were that to me.
Hamm	My house a home for you.
Clov	Yes. [*He looks about him.*] This was that for me. (*CDW* 110)

Hamm eventually tells an elaborate story about how a child, apparently Clov, came to be in his care. Near the play's end, another boy is spotted on the horizon, opening up the possibility that Hamm will assume custody of a new child. When Hamm responds, 'It's the end, Clov, we've come to the end. I don't need you any more' (*CDW* 131), the timing implies that Clov's replacement has arrived. With a line of succession seemingly in place, the play ends poised on the brink of possible regeneration.

Just as anxieties about bearing children spring from concerns surrounding Frank's death, so too do worries about being responsible for someone else's offspring. Beckett's concerns over future support for his fatherless niece and nephew worm their way into *Endgame*. As is often the case, the earlier drafts reveal Beckett's fundamental concerns more nakedly. The interlocking themes of death, sterility, regeneration and fosterage are laid bare in the manuscripts, where the personal sources of these anxieties are not yet expunged. Most revealing is the two-act version of the play, first extant as a conflated typescript in the Reading archives (UoR MS 1660). Gontarski's study of this manuscript in the third chapter of *The Intent of Undoing* remains the most extensive treatment, and I draw upon it heavily in the ensuing discussion.

In the two-act version the play's roots in death are tangibly acknowledged in the form of a coffin, uncommented upon by the characters A (later Hamm) and B (later Clov), but presiding over the entire play. At a few points a corpse's head peeks out from the coffin, as when A contemplates the possibility of introducing new characters to his story. Like the later *Endgame*, this version also contains a prayer, but not in this case to God but rather to Death [Thanatos].[19] The coffin is ultimately eliminated in revision, though it may well prefigure Beckett's later use of the ashbins. But as Gontarski notes, a residual reference to it remains in Hamm's line, 'Put me in my coffin', to which Clov replies, 'There are no more coffins' (*CDW* 130).[20] Moreover, the appearance of the corpse in this earlier version precisely at the moment when A – the Hamm figure – is concluding his story of the child's arrival implies a direct link between the death and fosterage motifs.

The competing attractions of Thanatos and Eros are also more explicit in the earlier typescript. The Noah source text is invoked directly, as A directs B to read from Genesis 8.21–2 and 11.14–19, that is, from God's covenant with Noah and from the chronicle of Noah's generations.[21] Though the latter passage is far from erotic, its reference to propagation has an aphrodisiac effect on A. Determined to prove his virility, he crudely calls for a woman: 'Mother, wife, sister, daughter, harlot. It's the same to me. A woman. Two breasts and a vulva'.[22] Instead of procuring an actual woman, B assumes the teasing voice and guise of 'Sophie'. 'Go get me Sophie', responds A, 'I'm going to beget'.[23] This recipe for reproduction is obviously doomed to fail, as Gontarski summarizes: 'But to Sophie's eagerness, A detumescently demurs. He fears procreation and refuses Sophie's advances'.[24] Here sexual groping and impotence are treated as the stuff of farce, but with successive revisions these themes become more grim and resentful in tone. An intermediary set of revision notes (held at Ohio State University) marks the transition. Gontarski highlights one line from these notes for its 'particularly cutting edge': 'No one sterile in our family'.[25] Considering the play's personal sources, one can well imagine why such a line would be excised from the final version as cutting too close to home.

The most intriguing personal reference in the two-act typescript, later suppressed from the final play, concerns the arrival of the new boy at play's end. In *Endgame*, there is an inkling of doubt as to whether Clov's sighting of a boy in the distance is accurate: 'You don't believe me? You think I'm inventing?'(*CDW* 131). In this earlier version, however, all doubt is removed: B is definitely inventing. Just as the play is about to end, the closing curtain is suspended and raised back up, and B enters disguised as the new boy. He speaks in a child's voice, begs to be fed, and begins ingratiating himself as A's servant. Gontarski notes A's response, 'It will never end', and comments, 'And so it does not. Another cycle begins, but with slight variation. B is simply playing the role of a younger servant'.[26] In spite of everything, regeneration of a kind has taken place, and now the farce is doomed to continue, along with all the responsibilities that inevitably ensue. But I have saved the most striking detail of this scene for last. When B enters, assuming the wardrobe and speech of a child, he also assumes a new identity, announcing that his name is *Edward*. Edward! So the representative of regeneration – he who ensures that the routines of servitude, dependence and abjection will continue – just happens to bear the same name as Beckett's own nephew. The early two-act version of the play concludes with the pronouncement of an heir apparent; but rather than providing resolution to the play's problems, this new complication only assures the continuation of a dreadful cycle, and only adds to the responsibilities of the survivors.

Even after the so-called Edward is written out of the final version of *Endgame*, echoes remain in Hamm's final speech. There he returns to the story of how the first child (probably young Clov) arrived in the shelter. But whereas his first telling featured the father begging Hamm to take the child, this new retelling has the father begging to keep the child. Hamm reprimands the father, in words that may be directed more at himself for clinging to Clov for too long: 'You don't want to abandon him? You want him to bloom while you are withering? Be there to solace your last million last moments? [*Pause.*] He doesn't realize, all he knows is hunger, and cold, and death to crown it all. But you! You ought to know what earth is like, nowadays. Oh, I put him before his responsibilities!' (*CDW* 133). All the blame – for having a child only to abandon it, for forcing a child to suffer through ones own inevitable demise, for blindly expecting a child to bloom in an atmosphere of decay, for even conceiving a child into such a wretched, preposterous, dying world – all these raw accusations remain intact in *Endgame*, but by the final version their original sources are obscured.

Edward Beckett was only 11 years old at the time of his father's death. To his credit, as Knowlson's biography amply shows, Beckett was a highly supportive uncle to both his niece and nephew. In turn, and true to the script, Edward Beckett has served dutifully as executor of Beckett's literary estate ever since Jérôme Lindon's death. With the advantage of hindsight, we can see that family obligations were accepted, debts were paid, the legacy has been preserved and the estate has flourished. During the immediate aftermath of Frank's death, however, anxieties and recriminations – not only over death, but also over the responsibilities left behind in the dead one's absence – haunted Beckett's imagination. Even though the more personal ghosts were eventually relegated to the archives, they remain palpable in the stage play that survives.

'... sucked in by this exquisite morass...'

Palpable, too, is Beckett's despair over other responsibilities of his own making. It is no coincidence that the most intense letters written during this period are to Pamela Mitchell. He first met her in a business capacity in September 1953. When Mitchell moved to Paris in April 1954 for a nine-month stay, their relationship intensified, but so, too, did Beckett's scruples about conducting an affair under Suzanne's nose. As Knowlson characterizes it, 'The affair, although brief, was intense, both romantic and sexual. But it was brusquely interrupted'.[27] Beckett's abrupt removal to Killiney gave him occasion to reconsider the affair from a distance. Weighed down with worries, he would regularly take long walks up and down the beach. He reported to Mitchell that 'the nights are still long and fairly good with the old sea still telling the old story at the end of the garden and I can slip out of an evening and prowl without disturbing anyone' (*Letters 2* 493). While 'revolving it all' (*CDW* 400) on Killiney strand, he determined that the affair was doomed: 'Soon the leaves will be turning, it'll be winter before I'm home, and then? It'll have to be very easy whatever it is. I can't face any more difficulties, and I can't bear the thought of giving any more pain' (*Letters 2* 493–4n.1). According to Knowlson he did not definitively break off the affair as such until November, but he seems to have decided upon this course of action during his dark ruminations in Ireland.

Killiney becomes for Beckett and his characters what the heath is for Lear or, what Sandymount Strand is for Stephen Dedalus. This stretch of shoreline expands to existential proportions and serves as a stage for wrestling with mortality; the death of specific loved ones, but more broadly the death of love itself. This is where he spent his childhood summers with Bill, May and Frank Beckett, all dead or dying. This is where he had dated Peggy Sinclair, who died a few years later in May 1933, where he decided to break Pamela Mitchell's heart, where he would later grieve over the passing of his beloved friend Ethna McCarthy, who died in May 1959. Walking into mortality on Killiney strand, his private 'stations of a mourner's cross', Beckett and his characters confront being and nothingness, contemplate responsibilities and regret choices and mourn past losses, as well as those to come, including his own. The allure of the sea of oblivion, to choose not to be, is ever present. Beckett was ruminating on more than Frank's looming death when he wrote Mitchell, 'Sometimes feel like letting myself be sucked in by this exquisite morass, just lie down and give up and do nothing more. Always felt that temptation here but never so strong as these last weeks' (*Letters 2* 487n. 3). He betrays suicidal thoughts in this passage, welcoming the prospect of death as preferable to taking up arms against a sea of troubles. He sounds a similar refrain in another letter to Mitchell, equating, 'the sound of the sea on the shore, and my father's death, and my mother's, and the going on after them'.[28] The ambiguity of 'going on after them', meaning either to continue living or else to follow them into death, is surely intentional.

Beckett eventually conferred his personal associations between Killiney and watery death to the characters in his post-1954 plays. For instance, Henry's father in the 1958 radio play *Embers* commits suicide in the sea at Killiney, and Henry himself is constantly lured back to the sea with the temptation of following in his father's footsteps. Hamm expresses a similar desire in *Endgame*, pining, 'If I could drag myself down to the sea! I'd make a pillow of sand for my head and the tide would come' (*CDW* 122). The most evocative treatment of

Killiney appears in the 1965 teleplay *Eh Joe*. Driven to despair by Joe's heartless jilting, his former lover sneaks out of her bedroom, much as Beckett did for his nightly walks, and wanders down to the sea. There she commits suicide, cupping out a place for her head in the shingle, and allowing the tide to wash her into oblivion just as Beckett had fantasized in his letters. As Eoin O'Brien first noted, specific geographical references to 'the viaduct' (*CDW* 365) and 'the Rock' (*CDW* 366) locate the lover's suicide near Whiterock Cove on Killiney strand.[29] Elsewhere I have elaborated upon Beckett's incorporation of Peggy Sinclair's untimely death and Ophelia's suicide in *Hamlet* as sources for *Eh Joe*.[30] Additionally, the published letters now make it readily apparent how Frank's pending death, the rejection of Pamela Mitchell's love and Beckett's own near-suicidal despair in Killiney likewise contribute seminally to the creation of *Eh Joe*.

'... cast a cold eye ...'

The confluence of Killiney associations is best captured in a 1956 letter to Aidan Higgins in which Beckett expresses bafflement at his friend's upcoming vacation to Ireland: 'Queer the way you all go to Ireland when you get a holiday. Piss on the White Rock for me and cast a cold eye on the granite beginning on the cliff face. Never been so miserable as on that strand, not even at Shankill, no solution and it unrealizable but just to walk out into the sea and not come back' (*Letters 2* 633). His associations with Ireland gravitate instinctively to Killiney, to the dark nights of the soul he spent there and the temptation to end all his problems by simply walking into the sea. Of course, instead of ending his problems and his life, Beckett instead began *Endgame*. The allusion to Yeats in the letter above ('cast a cold eye') is at once morbid and inspirational, in that it points the way through death towards art. Yeats's famous gravestone epitaph reads in full, 'Cast a cold Eye / On

Life, on Death. / Horseman pass by!'[31] Obviously death cannot be avoided and must eventually be confronted, and this is no less true for great artists like Yeats and Beckett. But if an artist has the courage and discipline to 'cast a cold eye' on both life and death, then he might produce honest and lasting works of art, even from the most wretched personal experiences.

Knowlson shares an insight into Beckett's creative process gleaned from conversation with the author: 'It was one of the key features of Beckett's aesthetic that what he once described to me as "the cold eye" had to be brought to bear on a personal experience before it could be used in a work of art'.[32] By casting a critical eye at Beckett's letters and manuscripts in relation to his final published works, one can reconstruct how 'the cold eye' method worked. Rather than succumbing to total despair over the series of personal devastations he faced in the early 1950s, he instead drew upon these experiences as a creative launchpad from the mid-1950s onward. Beckett transformed his encounters with death and loss into important new works of art, including the masterpiece *Endgame* and several other innovative works that followed closely on its heels. Hamm laments, 'The end is in the beginning and yet you go on' (*CDW* 126). For Beckett, the opposite proved equally true: endings inaugurated creative new beginnings. Just when his letters would seem to indicate that his creativity was entirely spent, he managed to find inspiration from his own desolation. In so doing, Beckett followed his own advice to the struggling young French writer Robert Pinget: 'Don't lose heart: plug yourself into despair and sing it for us' (*Letters 2*, 605).

Notes

1 Deirdre Bair, *Samuel Beckett: A Biography* (New York: Harcourt Brace Jovanovich, 1978), x.

2 James Knowlson and Elizabeth Knowlson (eds), *Beckett Remembering/ Remembering Beckett* (New York: Arcade, 2006), 136.
3 S. E. Gontarski, *The Intent of Undoing in Samuel Beckett's Dramatic Texts* (Bloomington: Indiana University Press, 1985), 2.
4 Samuel Beckett, *The Letters of Samuel Beckett. Volume 2: 1941–1956*, edited by George Craig, Martha Dow Fehsenfeld, Dan Gunn and Lois More Overbeck (Cambridge: Cambridge University Press, 2011), lxxvi. Subsequent references made parenthetically as *Letters 2*.
5 Beckett originally composed this play in French as *Fin de partie*, first published by Éditions de Minuit in 1957. He translated the play into English in 1957 as *Endgame*, which first appeared with Grove Press in 1958. References in the present essay draw from the standard English edition of *Endgame* in *The Complete Dramatic Works* (London: Faber and Faber, 1986), 89–134. Subsequent references to this volume are made parenthetically as *CDW*. When consulting *Fin de partie* manuscripts, I use S. E. Gontarski's English translations in *The Intent of Undoing*.
6 James Knowlson, *Damned to Fame: The Life of Samuel Beckett* (New York: Simon & Schuster, 1996), 46.
7 Ibid., 89.
8 For a fuller account of Beckett's publishing history, see *Publishing Samuel Beckett*, edited by Mark Nixon (London: British Library, 2011).
9 Samuel Beckett, *The Letters of Samuel Beckett, Volume 1: 1929–1940*, edited by Martha Fehsenfeld and Lois More Overbeck (Cambridge: Cambridge University Press, 2009), 111–12. Subsequent references made parenthetically as *Letters 1*.
10 The dates, sequence and titles of these rejected drafts are notoriously difficult to pin down with certainty. The manuscripts include pieces sometimes referred to by critics as 'Mime du rêveur, A', 'Avant *Fin de partie*', 'Ernest et Alice', 'A et B' and 'X et F'. The most thorough analysis remains Gontarski's *The Intent of Undoing*. See also the scrupulous overview in Ruby Cohn, *A Beckett Canon* (Ann Arbor: Michigan University Press, 2001), 220–5.
11 C. J. Ackerley and S. E. Gontarski, *The Grove Companion to Samuel Beckett* (New York: Grove Press, 2004), 196.
12 Knowlson, 363.

13 The most thorough considerations of *Endgame* in light of the Noah parallels remain those of Cohn and Cavell. See Ruby Cohn, *Samuel Beckett: The Comic Gamut* (New Brunswick, NJ: Rutgers University Press, 1962), 226–42; and Stanley Cavell, 'Ending the Waiting Game: A Reading of Beckett's *Endgame*', in *Must We Mean What We Say?* (Cambridge: Cambridge University Press, 1976), 115–62.

14 There are certainly other inspirations that lie beyond the scope of the present esssay. For instance, Gontarski emphasizes the ruins around Saint-Lô, where Beckett volunteered as an ambulance driver in 1945, as an important inspiration for the decimated environment of *Endgame* (Gontarski, 33–7). More recently, Peter Fifield has made a compelling intertextual case for Beckett's influence from Georges Bataille's *Histoire de l'œil*. See Peter Fifield, '"Accursed progenitor!": *Fin de partie* and Georges Bataille', *Samuel Beckett Today/Aujourd'hui* 22 (2010): 107–21.

15 Knowlson notes with discretion, 'Neither he nor Suzanne had ever wanted children' (Knowlson, 382). John Calder asserts this fact more forcefully as an extension of Beckett's philosophical beliefs: 'As Beckett speculated about the creation of the world, he increasingly envisaged the creator as a monster, but not necessarily a conscious one. The only way to frustrate that God (or nature) was to produce no children, and Beckett was true to his own principle' (Calder 130). Lawrence Shainberg professes more personal insight into Beckett's childlessness, offering this anecdote: 'The utter skepticism and despair about relationships in general and sexuality in particular which he has explored throughout his life has had as its counterpoint his marriage, which has lasted forty years. But lest one suspect that the continuity and comfort of marriage had tilted the scales so far that the dream of succession had taken root in his mind, "No", he replied, when I asked him if he had ever wanted children, "that's one thing I'm proud of"' (Shainberg).

16 Paul Stewart provides a comprehensive examination of these themes across Beckett's oeuvre in his admirable study, *Sex and Aesthetics in Samuel Beckett's Work* (Houndmills, Basingstoke/New York: Palgrave Macmillan, 2011).

17 For an excellent analysis of Beckett's concerns with sterility and reproduction within the broader social context of Irish Protestantism, see Seán Kennedy, "'A Lingering Dissolution': *All That Fall* and Protestant Fears of Engulfment in the Irish Free State', in *Drawing on Beckett: Portraits, Performances, and Cultural Contexts*, edited by Linda Ben-Zvi (Tel Aviv: Assaph, 2003): 247–61.

18 Just as anxieties over regeneration led Beckett to the Noah story as a model source text, his anxieties with respect to lineage and succession would naturally have led him to *King Lear*. A thorough analysis of Beckett's intertextual dialectic with Shakespeare is beyond the scope of this essay. The classic comparative analysis remains Jan Kott, '*King Lear*, or *Endgame*' in *Shakespeare Our Contemporary* (New York: Norton, 1974), 127–68.

19 Gontarski, 50.

20 Ibid., 51. Beckett, *Endgame*, 130.

21 Samuel Beckett, *The Theatrical Notebooks of Samuel Beckett, Volume IV: The Shorter Plays*, edited by S. E. Gontarski (London: Faber and Faber, 1999), 57n.605.

22 Gontarski, 48.

23 Ibid., 49.

24 Ibid., 40.

25 Ibid., 52.

26 Ibid., 49.

27 Knowlson, 361.

28 Ibid., 362.

29 Eoin O'Brien, *The Beckett Country* (Dublin: Black Cat Press, 1986), 97.

30 I presented a version of this talk at the 'Samuel Beckett: Debts and Legacies' lecture series on 24 May 2011. An expanded version is published as 'Mourning Becomes Electric: Mediating Loss in *Eh Joe*', in *Beckett and Pain*, edited by Mariko Hori Tanaka, YoshikiTajiri, and Michiko Tsushima (Amsterdam: Rodopi, 2012), 43–65.

31 W. B. Yeats, 'Under Ben Bulben', in *The Collected Poems of W. B. Yeats*, Second Revised Edition, edited by Richard J. Finneran (New York: Scribner, 1996), 328, ll.92–4.

32 Knowlson, 347.

Works cited

Ackerley, C. J. and S. E. Gontarski. *The Grove Companion to Samuel Beckett* (New York: Grove Press, 2004).

Bair, Deirdre. *Samuel Beckett: A Biography* (New York: Harcourt Brace Jovanovich, 1978).

Beckett, Samuel. *The Complete Dramatic Works* (London: Faber and Faber, 1986).

—. *The Theatrical Notebooks of Samuel Beckett, Volume IV: The Shorter Plays*, edited by S. E. Gontarski (London: Faber and Faber, 1999).

—. *The Letters of Samuel Beckett. Volume 1: 1929–1940*, edited by Martha Fehsenfeld and Lois More Overbeck (Cambridge: Cambridge University Press, 2009).

—. *The Letters of Samuel Beckett, Volume 2: 1941–1956*, edited by George Craig, Martha Dow Fehsenfeld, Dan Gunn, and Lois More Overbeck (Cambridge: Cambridge University Press, 2011).

Calder, John. *The Philosophy of Samuel Beckett* (London: Riverrun Press, 2003).

Cavell, Stanley. 'Ending the Waiting Game: A Reading of Beckett's *Endgame*', in *Must We Mean What We Say?* (Cambridge: Cambridge University Press, 1976): 115–62.

Cohn, Ruby. *Samuel Beckett: The Comic Gamut* (New Brunswick, NJ: Rutgers University Press, 1962).

—. *A Beckett Canon* (Ann Arbor: University of Michigan Press, 2001).

Fifield, Peter. '"Accursed progenitor!": *Fin de partie* and Georges Bataille', *Samuel Beckett Today/Aujourd'hui* 22 (2010): 107–121.

Gontarski, S. E. *The Intent of Undoing in Samuel Beckett's Dramatic Texts* (Bloomington: Indiana University Press, 1985).

Herren, Graley. 'Mourning Becomes Electric: Mediating Loss in *Eh Joe*', in *Beckett and Pain*, edited by Mariko Hori Tanaka, Yoshiki Tajiri, and Michiko Tsushima (Amsterdam: Rodopi, 2012), 43–65.

Kennedy, Seán. '"A Lingering Dissolution": *All That Fall* and Protestant Fears of Engulfment in the Irish Free State', in *Drawing on Beckett: Portraits, Performances, and Cultural Contexts*, edited by Linda Ben-Zvi (Tel Aviv: Assaph Books, 2003), 247–61.

Knowlson, James. *Damned to Fame: The Life of Samuel Beckett* (New York: Simon & Schuster, 1996).

Knowlson, James and Elizabeth Knowlson (eds). *Beckett Remembering/ Remembering Beckett* (New York: Arcade, 2006).

Kott, Jan. 'King Lear, or Endgame' in *Shakespeare Our Contemporary*. 3rd edn (New York: Norton, 1974): 127–68.

Nixon, Mark (ed.). *Publishing Samuel Beckett* (London: British Library, 2011).

O'Brien, Eoin. *The Beckett Country* (Dublin: Black Cat Press, 1986).

Shainberg, Lawrence. 'Exorcising Beckett', *Paris Review* 104 (Fall 1987). www.samuel-beckett.net/ShainExor1.html (Accessed 19 August 2012).

Stewart, Paul. *Sex and Aesthetics in Samuel Beckett's Work* (Houndmills, Basingstoke/New York: Palgrave Macmillan, 2011).

Yeats, W. B. 'Under Ben Bulben', in *The Collected Poems of W. B. Yeats*. Second Revised Edition, edited by Richard J. Finneran (New York: Scribner, 1996): 325–8.

6

'Close your eyes and listen to it':
Embers and the Difficulties of Listening

Julie Campbell
University of Southampton

Critics of Samuel Beckett's work have commented on *Embers*'s complexity and the difficulties the play presents to its listeners. Hugh Kenner, in 1961, described the play as 'Beckett's most difficult work'.[1] Ronald Hayman expressed his doubts as to 'whether anyone could assimilate' the multiple levels of the play 'just from hearing [it] once on the radio'.[2] Anthony Cronin describes the play as 'a hauntingly beautiful but obscure work whose narrative development is difficult enough to follow on the page and was, in spite of Donald McWhinnie's best efforts, still more difficult to follow as a broadcast'.[3] Marjorie Perloff considers that the play becomes 'progressively less well understood', because there is too much 'noise' blocking the listener's ability to decode the sounds of the play.[4] These views help to substantiate the fact that as a radio play it could be said to be asking a little bit too much of the listener, and certainly a first-time listener.

This essay will be exploring some of the difficulties encountered by listeners to *Embers* (1959). It will consider the causes of these difficulties, how these difficulties can hamper listeners encountering the play for the first time and will contrast responses of listeners who lack the experience of listening to audio drama with those of more 'informed' listeners. The discussion will suggest that the problems facing listeners to this play are in fact essential to the play's effect, which can misfire. A great deal is expected from a new listener to this play: an openness and a quite astonishing receptivity. A single listening will be beset with difficulties, as the play resists accessibility, just as it resists interpretation, and thus the very impediments to reception, fundamental to the play, have proved insurmountable for many listeners.

An essential question to begin with is: why is *Embers* a difficult play? One reason is that it is a radio play, and listening to a radio play requires very particular skills: the skills of attentive and creative listening, which need to be acquired. The difficulties in the reception of radio drama include the fact that it is a temporal medium that, unlike the reading process, does not allow listeners to take a break and think about what they are presented with, or turn back to revisit a complex passage. Listening to radio drama requires concentration, a strong visual imagination, a good memory (both short- and long-term) and the ability to become creatively involved in what is being listened to. *Embers* was Beckett's second radio play and his exploration of what the medium can be pushed to do has been taken far further than in *All That Fall* (1957). In the process, the play has moved further away from listeners' expectations, and thus further away from accessibility within a medium that has only sound and silence to offer.

The radio playwright needs to be aware of many factors that will encourage, and enable, the listener to become involved in the creation of the drama they are listening to, with only sounds and silence to prompt them. There are dangers involved: too many sounds, or too few, can confuse the listener. Sounds in themselves can be confusing, and often require dialogue to clarify them. In the BBC's advice for writing radio drama, the prospective playwright is told that 'Good radio is very difficult to write', and that 'it is in the dialogue that the writer will provide most of the essential information and this means that radio dialogue must often be more explicit than that written for a visual medium'.[5] It is dangerous to have too many characters, as listeners can only hold so many in their heads at a time, and in order for characters to be made 'present' to the listener they need to be named and heard.[6] Much radio drama is realistic, attempting to create the illusion of a believable world, with familiar characters, familiar settings and credible events taking place. In this way many of the difficulties inherent in the medium can be overcome: there is less possibility of confusing the listener if the visual world they are invited to imagine is a familiar one, and memories can be brought into play, alongside logical inferences concerning causation and probability. Martin Esslin recommended that a radio play should be structured 'so that the listener always knows exactly where he stands within the structure at any given moment'.[7] Yet, with *Embers*, the listener can be very confused about where s/he stands at certain moments in the play. Esslin advocated 'clarity and transparency of structure'; *Embers* can be described as very definitely lacking these attributes. Beckett is breaking Esslin's 'rules', albeit outlined retrospectively, and yet doing so in such a way as to fully exploit radio's ability to obscure and confuse – the very pitfalls that Esslin advised against. He declared that 'In radio, too much confusion is deadly', and stressed the importance of grabbing the listener's attention and keeping it, as it is so easy to switch off.[8] Yet *Embers* is, very definitely, confusing. The listener is taken out of a familiar world. There is a familiar setting, a seashore with a shingle beach, yet the listeners spend much of their time inside the character Henry's head. The listener shares his thoughts as the reader shares a character's thoughts when reading focalized narrative or an internal monologue. But the difference is glaring and of great significance: the listener *hears* Henry's thoughts, *hears* the one-sided conversation he has with his father, and *hears* both sides of the conversation he has with his wife, as well as the memories he summons up from the past and the fictional story he is inventing. The play demands unwavering attention, as there are sudden shifts in time and jumps from one diegetic level to another, with little or no signposting.

The different diegetic levels and temporal shifts are not clearly signalled. There is what we could term the 'narrative situation': the listener is placed in what must be the present of the drama, with Henry on the beach. He is speaking, and it seems valid to suggest that he is speaking out loud. But there are sudden shifts when the listener is suddenly conveyed, through Henry's memory, into the past. At one point there is the stage direction: '*Twenty years earlier* [. . .]', but the listener can have no clear idea of this time shift.[9] In the BBC's advice to writers of radio drama they are cautioned that '"stage directions" for the producer's or actor's benefit are to be avoided. If it is important it should be there in the dialogue'.[10] If it is not in the dialogue the listener will not receive such information. There is the diegetic present, on the beach, flashbacks to earlier times and there are also movements, on two occasions, to a metadiegetic level, into Henry's apparently fictional story of Bolton and Holloway. The clear distinction between the diegetic and metadiegetic levels is confused when Holloway is mentioned within the diegesis as if he is a 'real' rather than fictional character. This blurring of 'real' and imagined also occurs when Henry speaks to his father, who is presumed dead by drowning. Ada, Henry's wife, appears to be from a distinctly different level, as the listener does not hear her steps on the shingle, or the sound of her sitting down: '*No sound as she sits*' (*CDW* 257). The alert listener will pick this up, along with her '*Low remote voice throughout*' (*CDW* 257) which is another clue, but one that could be misconstrued. There is a great deal that needs careful attention, and much that can be missed by the listener. This play has just one definitely 'living' character, and the listener is as if inside his head, which is peopled by characters who are presumably not living, not 'there': dead or absent or fictional. On a first listening it is very difficult to discern what is 'real' and what is not. Henry repeatedly demands 'Listen to it!' and once even pleads 'Close your eyes and listen to it' (*CDW* 255), but a listener can choose not to, and choose not to listen attentively. Beckett, with this play, was expecting a great deal from his listeners.

The BBC's advice to prospective writers warns: 'Beware of boring the listener. Radio is fatally easy to turn off'.[11] Yet first listeners can easily be bored by this play; its complexity can form an impermeable barrier for those not accustomed to concentrated listening. I played the original BBC production to students studying the module 'Drama since World War II'.[12] Thirty two students listened to the play. They had not read the play or read any critical responses to it. They were second-year students who had studied two stage plays by Beckett: *Waiting for Godot* in the first year, and *Play* in the second year, just before they listened to *Embers*. None of them were accustomed to listening to radio drama, which is generally the case with contemporary students, who, if they have radios, listen to the music channels only. They did have a short introduction concerning attentive listening, and how useful a skill it is to acquire for their studies at university, as well as for life in general. The introduction also mentioned how listening to radio drama encourages the listeners' imaginations to create the visual images of the play. They were asked to concentrate, to practise attentive listening while they listened to *Embers*, and immediately afterwards the students put their responses on evaluation sheets. The results demonstrate the difficulties in listening to this play for the first time, the variety of responses it elicits, as well as testifying to the decline in attentive listening skills in our visually dominant contemporary culture. Here are their ratings:

Students' Evaluations						
	5	4	3	2	1	
Very well worth hearing	0	5	8	14	2	Not worth hearing at all
Story very interesting	0	3	10	11	5	Not at all interesting
Characters very interesting	2	5	9	11	1	Not at all interesting
Very clear	0	0	4	14	12	Very confusing
Performance excellent	1	11	12	5	0	Performance poor

It is useful to have the responses of a first listening: the kind of listening that can never be returned to. Responses to the play are necessarily modified as a result of repeated listenings, reading and rereading the text, and reading critical exegeses of the play, and, in the process, the memory of the original and 'untainted' listening is no longer accessible.

The widest spread of responses concerned the characters, and the comments showed that many did imagine them visually, and often quite vividly. Eight-six per cent of the students found the play confusing or very confusing. Interestingly, the performance (the acting and the production values) rated highest of all, and none gave this the lowest score. The varied responses could be evaluated as caused by some students already having strong visual imaginations, while others clearly felt very lost, even bored, and most were very definitely confused.

In describing their visualization of Henry just about every student called him 'old' and added words such as 'weak' and 'frail'; he was also often 'seen' as 'bent over' or 'hunched'. He was also described as 'crazy', 'mad' or as having 'some sort of mental health issues' by some. It was pleasing to see quite a few students describing him as 'bitter' (which he surely is). Sometimes there were some very impressive details, and one student visualized him as 'talking to himself', which is essentially what he is doing. One placed him 'sat on the stones [. . .] fixed gaze always on the sea'. There is a double viewpoint encouraged by the play, in that the listener can visualize Henry externally, walking and then sitting on the shingle beach, but there is also the shared viewpoint, from inside Henry's mind, seeing what he sees; imagining what he imagines.

Henry's father (who is not 'there', except in Henry's mind) was visualized with far more variation, even though he does not speak or make any noise (which is unusual for a character in a radio play) he is given an existence for the listener, through Henry addressing him. It is significant, however, that the ability to accurately pinpoint Henry's father's imaginary presence is enabled by reading the script, which is of course a very different process from the listening experience. Henry speaks of his presence/non-presence: 'Who is beside me now? [*Pause.*] An old man, blind and foolish. [*Pause.*] My father back from the dead to be with me. [*Pause.*] As if he hadn't died' (*CDW* 253). And yet, the fact that he is dead is soon questioned; Henry speaks to him as if he was there, and tells him that 'We never found your body, you know [. . .] there was nothing to prove you hadn't run away from us all and alive and well under a false name [. . .]' (*CDW* 253–4). The attentive listener will have the image of a dead father, as if haunting Henry, and then the image of an absent father, with his death now uncertain. Only two students realized that he was very likely dead, while another queried this, obviously strongly sensing the possibility. In Henry's memories he is authoritarian, and this was noted by some; two described him as wearing a red dressing gown, which, in fact, Henry's fictional character Bolton is spoken of as wearing. There was less noted in relation to this 'character' than Henry or Ada, which reflects the fact that he does not speak and is not referred to very often.

Ada, Henry's wife, was 'seen' by all the students; surely due to the fact that her voice is heard alongside Henry's. However, it is questionable just how much she is really 'there'. The listener hears her, and clearly the sense is given that Henry hears and sees her in his mind. This 'ghostly' quality is presented indirectly, and is an example of the kind of ambivalent presence that can be achieved in the radio medium, but not so easily on stage. Her '*Low remote voice*' will be a strong signal, but can easily be misconstrued, and the fact that she makes '*No sound as she sits*' is such a subtle signal that it can easily be missed (*CDW* 257). There was some interesting detail in the students' visualizations of Ada. One student described her as 'Sinister, like a spirit', which shows that her 'ghostly' quality was recognized in this instance. She was often described as quiet, but details such as age, hair colour, dress, etc. were extremely diverse.

Addie, Ada and Henry's daughter, is remembered by Henry, but we do also hear her, albeit briefly: we must be hearing Henry's memories of her, or perhaps he is imagining moments in her past. The listener can 'see' what he 'sees': what he 'really' sees, as well as what is going on in his head: his imaginings, his memories and his fictionalizing. This is one of the reasons this kind of 'inner' drama works so well on radio: the listener 'sees' in her or his head, with the play encouraging the listener to 'see' inside Henry's head. There was less detail from the students concerning Addie than with Henry and Ada, as her 'appearances' are very brief. She was visualized as young, and often her dress was described, but, like Ada, there was wide variation when students suggested her age, her hair colour and how she was dressed.

The Music Master, heard for seconds only, also had very little description, but was often called 'angry' and 'impatient' by students. The Riding Master, also heard for a very short time, was usually not described at all by the students, or with little detail, with 'good posture' and related terms recurring.

In relation to Henry's fictional characters, Bolton and Holloway, three students recognized that Bolton was wearing a red dressing gown (colour is a useful prompt for visualization, and Henry speaks of the 'old red dressing-gown' three times in the play (*CDW* 254, 255)). Bolton was often described as 'standing by fire', and the repetition of the words 'standing' and 'fire' in a short space of time early in the play will have helped this to be pictured and retained (*CDW* 254). One student described him as 'cowering in a corner', but this action is not narrated, but was no doubt summoned up by the ominous atmosphere of the 'ghastly scene' (*CDW* 264). Holloway was visualized as a doctor by three students, and one student recognized his 'existence' on different diegetic levels: Ada mentions him, in what we could call the narrative situation, on the beach with Henry, so he is given a stronger sense of 'reality' beyond Henry's fictional story. He was often described by the students as tall and well-built, and this will have been prompted by the direct nature of Henry's description of him: 'fine old chap, six foot, burly' (*CDW* 255), in marked contrast to the general obscurity and lack of clarity that pervades the play.

In visualizing the set, students were often confused by the different diegetic levels: the beach on which Henry sits and the room in which Bolton and Holloway are imagined were not always distinguished. The sound of the sea is always heard when no one is speaking, a clue that the story of Bolton and Henry is being told in the narrative situation of the beach, but many failed to tune into the disparate diegetic levels. Some sketched what they 'saw' (the sketches were greatly varied), and some recognized the visualization as a memory of a known seascape. The details included reflected the way in which listening to radio drama, as well as reading fiction, can encourage the imagination to create settings in response to the way they are described, and can also summon up memories of similar settings (in this case perhaps from holidays by the sea) and often there is a combination of both. In the past I have read Beckett's short piece *Still* to students, and the visualizations the students reported often involved memories fused with imagination, particularly in relation to the view from the window.

There were comments by students that brought home with real force just how difficult this play is for a first listener. Here is one student's conclusion: 'Confusing to the extreme. The delivery was both disturbing and irritating. Could not make out most of what was being said. Very repetitive and annoying. Very melodramatic'. Another's student commented: 'I do not think this play works well for radio [...] we rely on the words of a man whose voice is cracked and borderline incomprehensible. In moments it bordered on cacophony, genuinely unsettling at times'.

The students' evaluations (modern listeners' responses, albeit a set of listeners lacking practice in attentive listening skills) are in many ways in great contrast with those reported by members of the original audience of this play on the BBC Third Programme (Wednesday, 24 June 1959, 8.00–9.00 p.m.), and yet there are also some parallels, which serve to underscore the challenging nature of the play for first listeners.

The BBC Audience Research Report				
A+	A	B	C	C–
%	%	%	%	%
16	19	27	24	14

The BBC Audience Research Report is a useful document concerning the very first listening of the play, by listeners who would have had developed skills of attentive listening.[13] And yet, despite the significant difference in the two audiences, there are certain similarities. For example, the summary reports that it 'was a considerable disappointment for many listeners in the sample audience. A rather small minority only were able to give it unstinted praise'. But this table does show a substantially greater readiness on the part of the original listeners to praise the play above the middle grade: 35 per cent, whereas only 18.6 per cent of the undergraduate responses did. Although the tables are not quite the same it suggests that the original audience was twice as ready to find quality in the play. The Third Programme listening panel would have been made up of skilled radio listeners while the students' skills are in textual analysis rather than in the concentrated listening activity the play demands. The report, however, continues by recording that a 'not inconsiderable number [...] could find nothing at all to commend in the broadcast. They dismissed it as boring, incomprehensible, or depressing and regretted the time they had spent listening to it'. Although 'the largest group found much to interest and even entertain them in the play [they] remained far from enthusiastic. Beckett, they admitted, had a compelling and disturbing power; his work was full of starkly beautiful poetry and his command of language was sure and economically expressive'. Most members of the listening panel were both articulate and thoughtful in their responses, with only some dismissing it out of hand. And some also commented on its radiophonic qualities: 'several remarked that this play had been admirably conceived as a radio work, taking full advantage of all the resources of the medium'.

In relation to the actors, 'the great majority were full of praise for all those taking part', although some complained about Jack McGowran as Henry, finding his 'unintelligible mumble' and 'ear-splitting shouts [. . .] difficult to follow'; others gave his performance high praise. Ada's voice was 'generally [. . .] considered a very effective "spirit" voice'. There was also a variety of comments on the sound effects: some had to 'continually [. . .] adjust their volume control', and this is certainly a problem with the recording: MacGowran can be very loud; Kathleen Michael as Ada speaks very softly. Others found the 'production overloaded with contrived and artificial-sounding effects and suggested that a cult of "effects for effects' sake" was growing up'. This can be a problem, and was commented on by the students: one thought that the hum accompanying the sound of the sea on the shingle was an aeroplane, while another thought that the beach must have been close to a dual carriageway! A Third Programme listener described it as 'like my Hoover'. However the 'incessant sound of the sea' was appreciated by most listeners.

The 'effects for effects' sake' view does have credibility. The radiophonic workshop was an innovative BBC venture. Donald McWhinnie decided that the sea sound should be overlaid with an electronic hum which proved problematic for some listeners. No doubt his choice of defamiliarizing the sound of the sea was prompted by Henry's apparent need to clarify the sound of the sea to his father (and thus, of course, to the listener): 'The sound you hear is the sea, we are sitting on the strand. [*Pause. Louder.*] I say that sound you hear is the sea, we are sitting on the strand. [*Pause.*] I mention it because the sound is so strange, so unlike the sound of the sea, that if you didn't see what it was you wouldn't know what it was' (*CDW* 254). It could be claimed that McWhinnie took this too literally. Henry is explaining the sound to his blind father (surely quite unnecessarily, considering his love of the sea), and thus also to the 'blind' listener. This is what in film would be called an establishing shot. It is clarifying the sea and the strand as the situation in which the play is set. It is a strange explanation, but it is not necessary to estrange the actual sound of the sea, as the 'real' sea sound in Katharine Worth's production is markedly effective.[14] Everett Frost's production uses an actual recording of the sea.[15] McWhinnie's choice of defamiliarizing the sea sound creates a further difficulty for a radio play that is already placing an unusual burden on the listening skills of its audience, although repeated listenings do minimize the distracting quality of these sound effects. Alongside this, reading the text of the play, although it does not eliminate the difficult nature of the play, allows greater insight into the temporal shifts and the metalepses between the diegetic and metadiegetic levels.

Embers has had a surprisingly wide range of critical responses, and thus is a play that underlines the fact that with radio drama, and certainly with this particular Beckett play, 'each listener will construe it differently'.[16] Beckett had his own reservations about the play: 'It's not very satisfactory, but I think it's just worth doing'; 'I think it just gets by on radio'.[17] It is interesting to note that his first comment predates, and the second postdates, the BBC production. Roger Blin, in 1964, considered that *Embers* was 'Beckett's finest' play but his was a lone voice, although Paul Lawley has discussed it convincingly as an unrecognized 'achievement'.[18] Kenner, writing in 1973, was clearly disappointed with the BBC production, but considered that the 'script is fascinating'.[19] The more time spent considering the script, alongside re-listening to the production, certainly increases its fascination. But not everyone would agree: John Pilling, in 1976, contended that it was 'the first of Beckett's dramatic works that seems to lack a real centre; it relies very considerably on repeating a cluster of phrases [...] and it has a structural slackness deriving from the two main topics failing to blend'.[20] The 'remarkably complex' structure which Pilling points out is clearly working against the structural clarity Esslin recommends.[21] But Pilling adds that 'it is, despite this a very moving work', and is 'one of Beckett's most interesting confrontations of the configuring mind of the artist with the atoms of aesthetic material that he tries to make sense of'.[22] Worth, in 1981, commented on the fact that the original recording of *Embers* was not repeated by the BBC for 18 years (although there were repeat broadcasts in 1959 on 16 July and 28 November), and had less critical exegesis than *All That Fall*: 'One can only guess at the reasons; perhaps it has been considered a more rarified piece than its predecessor, less strong in variety of human interest'.[23] It is definitely less accessible than *All That Fall*, but does grow in depth and interest when re-listened to, but the original recording was unavailable until 2006. Worth produced her own audio performance of the play for the University of London, because of this lack of availability.

What does listening involve? According to Dan Sperber and Deirdre Wilson relevance plays an essential part. They write of how '[h]uman beings are efficient information-processing devices'.[24] To facilitate efficient processing a listener brings to a communication a set of assumptions from their 'cognitive environment'.[25] In the activity of listening 'much more information [is monitored] than central conceptual abilities can process', and for the sake of efficiency listeners process what seems to have most relevance to them.[26] If the communication being processed does not seem to have relevance in relation to existing assumptions, or cannot be connected to them, they will 'not bother to process it at all'.[27] In the everyday world 'the faculty of auditory perception handles a great number and variety of noises, few of which reach the level of attention'.[28] Much that is deemed irrelevant is filtered out, and 'the relevance of a phenomenon to an individual [is] the relevance achieved when it is optimally processed'.[29]

This idea of efficiency and optimal processing is without doubt very pertinent to everyday communication, but what of art? Sperber and Wilson do discuss explicit and implicit communication, and how much the listening ability can be slowed down and made more difficult by poetic effects.[30] The economy and efficiency of direct and explicit communication is lost. Poetic effect is defined as 'the particular effect of an utterance which achieves most of its relevance through a wide array of weak implicatures'.[31] Responding to art requires more effort – 'an effort of imagination'.[32] Art requires more than efficiency, and it can be suggested that art thrives on inefficiency, but this entails that it can also fail for those readers, spectators or listeners who resist the effort involved and find that the communication fails to connect with their existing assumptions.

Embers, unlike the vast majority of radio plays, is not concerned with facilitating the listening experience by minimizing the radio medium's inherent difficulties. On the contrary, it is, in fact, built upon the medium's very particular qualities – its ability to confuse, to obscure, to puzzle – and is focused on exploiting the very effects that result from the listener experiencing a dramatic world through sound and silence alone. In comparison with habitual perception, much is hidden, ambivalent and unclear, with the listener encouraged to imagine, invent and create. Beckett has not diminished the strangeness, but has made it a central element of the drama. He has taken on board the fact that the listener cannot see, and thus cannot use the visual sense to clarify or resolve the ambivalences, and has intensified the resultant effects rather than compensating for the medium's comparative limitations in relation to audience perception. The radio medium, the 'blind' medium, defamiliarizes, and Beckett has chosen to accentuate this. As Viktor Shklovski contends, defamiliarization is concerned with bringing a new perception to the reader, spectator or listener. It is in great contrast with Sperber and Wilson's model of efficiency as it is directly involved in overturning assumptions, and encouraging attention to what is filtered out in everyday, habitual perception:

> This new attitude to objects in which, in the last analysis, the object becomes perceptible, is that artificiality which, in our opinion, creates art. A phenomenon, perceived many times, and no longer perceivable, or rather, the method of such dimmed perception, is what I call 'recognition' as opposed to 'seeing'. The aim of imagery, the aim of creating new art is to return from 'recognition' to 'seeing'.[33]

The radio medium is an essentially artificial one, disrupting habitual perception through its lack of a visual dimension, yet listening without seeing can provoke, paradoxically, not 'dimmed perception' but a new way of 'seeing' – an interior 'seeing'. Shklovski's contention is valid in relation to habitual perception, which *Embers* is certainly engaged in problematizing, but repeated listenings to this play, intriguingly, do not encourage the 'dimmed' habituated perception, as the play continues to evade easy solution, and the listener continues to 'see' rather than merely recognize, in increasing depth – in effect, to 'see' what, in reality, cannot be seen.

In H. Porter Abbott's discussion of the 'cognitive sublime' the experience of difficult art is firmly differentiated from the cognitive efficiency of everyday, habitual perception. He begins by contrasting two ways of considering the 'conditions of reader resistance' and 'difficulty': defamiliarization and veiling. The 'veiled' narrative 'leads in one direction: to cognitive darkness', a darkness of course applicable to the radio medium: 'The insight acquired is a lack of sight, the revelation of an inescapable condition of unknowing that is unacknowledged or pasted over in conventional texts as it is in our lives outside the text'.[34] A radio listener lacks the sight of what is being presented, and staging *Embers* would enable a far more efficient assessment of what is 'happening' in the play, but at the same time would disambiguate elements in the play that need to remain a mystery: the ambiguity achieved by the veiling that is an essential element of the 'blind' medium would be unveiled. The veiled elements are crucial to *Embers*; it is deliberately making use of what could be seen as the limitations of radio drama, and showing just how these very limitations paradoxically create the ability to go further than is possible in audio/visual media – taking the listeners beyond the known, the recognizable, the already assimilated. Abbott defines his term the 'cognitive sublime' as achieved by 'an immersion in a state of bafflement'; 'an immersion in a state of unknowing'.[35] This recalls Stanley Fish's advocation of the unsolvable, the uninterpretable in difficult art: 'There are problems that apparently can't be solved [. . .] What I would like to argue is that they are not *meant* to be solved, but to be experienced [. . .]'.[36] Abbott's use of the word 'bafflement' recalls Beckett's striking phrase in his essay on Marcel Proust: 'baffled ecstasy', a useful term in relation to some listeners' responses to *Embers*.[37] Turning to *Proust* (1931) can help to explain the puzzling nature of *Embers*, and the particular listener response which this play, it can be suggested, is attempting to achieve. Beckett's discussion of 'Habit' (that 'great deadener' [*CDW* 84]) shows how it incapacitates the ability to deal with that which is mysterious or 'strange' (*Proust* 20); it is 'a minister of dullness' and 'an agent of security' (*Proust* 21). Listening is shown as able to circumvent habit, as when Marcel hears his Grandmother's voice on the telephone 'in all its purity' and strangeness (*Proust* 26–7), and in the discussion of music, which is described as 'an art that is perfectly unintelligible and perfectly inexplicable' (*Proust* 92). Radio drama disrupts habitual perception in that it is to be listened to, and only listened to. Sounds and silence abstracted from sight cause an immediate estrangement. *Embers* encourages the listener to enter into a strange, dark and inexplicable place – the interior – to circumvent the habitual and discover/uncover the hidden and the strange. It is a challenging play, especially for first listeners, but given time it is a play that grows and grows in depth and richness without ever relinquishing what really matters: its difficulty, and thus its mystery and its magic.

Acknowledgements

Many thanks to the BBC Written Archives for permission to quote from their files, to Louise North (WAC) for all her help with my research and to John McGavin, Angela Moorjani and Porter Abbott for their useful comments and suggestions. I also wish to thank all the students who listened to the play and reported their responses.

Notes

1 Hugh Kenner, *Samuel Beckett* (London: John Calder, 1962), 174.
2 Ronald Hayman, *Samuel Beckett* (London: Heinemann, 1980), 54.
3 Anthony Cronin, *Samuel Beckett: The Last Modernist* (London: HarperCollins, 1996), 489.
4 Perloff, Marjorie, 'The Silence that is not Silence: Acoustic Art in Samuel Beckett's *Embers*'. http://wings.buffalo.edu/epc/authors/perloff/beckett.html (Accessed 20 June 2012), 7.
5 *Writing Drama for BBC Radio*. www.dswilliams.co.uk/ete/Writing%20Drama%20For%20BBC%20Radio.htm (Accessed 20 June 2012).
6 Ibid.
7 Martin Esslin, *Mediations: Essays on Brecht, Beckett and the Media* (London: Eyre Methuen, 1980), 179.
8 Ibid., 180.
9 Samuel Beckett, *The Complete Dramatic Works* (London: Faber and Faber, 1990), 260. Subsequent references are made parenthetically as *CDW*.
10 *Writing Drama for BBC Radio*.

11 Ibid.
12 Samuel Beckett, *Works for Radio: The Original Broadcasts* (British Library Board, 2006).
13 The subsequent references are to the Audience Research Report, *Embers*.WAC LR/59/1090. 9 July 1959. BBC Written Archives, Caversham. The Third Programme featured many non-mainstream and experimental plays by playwrights such as Jean Anouilh, Bertolt Brecht, Albert Camus, Jean Cocteau and Eugene Ionesco, and the radio broadcast would usually precede any theatre performance in the United Kingdom. See Kate Whitehead, *The Third Programme: A Literary History* (Oxford: Clarendon Press, 1989), 138.
14 See Katharine Worth, 'Beckett and the Radio Medium', in, *British Radio Drama*, edited by John Drakakis (Cambridge: Cambridge University Press, 1981), 191–217.
15 See Everett Frost, 'Fundamental Sounds: Recording Samuel Beckett's Radio Plays', *Theatre Journal* 43 (1991): 361–76 for a discussion of his production.
16 Donald McWhinnie, *The Art of Radio* (London: Faber & Faber, 1959), 26.
17 Quoted in Clas Zilliacus, *Beckett and Broadcasting: A Study of the Works of Samuel Beckett for and in Radio and Television* (Abo: Abo Akademi, 1976), 76.
18 Quoted in Beryl Fletcher, John Fletcher, Barry Smith and Walter Bachem, *A Student's Guide to the Plays of Samuel Beckett* (London: Faber & Faber, 1978), 95. Paul Lawley, 'Samuel Beckett's Relations' *Journal of Beckett Studies* 6.2 (1997), 1.
19 Quoted in ibid., 127.
20 John Pilling, *Samuel Beckett* (London: Routledge & Kegan Paul, 1976), 98.
21 Ibid., 101, 180.
22 Ibid., 98–9.
23 Worth, 202.
24 Dan Sperber and Deirdre Wilson, *Relevance: Communication and Cognition* (Oxford: Basil Blackwell, 1986), 46.
25 Ibid., 46.
26 Ibid., 47.

27   Ibid., 142.
28   Ibid., 151.
29   Ibid., 152.
30   Ibid., 218.
31   Ibid., 222.
32   Ibid., 223.
33   Viktor Borisovich Shklovski, *Mayakovsky and his Circle*, edited and translated by Lily Feiler (New York: Dodd, Mead, 1972), 101.
34   H. Porter Abbott, 'Immersions in the Cognitive Sublime: The Textual Experience of the Extratextual Unknown in Garcia Márquez & Beckett', *Narrative* 17.2 (2009), 131.
35   Ibid., 3, 14.
36   Stanley Fish, 'Interpreting the *Variorum*', in *Reader-Response Criticism: From Formalism to Post-Structuralism*, edited by Janet Tompkins (Baltimore: The Johns Hopkins University Press, 1980), 164.
37   Samuel Beckett, *Proust and Three Dialogues with Georges Duthuit* (London: John Calder, 1987), 76. Subsequent references are made parenthetically as *Proust*.

Works cited

Abbott, Porter H. 'Immersions in the Cognitive Sublime: The Textual Experience of the Extratextual Unknown in Garcia Márquez & Beckett', *Narrative* 17.2 (2009): 131–42.
Audience Research Report. *Embers*. LR/59/1090. 9 July 1959. BBC Written Archives, Caversham.
Beckett, Samuel. *Proust and Three Dialogues with Georges Duthuit* (London: John Calder, 1987).
—. *The Complete Dramatic Works* (London: Faber and Faber, 1990).
—. *Works for Radio: The Original Broadcasts*. Audio recording (London: British Library Board, 2006.)
Cronin, Anthony. *Samuel Beckett: The Last Modernist* (London: HarperCollins, 1996).

Drakakis, John. *British Radio Drama* (Cambridge: Cambridge University Press, 1981).

Esslin, Martin. *Mediations: Essays on Brecht, Beckett and the Media* (London: Eyre Methuen, 1980).

Fish, Stanley. 'Interpreting the *Variorum*', in *Reader-Response Criticism: From Formalism to Post-Structuralism*, edited by Janet Tompkins (Baltimore: The Johns Hopkins University Press, 1980), 164–84.

Fletcher, Beryl, John Fletcher, Barry Smith and Walter Bachem. *A Student's Guide to the Plays of Samuel Beckett* (London: Faber & Faber, 1978).

Frost, Everett. 'Fundamental Sounds: Recording Samuel Beckett's Radio Plays', *Theatre Journal* 43 (1991): 361–76.

Hayman, Ronald. *Samuel Beckett* (London: Heinemann, 1980).

Kenner, Hugh. *Samuel Beckett* (London: John Calder, 1962).

Lawley, Paul. 'Samuel Beckett's Relations', *Journal of Beckett Studies* 6.2 (1997): 1–61.

McWhinnie, Donald. *The Art of Radio* (London: Faber & Faber, 1959).

Perloff, Marjorie. 'The Silence that is not Silence: Acoustic Art in Samuel Beckett's *Embers*'. http://wings.buffalo.edu/epc/authors/perloff/beckett.html (Accessed 20 June 2012).

Pilling, John. *Samuel Beckett* (London: Routledge&Kegan Paul, 1976).

Shklovski, Viktor Borisovich. *Mayakovsky and his Circle*, edited and translated by Lily Feiler (New York: Dodd, Mead, 1972).

Sperber, Dan and Deirdre Wilson. *Relevance: Communication and Cognition* (Oxford: Basil Blackwell, 1986).

Whitehead, Kate. *The Third Programme: A Literary History* (Oxford: Clarendon Press, 1989).

Worth, Katharine. 'Beckett and the Radio Medium', in, *British Radio Drama*, edited by John Drakakis (Cambridge: Cambridge University Press, 1981), 191–217.

Writing Drama for BBC Radio. www.dswilliams.co.uk/ete/Writing%20Drama%20For%20BBC%20Radio.htm (Accessed 20 June 2012).

Zilliacus, Clas. *Beckett and Broadcasting: A Study of the Works of Samuel Beckett for and in Radio and Television* (Abo: Abo Akademi, 1976).

7

Somnambulism, Amnesia and Fugue: Beckett and (Male) Hysteria

Ulrika Maude
University of Reading

Hysteria was a fashionable disease in the last decades of the nineteenth century, so much so that it 'was covertly identified with something like an art [form], close to theatre and painting'.[1] Jean-Martin Charcot's famous Tuesday lectures, held at his neurology clinic at the Salpêtrière Hospital in Paris – the first clinic of its kind in Europe, established in 1882 – were crowd-pullers and references to the lectures frequently appeared in popular newspapers and magazines. At the Tuesday lectures, Charcot would develop his case studies and demonstrate the symptoms of his patients in front of admiring crowds, much in the manner portrayed in André Brouillet's well-known painting, 'Une leçon clinique à La Salpêtrière' (1887), which features a swooning female patient, known as 'Blanche', being supported by Charcot's student, Joseph Babinski, while the neurologist himself is lecturing to what were later to become his many celebrity students. The painting, as the medical historian, Mark S. Micale has pointed out, offers a classic gendered representation: 'sober, active, authoritative male science, bearded and clad formally in black, on one side of the image, and passive, vulnerable but voluptuous femininity, highlighted with crimson lipstick, on the other side'.[2] Charcot and his disciples were considered the medical avant-garde of Paris, and a number of them, including Sigmund Freud, Georges Gilles de la Tourette, William

James, Pierre Janet and Joseph Babinski, went onto have illustrious careers of their own. But in the popular culture of the period, many of Charcot's female patients (including 'Blanche', whose real name was Marie Wittman), also acquired celebrity status. As Asti Hustvedt has recently argued, they were sculpted, painted, photographed and fictionalized, and a number of the patients even went on to have successful careers on the stage.[3]

What has been observed less often is that Charcot also had a serious interest in male hysteria, which he studied for the last 15 years of his life, from 1878 to 1893. The Salpêtrière had been a female institution since its inauguration in the seventeenth century, and had housed between five and eight thousand female patients at any one time. In 1882, partly in order to pursue his interest in male hysteria, Charcot inaugurated the Hospital's *'service des hommes'*, dedicated to 'the study and treatment of [male] subjects suffering from transient nervous and neurological disorders'.[4] During the 1880s, Charcot wrote 61 detailed case studies of male hysteria, took notes on 30 additional cases and treated numerous other male patients who suffered from what was then called hysteria.[5] In his preface to *Clinical Lectures on Certain Diseases of the Nervous System*, written in 1888, Charcot noted that 'Male hysteria belongs truly to every-day medical practice, and not to know it, not to be aware that it exists in both men of culture and in the working man devoted to manual labour, is to render one's self liable to frequent mistakes, and mistakes which may be quite serious from a professional point of view'.[6] By the time of Charcot's death, in 1893, male hysteria 'was widely accepted within mainstream European medical communities' as a diagnostic category, but the publication of Freud and Breuer's *Studies in Hysteria* in 1895, and Freud's subsequent work on the topic, revived the gendered bias of hysteria as a female affliction.[7]

Charcot's interest in male hysteria had a number of triggers. In part, it was instigated by 'a broad cultural process occurring in many scientific and non-scientific areas of late nineteenth-century European thought, whereby traditional definitions of masculinity and femininity underwent extensive reformulation.'[8] Charcot, however, was not the first physician to write about male hysteria. Although the disorder is by its name a female one (from the Greek *hystera*, for womb) Charles Lepois, as early as 1618, suggested that both men and women suffered from the disorder and that both exhibited almost all of its known symptoms. The shift witnessed in the seventeenth century in the understanding of mental illness as a problem not of the reproductive organs but of the brain and nerves, also triggered other writings on male hysteria in the early modern period, but the late-eighteenth and early-nineteenth centuries revived the gyneacological theories of nervous and mental illness, and with them the gendered notion of hysteria as a female affliction. However, in 1859 Pierre Briquet argued in his *Traité Clinique et thérapeutique de l'hystérie* that 'hysteria was a disorder of the higher nervous system' and he insisted on its 'reality in both sexes'.[9] His book had little impact on his contemporaries, but it proved crucial to Charcot and the Salpêtrians a few decades later, in the 1880s.

Hysterical and epileptic patents at the Salpêtrière frequently described their behaviour as mechanical and automatic. The convulsive movements they experienced gave rise to the concept of the 'corporeal unconscious': 'the lower, automatic and instinctual level of life', which was seen to predominate in patients who suffered from pathologies of the nervous system.[10] Popular interest in these disorders was rife. In addition to being disseminated through the Tuesday lectures and the popular publications of its time, the work of Charcot and his students was brought to public attention through the journal *Nouvelle iconographie photographique de la Salpêtrière*, which distributed images of hysterics and epileptics as well as of sufferers of other neurological disorders, and which ran from 1888 to 1918 and had Gilles de la Tourette as one of its founders. So pervasive was Charcot's work and its impact that it rapidly influenced the performance style of the Parisian cabaret and vaudeville 'with a new repertoire of movements, grimaces, tics and gestures'.[11] Comedians in particular sported convulsive and marionette-like gaits and movements, and mime troupes and singers followed suit in performances that seemed to cast doubt over received notions of the body's functioning and by implication, the wider questions of agency and free will. Many cabaret and music hall performers went on to have successful careers in silent film, which, as a genre, adopted the frenetic, convulsive and automatic performance style of vaudeville and cabaret. As Rae Beth Gordon writes: 'There is a continuous line and directing force running from the cabaret and café-concert performances of the last quarter of the nineteenth century, through the films of Georges Méliès and the musicals of Ernst Lubitsch in the 1930s [...]. The uniting element is hysterical gesture and gait'. Henri Bergson's *Le Rire*, published in 1899, centred itself around the notion of 'automatic gesture and word', and one can trace a direct genealogy between Charcot's work, the popular culture of the period and Bergson's theory of comedy.[12] So fashionable and intriguing did hysteria prove at the turn of the century that it generated, besides a new performance style, a number of songs and literary works, such as Guy de Maupassant's short story, 'Le Tic' ('The Spasm'), from 1884. Tracing the development and manifestations of an involuntary spasm in a father whose daughter has been buried alive, the story can be read as a curious demonstration of what would later be called conversion hysteria. The spasm the father experiences each time he reaches for an object is described as 'a sort of zigzag' – a pattern that according to Charcot presented in the visual scotoma of hysterical patients, and that features as a trope for nervous disorders in films like Robert Wiene's *Das Kabinet des Dr Caligari* (*The Cabinet of Dr Caligari*), from 1920, and Ernst Lubitsch's *Die Puppe* (*Doll*), from 1919.

We do not know whether Samuel Beckett read Maupassant's story, but we do know that Maupassant was one of the authors

Beckett studied for his degree in French and Italian at Trinity College, Dublin. We also know that in 1931, Beckett came across direct references to Charcot's work on male hysteria in his reading of Max Nordau's *Degeneration*, translated in 1895 from the 1892 original, *Entartung*. He made a note in his '*Dream* Notebook', for instance, of Charcot's conception of '*Folie à deux*', by which Charcot meant, in Nordau's formulation, that 'a deranged person completely focuses his ideas on his companion; among the hysterical it assumes the form of close friendships, causing Charcot to repeat at every opportunity: "Persons of highly-strung nerves attract each other"; and finally authors found schools'.[13] Nordau is here referring to the notion of contagion by imitation, a recurrent fear surrounding nervous disorders in the nineteenth century, and proposing nervous imitation as the raison d'être of artistic schools. But the notion of nervous imitation and 'sympathy' was a pervasive one, and Bergson himself argued that an artist aims to communicate to us the emotion he himself has felt,

> enabling us to experience what he cannot make us understand. This he will bring about by choosing, among the outward signs of his emotions, those which our body is likely to imitate mechanically, though slightly, as soon as it perceives them, so as to transport us to the indefinable psychological state which called them forth.[14]

Such imitation, it was feared, could precipitate a habitual action, and trigger hysteria (or epilepsy) in the otherwise unaffected subject. This idea of somatic imitation is at play for instance in T. S. Eliot's early poem, 'Hysteria' (1915), where the speaker is transfixed by the sight of a woman suffering from a hysterical attack: 'I was drawn in by short gasps, | inhaled at each momentary recovery, lost finally | in the dark caverns of her throat, bruised by | the ripple of unseen muscles'.[15] Eliot's poem, in its staging of the 'contagious' nature of hysteria, is an example of the somatic identification that Bergson outlined.

Like Maupassant's story, it also represents male subjects affected or afflicted by hysteria.

Beckett would also have read, in Nordau's book, of 'the researches of the Charcot school into the visual derangements in degeneration and hysteria. The painters who assure us that they are sincere, and reproduce nature as they see it, speak the truth. The degenerate artist who suffers from *nystagmus*, or trembling of the eyeball, will, in fact, perceive the phenomena of nature trembling, restless, devoid of firm outline'.[16]

Beckett took a note of this passage in his '*Dream* Notebook' and it would have intrigued him greatly, not least because he had an avid interest in painting as we know from his correspondence and his critical writings. But Beckett also had an interest in the kinds of visual 'derangements' that Nordau outlines. The visual effects of blurring or a loss of firm outline appear regularly in Beckett's prose, for instance in the novella *The Calmative* (1946), which can be said to focus on fallible and fleshly human vision, and in which the narrator, fixing his eyes on a boy and a goat, remarks that 'soon they were no more than a single blur which if I hadn't known I might have taken for a centaur'.[17] Blurring, or the loss of a firm outline also figures prominently in Beckett's *Film* (1964), where the effect is achieved through the use of a gauze filter on the camera lens. Both works also profitably lend themselves to more comprehensive readings that focus on hysteria. Beckett was to encounter the very real effects of discourses of degeneration during his travels in Nazi Germany from October 1936 to April 1937. As he toured the various public galleries, he realized with disappointment, as he put it in a letter to Mary Manning Howe in November 1936, that all 'the best pictures are in the cellar'.[18] For the National Socialists, modern art was a manifestation of degeneracy, and hence best kept out of the public realm. On 30 July 1936, the Nationalgalerie in Berlin was forced to close the rooms housing its contemporary artworks. It was the first of many such closures to follow.[19]

Another of Beckett's early encounters with the notion of hysteria came in 1932, when he translated Louis Aragon and André Breton's 'The Fiftieth Anniversary of Hysteria' for the special Surrealist issue of *This Quarter*, published in 1932. Breton had himself studied neurology and psychiatry, and been a student of Pierre Janet, who had published *État mental des hystériques* in 1894 and had in turn studied with Charcot. Furthermore, Breton had also worked in the psychiatric wards during the First World War, and he would have witnessed first-hand the effects of shell shock, which was but another name for male hysteria. In the essay, Aragon and Breton advocate hysteria not as a 'pathological phenomenon' but as 'a supreme form of expression'. They associate the 'birth date' of hysteria with the year 1878, which is precisely when Charcot began to study male hysteria.[20] Beckett also translated passages from *The Immaculate Conception* by Breton and Paul Éluard, for the same special issue. The book's essays simulate mental illness, paralysis and other debilities for literary effect, 'maladies virtual in each one of us [that] could replace most advantageously the ballad, the sonnet, the epic, the poem without head or tail, and other decrepit modes'.[21] For the Surrealists, nervous disorders and madness liberated language from convention, which in turn enabled the linguistic experimentation endemic to modernist writing. As Daniel Albright has remarked, Breton's catch phrases – 'psychic automatism, convulsive beauty' – foreground the hysterico-epileptic aspect of Surrealism.[22] Although Beckett was not an advocate of the Surrealists' automatic writing, the connection between pathological language and linguistic creativity bears crucial relevance to his work.

In the 1930s, and especially after his father's death in 1933, Beckett himself suffered a number of symptoms that fit the description of hysteria. These included an arrhythmic heart (which Charcot would have called a 'hysterical heart'), shudders, panic attacks, night sweats, breathlessness and even, at its most extreme, paralysis. During what

Beckett himself called the 'bad years' of 1932 and 1933, he had a curious and memorable experience that he later recounted to his biographer, James Knowlson:

> I was walking up Dawson Street and I felt I couldn't go on. It was a strange experience I can't really describe. I found I couldn't go on moving. So I had to rush into the famous pub in Dawson Street, Davy Byrne's. I don't know where I was going, maybe to Harcourt Street [station]. So I went into the nearest pub and got a drink – just to stay still. And I felt I needed help.[23]

After the incident, Beckett consulted a close friend from his days at Portora Royal School, Geoffrey Thompson, who had trained as a doctor and who duly recommended that Beckett have analysis. This, however, was illegal in Ireland at the time, due in part to its connotations as a secular form of confession, and Beckett travelled to London where he was analysed by Wilfred Bion at the Tavistock Clinic for a period of close to two years. During the period of his thrice-weekly sessions of analysis, in 1934 and 1935, Beckett read a number of books on psychology and psychoanalysis. Matthew Feldman has argued that the 'overriding impulsion' for this reading was 'attempted self-diagnosis'.[24] One of the volumes Beckett read was the 1931 edition of Robert S. Woodworth's *Contemporary Schools of Psychology*, which contained references to Charcot and his discoveries.[25] Another was Ernest Jones's *Treatment of the Neuroses*, from 1920; Jones's book was deeply Freudian, and Beckett humorously referred to Jones in his notes as 'Freudchen'. He took three pages of notes on the second chapter of the book, which is dedicated to hysteria. Among these are the following annotations:

> Hysteria, or, malingering.
> Common neurotic manifestations: oedemas, neuralgias, pseudoangina & other cardiac syndromes, bronchial asthma, enuresis, pavor nocturnus [night terror], gastric & intestinal disturbance, pollakiuria, spermatorrhoea, dysuria.

Central symptom of neurosis is interference with social capability. One of the functions & meanings of a neurosis the provocation of distress in the subject's entourage (hence resentment & scepticism of 'normal' people).
Neuroses represent a conflict between the individual and society, other diseases a conflict between man & nature.
Hysteria almost as incurable as cancer.
Three simple or actual neuroses: neurasthenia, anxiety neurosis & hypocondria [sic]; & four psychoneuroses: conversion-hysteria, anxiety-hysteria, fixation-hysteria & the obsessional neurosis.[26]

Many of these symptoms later enter Beckett's work, and the author himself suffered from a number of them. For Matthew Feldman, in fact, this 'excerpt is in closest proximity to Beckett's own self-conception'.[27] Beckett also wrote the following definition of conversion hysteria in his notebook: 'an afferent impulse which is inhibited from finding its normal expression, corresponding to an emotional manifestation, flows along other neural paths, producing motor effects appropriate to the latter'.[28] In addition to shedding light on Beckett's pervasive interest in the involuntary tics and automatisms that figure so prominently in his work, this annotation registers the close connection between neurology and psychology in the period. Beckett is taking his notes in the early heyday of psychoanalysis, but Jones's book is written in 1920, when psychoanalysis was just taking over from neurology as the dominant discourse on problems of the mind and the nervous system.

In Beckett studies, there has been a tendency to see female characters such as Maddy Rooney in *All That Fall* (1956), Winnie in *Happy Days* (1961), W1 and W2 in *Play* (1963), Mouth in *Not I* (1972), May in *Footfalls* (1975) and W in *Rockaby* (1980) as hysterics. For some critics, this has supported claims of Beckett's misogyny. Beckett's male characters, on the other hand, have on more than one occasion been deemed schizophrenics.[29] Although it is true that

Mr Endon in *Murphy* (1938) is described as 'a schizophrenic of the most amiable variety', and Victor Krap in *Eleutheria* (1947) also suffers, according to Dr Piouk, from 'schizophrénie', this stark critical division into female hysteria and male schizophrenia may nonetheless be an appropriation or internalization of normative gender representations and encoded ideas of masculinity that are reproduced in critical practice.[30] In *Beckett, Literature and the Ethics of Alterity* (2006), however, Shane Weller responds compellingly to the received division in Beckett criticism of female hysteria and male schizophrenia by proposing that these two disorders, whose symptomatology is often strikingly similar, form a kind of pseudocouple. Weller writes: 'this pseudocouple is not static but itself disintegrative, disintegrating the difference between schizophrenia and hysteria – which is to say, disintegrating the difference between what, for Freud, are two distinct modes of disintegration.'[31] If we date these disorders back to the nineteenth century, in fact, the distinction between hysteria and dementia praecox, a mental illness identified by Emile Kraepelin in 1887 (the term 'schizophrenia' was not coined until 1911, by Eugen Bleuler), would have been less significant than the distinction between hysteria and epilepsy, which were themselves closely linked in the medical understanding of the nineteenth century. Nor is there a clear-cut division in the period between psychiatry, neurology and the emerging discourse of psychoanalysis, nor, by proxy, between neurosis and psychosis, and there is a notable diagnostic and discursive slippage between the various branches of study and the two types of mental disturbance. Freud and Breuer published their 'Psychical Mechanism of Hysterical Phenomena: A Preliminary Communication' in 1893, followed by *Studies on Hysteria* in 1895, which heralded a return to gendered notions of hysteria. But hysteria as a performance style and as a disorder that captured the popular imagination on a wide scale was already well-established by this time and Rae Beth Gordon has described in some detail the various forms that this fascination took, from cartoons, hysterical songs, mime groups, music hall performances and medical plays to short stories and film.[32] In other words, in the period these disorders entered performance culture and the popular imagination, the gendered distinctions were not as stark as they were to become in the twentieth century.

Beckett would also have been intimately familiar with the performance style of early film, especially silent comedy, which was deeply indebted to cabaret, vaudeville and music hall performances, which were themselves in turn influenced by the discoveries and debates surrounding nervous disorders. Early film, furthermore, inherited a number of its stars from music hall and vaudeville, which in part helps explain the clear affinities between music hall and vaudeville aesthetic, on the one hand, and silent film, on the other. Beckett, born in 1906, had been an avid fan of cinema since his childhood in Dublin, and during his undergraduate years at Trinity College Dublin and his period as *Lecteur* at the École Normale Supérieure in Paris from 1928 to 1930, he had continued to see films regularly, as James Knowlson asserts, adding that Beckett was also 'very familiar with Expressionist and Surrealist cinema.'[33] He particularly enjoyed the silent films of Buster Keaton and Charlie Chaplin, and it was in Paris that he would have seen a number of avant-garde films, including Luis Buñuel and Salvador Dalí's *Un Chien andalou* (1928) and *L'Age d'or* (1930), whose iconography left traces both in Beckett's prose and in his drama. Although we do not know for certain which German Expressionist films Beckett saw, it is unlikely he would have missed Robert Wiene's *Das Kabinet des Dr Caligari*. The same could be said for Murnau's *Nosferatu*, from 1922, as well as a number of Fritz Lang films, such as the Dr Mabuse films, which feature Mabuse as a mesmerist or mind doctor who manipulates people into acting to the dictates of his will. What all of these films have in common, firstly, is the prominent medical references they contain, most markedly to mesmerism or hypnosis (an early treatment for hysteria at the Salpêtrière), and to such disorders as somnambulism, dyskinesia, amnesia, fugue and mental breakdown, all of which were classified as symptoms of hysteria in the period. Secondly, they all share a highly stylized performance style, reminiscent of cabaret and music hall performances, and they also often feature the iconography of hysteria, such as the zigzag patterning reminiscent of the scotoma that Charcot's hysterical patients suffered from. Thirdly, they represent a pervasive thematic concern and anxiety over loss of agency and autonomy: in other words, of the self (body and mind) acting at the dictates of forces beyond its control. The hysterics in early cinema, however, tended to be men, and the wider point I would like to make here is that although the iconography of hysteria in the last decades of the nineteenth century centred around the fetishization of female patients there is also an iconography of male hysteria which is recorded most prominently in silent film. As the avant-garde film maker, Jean Epstein observed about one of the greatest stars of the silent era, Charlie Chaplin: 'his entire performance consists of the reflex actions of a nervous, tired person'. Epstein characterised Chaplin's performance style as one of 'photogenic neurasthenia'.[34]

The importance of silent film to Beckett's aesthetic can be seen in the many motifs of early film that repeat themselves in his work, and in the performance style of his drama, particularly in the prominence of dyskinesia – the curious gait of the characters and the tics, trembling, convulsions and grimaces that repeat themselves throughout his stage and television plays, as I have argued elsewhere. It can also be seen in the many motifs of silent film that one encounters in his work. Among the most striking are somnambulism, amnesia and fugue, which were all considered symptoms of hysteria at the turn of the twentieth century. These are particularly prominent in Beckett's drama, although not exclusive to it, perhaps since, as Phil Baker argues, 'The art that hysteria particularly resembles is drama, because the feature that distinguishes hysteria is the conversion of psychic material into bodily actions and symptoms'. As Baker adds, hysteria 'somatises or dramatises the psychic by (re)enacting it, converting it into a somatic/dramatic form'.[35]

The protagonists of Beckett's television plays, in particular, in their curiously 'absent present' nature, often seem to resemble somnambulists: players acting, as if in a deep hypnotic trance, at the dictates of forces beyond their control. *Eh Joe*, Beckett's first television play, from 1966, features a protagonist haunted by a female voice from the past, 'Low, distinct, remote, little colour, absolutely steady rhythm, slightly slower than normal', which compels Joe to look behind a window and pallet in a vain attempt to locate its source.[36] The voice in the BBC production was Siân Phillips's: 'it was picked up by a long, slim microphone almost in her mouth. The sound was processed: high and low frequencies were cut off. This resulted in a kind of posthumous vocal colourlessness, as suggested by the author's directions'.[37] For Jack MacGowran, the actor who played the part of Joe in the BBC production, Joe was 'listening to this voice in his head'. For him, the teleplay was essentially about 'photographing the mind', because 'the television camera photographs the mind better than anything else'.[38] This may be said to be a feature of Beckett's teleplays that bears striking affinities with German Expressionist films of the 1920s and 1930s, which repeatedly and obsessively stage the 'absent present' quality of somnambulism and night terror. *Ghost Trio*, from 1976, and *...but the clouds...* from 1977, are, like *Eh Joe*, memory plays, but in them, the protagonists, F and M, act even more mechanically, as if in the grip of a clockwork mechanism. The voiceovers in these two plays, furthermore, have a more clearly 'agential function, determining what takes place within the frame'.[39] Beckett's late plays for the screen and the stage are dominated by an acousmatic voice, a voice that is heard but not seen, 'a voice without a place'. A particularly striking feature of the television plays is that since the voice is 'inassimilable to diegesis' it provides 'a kind of technological mediation between presence and absence, and aural equivalent for the phenomenology of sleep'.[40] Paul Sheehan argues that 'by confounding the distinction between diegetic and non-diegetic sound, Beckett is also charting an in-between state that disturbs the division between presence and absence, just as sleep does'.[41] For Sheehan, Beckett's model for his television plays comes precisely from 'the silent cinema of the 1910s and 1920s, with its air of distant, yet deep-rooted melancholia': 'Ronald Pickup as F, the male figure [in *Ghost Trio*], seems to have wandered in from a German Expressionist film'.[42] Although devoid of the acousmatic voice, which here has been replaced by a hypnotic percussion, the four players in *Quad I* and *II* (1982) similarly seem to be acting under a compulsion not discernibly or understandably their own. These films bring to mind such classics as Wiene's *Caligari*, in which the somnambulist, Cesare, commits crimes under Caligari's mesmeric dictates. They also resemble Fritz Lang's Dr Mabuse films, precisely in the way that the protagonists seem to be acting under an agency not their own. Beckett's screen players (one hesitates to call them characters) are sleepwalkers ruined by grief and regret. They repeat the same actions over and over again, without release from their 'absent present' state. Stage plays that exhibit a similar pattern include *Footfalls* and *Rockaby*, which can be characterized as Beckett's deep sleep dramas. As V puts it to Amy in *Footfalls*: 'I heard you in my deep sleep. There is no sleep so deep I would not hear you there' (*CDW* 399). Phil Baker has argued that

> The physical hieroglyph of May [in *Footfalls*] presents her 'wheeling' in body as the somatic/dramatic equivalent of her 'revolving it all' in her mind, and is thus a definitively hysterical element within the play's obsessional ritual: her wheelings to and fro on the stage *embody* her 'revolving it all' endlessly in her 'poor mind'.[43]

Rockaby, which is often paired in performance with *Footfalls*, displays a similar ossification of affect. The play is structured around four movements, consisting of V's obsessional and repetitive enunciations and the near-autistic rocking of W in her chair, which for Baker becomes precisely a trope for the 'mechanization of human feeling'.[44] W's 'Huge eyes in white expressionless face' (*CDW* 433) only add to the compulsive, somnambulistic quality of the play.

One prominent category of transient mental illness studied at the medical faculty in Bordeaux and at the Salpêtrière Hospital in Paris was ambulatory automatism, a form of hysterical, dissociative fugue. In addition to France, cases of ambulatory automatism, also known as dromomania, *poriomanie* and *Wandertrieb*, were encountered in Italy, Germany and Russia. Ambulatory automatism became a diagnosable mental illness in 1887, and what was striking about it was that it was 'highly gender-specific', conceived of almost exclusively as a male disorder.[45] A major epidemic of ambulatory automatism was encountered in France between 1887 and 1909. Attacks were characterized by 'an episode of sudden, unexpected travel away from home or business with amnesia regarding the past and partial to total confusion about identity or assumption of a new identity'. A. Pitre, who studied the disorder in Bordeaux, described it in 1891 in the following way:

> By the term ambulatory automatism is understood a pathological syndrome appearing in the form of intermittent attacks during which the patient, carried away by an irresistible impulse, leaves his home and makes an excursion or journey justified by no reasonable motive. The attack ended, the subject unexpectedly finds himself on an unknown road or in a strange town. Swearing by all the gods never again to quit his penates, he returns home but sooner or later a new attack provokes a new escapade.[46]

Silent film appears to be centrally indebted to this epidemic, and Charlie Chaplin's tramp, for instance, was probably in part modelled on the sufferers of this disorder. But equally indebted to it seem to be Beckett's tramps, especially the narrators of the four novellas (*Premier amour, L'Expulsé, Le Calmant* and *La Fin*) from 1946. The same could be said for *Molloy*, whose protagonist forgets his name and place of origin, and who by some accounts is even doubled in the stern figure of Moran in the second part of the novel, in another classic symptom of hysteria. Attacks of ambulatory automatism were characterized by behaviour that did not seem intentional. The journeys of sufferers appeared agent-less and devoid of distinct goals. In a similar vein, *Molloy* although clearly drawing on the genre of quest narratives, repeatedly frustrates notions of questing precisely in its problematization of intentionality or goal-oriented behaviour. The novel also draws on the genre of *Bildungsroman*, but again, instead of identity, we encounter in Beckett's novel its progressive undoing – something that also seemed to occur in attacks of dissociative fugue. Ambulatory automatism is characterized by behaviour that is not directed by any normal sense of personality nor remembered after the fugue ends, and Molloy too suffers from amnesia in the novel. When at the beginning of the novel he unexpectedly finds himself in his mother's bed, he is forced to acknowledge that 'I don't know how I got there'.[47] The *fugueur*, furthermore, 'tended to lose touch with exactly those facts that bureaucrats use to identify us: proper name, place of birth, domicile, married or single?, relatives, educational history, job'.[48] When Molloy is arrested and taken to the police station for interrogation, we learn that

> the sergeant, content to threaten me with a cylindrical ruler, was little by little rewarded for his pains by the discovery that I had no papers in the sense that this word had a sense for him, nor any occupation, nor any domicile, that my surname escaped me for the moment and that I was on my way to my mother, whose charity kept me dying. As to her address, I was in the dark, but knew how to get there, even in the dark. (*Trilogy* 22)

Molloy's behaviour is also characterized by other manifestations of hysteria. He suffers from stiffness of the leg, a classic symptom of conversion hysteria, which he overcomes in the following way:

> Crippled though I was, I was no mean cyclist, at that period. This is how I went about it. I fastened my crutches to the cross-bar, one on either side, I propped the foot of my stiff leg (I forget which, now they're both stiff) on the projecting front axle, and I pedalled with the other. (*Trilogy* 17)

And some fugueurs did in fact travel by bicycle. In this sense, the narrators of the four novellas, as well as Molloy, Malone (who makes repeated albeit confused and uncertain references to his former travels), Didi, Gogo, Clov, Mercier and Camier and a number of other male protagonists in Beckett's work who experience fugue, amnesia, limping, stiffness of the joints and other symptoms of (conversion) hysteria, fit the bill of male hysterics.[49] Lucky's monologue, which has been read as an example of shell shock, can in turn in performance be seen to resemble what Charcot defined as the *grande attaque*, the most flamboyant expression of a hysterical attack, to which men as well as women were subject. In the case of men, the attacks were even more spectacular than in women, for 'Charcot believed that the athletic contortions of the fit came more naturally to boys and men than to women, and named one of the phases of the four-stage hysterical attack "clownisme", reflecting his own lifelong fascination with the circus'.[50] Beckett's characters also suffer variously from aboulia (loss of will), motor disturbances (*Watt*), delirium (*Malone*), fixed ideas (*Play*) and they display a range of speech pathologies that often characterize the language of hysterics, including a disorganization of speech (e.g. Lucky and Mouth) and loss of power to find the right word (*What Is the Word*). For Charcot, hysterical language disorders included a number of 'pathologies' that appear in Beckett's work, such as stuttering (*Watt, Ill Seen Ill Said*), telegraphic language (*The Unnamable*), aphonia and mutism (*The Calmative*) and coprolalia (*Krapp's Last Tape, the Trilogy*), accompanied by convulsive tics and obsessive daily thoughts and practices.[51]

Beckett, then, was intimately familiar with the notion of hysteria, and had come across numerous accounts of both male and female sufferers. Particularly prominent in Nordau's *Degeneration* and the work of the Surrealists were in fact the accounts of male hysteria, a motif that also permeates the iconography of silent film. Hysteria can be said to be pervasive in Beckett's work, leaving marks and traces throughout the oeuvre, but its centrality has often been concealed by the gendered interpretation of hysteria as a female affliction, which has obscured from critical view the centrality of hysterical motifs across Beckett's work.

Notes

1. Georges Didi-Huberman, *Invention of Hysteria: Charcot and the Photographic Iconography of the Salpêtrière*, translated by Alisa Hartz (Cambridge, MA: The MIT Press, 2003), xi.
2. Mark S. Micale, *Hysterical Men: The Hidden History of Male Nervous Illness* (Cambridge, MA: Harvard University Press, 2008), 2–3.
3. Asti Hustvedt, *Medical Muses: Hysteria in Nineteenth-Century Paris* (London: Bloomsbury, 2011).
4. Mark S. Micale, 'Charcot and the Idea of Hysteria in the Male: Gender, Mental Science, and Medical Diagnosis in Late Nineteenth-Century France', *Medical History*, 34 (1990), 372.
5. Ibid., 371.
6. Jean-Martin Charcot, 'Author's Preface' in *Clinical Lectures on Certain Diseases of the Nervous System*, translated by E. P. Hurd (Detroit: George S. Davis, 1888), ix.
7. Micale, 365.
8. Ibid., 365.
9. Ibid., 366–9.
10. Rae Beth Gordon, 'From Charcot to Charlot: Unconscious Imitation and Spectatorship in French Cabaret and Early Cinema', in *The Mind*

of Modernism: Medicine, Psychology, and the Cultural Arts in Europe and America, 1880–1940, edited by Mark S. Micale (Stanford: Stanford University Press, 2004), 108.
11 Ibid., 93.
12 Ibid., 111, 109.
13 Max Nordau, *Degeneration*, translated by George L. Mosse (Lincoln and London: University of Nebraska Press, 1993), 30.
14 Henri Bergson, *Time and Free Will: An Essay on the Immediate Data of Consciousness*, translated by F. L. Pogson (London: George Allen & Company, 1912), 18.
15 T. S. Eliot, *Complete Poems and Plays* (London: Faber, 2004), 32. Ll. 4–7.
16 Nordau, 27.
17 Samuel Beckett, *The Complete Short Prose 1929–1989*, edited by S. E. Gontarski (New York: Grove Press, 1995), 67.
18 Samuel Beckett, *The Letters of Samuel Beckett. Volume 1: 1929–1940*, edited by Martha Fehsenfeld and Lois More Overbeck (Cambridge: Cambridge University Press, 2009), 384.
19 Mark Nixon, *Samuel Beckett's German Diaries 1936–1937* (London: Continuum, 2011), 134.
20 Louis Aragon and André Breton, 'The Fiftieth Anniversary of Hysteria', translated by Samuel Beckett, in André Breton, *What Is Surrealism? Selected Writings*, edited by Franklin Rosemont (London: Pluto Press, 1978), 321.
21 André Breton and Paul Éluard, 'Introduction to the Possessions', translated by Samuel Beckett, in Breton, *What Is Surrealism? Selected Writings*, edited by Franklin Rosemont (London: Pluto Press, 1978), 51.
22 Daniel Albright, *Beckett and Aesthetics* (Cambridge: Cambridge University Press, 2003), 10.
23 James Knowlson and Elizabeth Knowlson (eds), *Beckett Remembering, Remembering Beckett: Uncollected Interviews with Samuel Beckett & Memories of those Who Knew Him* (London: Bloomsbury, 2006), 67.
24 Matthew Feldman, *Beckett's Books: A Cultural History of the Interwar Notes* (London: Continuum, 2006), 100.
25 In later editions of his book, Woodworth also makes mention of Charcot's studies in male hysteria, but there is no mention of Charcot's work on male hysteria in the edition Beckett read.

26 TCD MS 10971/8/21, cited in Feldman, 101.
27 Feldman, 101.
28 Ernest Jones, *The Treatment of the Neuroses* (London: Bailliere, Tindall and Cox, 1920), 120. See Samuel Beckett, 'Psychology Notes', TCD MS 10971/8/22.
29 See, for instance, Louis Sass, *Madness and Modernism: Insanity in the Light of Modern Art, Literature and Thought* (Cambridge, MA: Harvard University Press, 1992) and Benjamin Keatinge, 'Beckett and Language Pathology', *Journal of Modern Literature*, 31.4 (2008): 86–101.
30 Samuel Beckett, *Murphy* (London: Picador, 1973), 105; Samuel Beckett, *Eleutheria* (Paris: Minuit, 1995), 163.
31 Shane Weller, *Beckett, Literature, and the Ethics of Alterity* (Basingstoke: Palgrave Macmillan, 2006), 185.
32 Rae Beth Gordon, *Why the French Love Jerry Lewis: From Cabaret to Early Cinema* (Stanford: Stanford University Press, 2001).
33 John Haynes and James Knowlson, *Images of Beckett* (Cambridge: Cambridge University Press, 2003), 91.
34 Cited in Gordon, 'From Charcot to Charlot', 99.
35 Phil Baker, *Beckett and the Mythology of Psychoanalysis* (Basingstoke: Macmillan, 1997), 130–1.
36 Samuel Beckett, *Samuel Beckett: The Complete Dramatic Works* (London: Faber, 2006), 361–2. Subsequent references are made parenthetically as *CDW*.
37 Clas Zilliacus, *Beckett and Broadcasting: A Study of the Works of Samuel Beckett for and in Radio and Television* (Åbo: ÅboAkademi, 1976), 198.
38 Ibid., 198.
39 Paul Sheehan, 'Beckett's Ghost Dramas: Monitoring a Phenomenology of Sleep', in Ulrika Maude and Matthew Feldman (eds), *Beckett and Phenomenology* (London: Continuum, 2009), 159.
40 Ibid., 166.
41 Ibid., 165, 168.
42 Ibid., 165, 168.
43 Baker, 131. Adam Piette has argued that Pierre Janet's famous case study of Irène, a hysteric, informs *Footfalls*. See Adam Piette, 'Beckett, Early Neuropsychology and Memory Loss: Beckett's Reading of

Claparède, Janet and Korsakoff', *Samuel Beckett Today/Aujourd'hui*, 2 (1993): 41–8.
44 Baker, 144.
45 Ian Hacking, *Mad Travelers: Reflections on the Reality of Transient Mental Illness* (Cambridge, MA: Harvard University Press, 1998), 8, 13.
46 Cited in Ian Hacking, 'Automatisme Ambulatoire: Fugue, Hysteria, and Gender at the Turn of the Century', *Modernism/Modernity*, 3.1 (1996), 31.
47 Samuel Beckett, *The Beckett Trilogy: Molloy, Malone Dies, The Unnamable* (London: Picador, 1979), 9. Subsequent references are made parenthetically as *Trilogy*.
48 Hacking, 'Automatisme Ambulatoire', 33–4.
49 For a neuropsychlogical account of amnesia in Beckett's work, see Peter Fifield's fine essay, 'Beckett's Amnesiacs, Neuropsychology, and Temporal Moribundity'. Fifield draws attention to the ways in which Beckett's severe amnesiacs are 'unable to posit a future or to recall a past substantially different from present experience' (138). He compellingly argues that in Beckett's work, amnesia results in 'timelessness, when forgetting obliterates the movement of time itself' (143).
50 Elaine Showalter, *The Female Malady: Women, Madness and English Culture, 1830–1980* (London: Virago, 1987), 67.
51 In fact before 1885, sufferers of Tourette's symptom were classified as hysterics: for an analysis of Beckett's writing and Tourette's syndrome, see Ulrika Maude, '"A Stirring Beyond Coming and Going": Beckett and Tourette's', *Journal of Beckett Studies*, 17.1–2 (2008): 153–68.

Works cited

Albright, Daniel. *Beckett and Aesthetics* (Cambridge: Cambridge University Press, 2003).
Baker, Phil. *Beckett and the Mythology of Psychoanalysis* (Basingstoke: Macmillan, 1997).
Beckett, Samuel. *Murphy* (London: Picador, 1973).
—. *The Beckett Trilogy: Molloy, Malone Dies, The Unnamable* (London: Picador, 1979).

—. *The Complete Short Prose 1929–1989*, edited by S. E. Gontarski (New York: Grove Press, 1995).

—. *Eleutheria* (Paris: Minuit, 1995).

—. *The Complete Dramatic Works* (London: Faber, 2006).

—. *The Letters of Samuel Beckett. Volume 1: 1929–1940*, edited by Martha Fehsenfeld and Lois More Overbeck (Cambridge: Cambridge University Press, 2009).

Bergson, Henri. *Time and Free Will: An Essay on the Immediate Data of Consciousness*, translated by F. L. Pogson (London: George Allen & Company, 1912).

Breton, André. *What Is Surrealism? Selected Writings*, edited by Franklin Rosemont (London: Pluto Press, 1978).

Charcot, Jean-Martin. 'Author's Preface', in *Clinical Lectures on Certain Diseases of the Nervous System*, translated by E. P. Hurd (Detroit: George S. Davis, 1888).

Didi-Huberman, Georges. *Invention of Hysteria: Charcot and the Photographic Iconography of the Salpêtrière*, translated by Alisa Hartz (Cambridge, MA: The MIT Press, 2003).

Eliot, T. S., *Complete Poems and Plays* (London: Faber, 2004).

Feldman, Matthew. *Beckett's Books: A Cultural History of the Interwar Notes* (London: Continuum, 2006).

Fifield, Peter. 'Beckett's Amnesiacs, Neuropsychology, and Temporal Moribundity', in *Beckett and Death*, edited by Stephen Barfield, Matthew Feldman and Philip Tew (London: Continuum, 2009), 128–46.

Gordon, Rae Beth. *Why the French Love Jerry Lewis: From Cabaret to Early Cinema* (Stanford: Stanford University Press, 2001).

—. 'From Charcot to Charlot: Unconscious Imitation and Spectatorship in French Cabaret and Early Cinema', in *The Mind of Modernism: Medicine, Psychology, and the Cultural Arts in Europe and America, 1880–1940*, edited by Mark S. Micale (Stanford: Stanford University Press, 2004), 93–124.

Hacking, Ian. '*Automatisme Ambulatoire*: Fugue, Hysteria, and Gender at the Turn of the Century'. *Modernism/Modernity*, 3.1 (1996): 31–43.

—. *Mad Travelers: Reflections on the Reality of Transient Mental Illness* (Cambridge, MA: Harvard University Press, 1998).

Haynes, John and James Knowlson. *Images of Beckett* (Cambridge: Cambridge University Press, 2003).

Hustvedt, Asti. *Medical Muses: Hysteria in Nineteenth-Century Paris* (London: Bloomsbury, 2011).

Jones, Ernest. *The Treatment of the Neuroses* (London: Bailliere, Tindall and Cox, 1920).

Keatinge, Benjamin. 'Beckett and Language Pathology', *Journal of Modern Literature*, 31.4 (2008): 86–101.

Knowlson, James and Elizabeth (eds). *Beckett Remembering, Remembering Beckett: Uncollected Interviews with Samuel Beckett & Memories of those Who Knew Him* (London: Bloomsbury, 2006).

Maude, Ulrika. '"A Stirring Beyond Coming and Going": Beckett and Tourette's', *Journal of Beckett Studies*, 17.1–2 (2008): 153–68.

Micale, Mark S. 'Charcot and the Idea of Hysteria in the Male: Gender, Mental Science, and Medical Diagnosis in Late Nineteenth-Century France', *Medical History* 34 (1990): 363–411.

—. *Hysterical Men: The Hidden History of Male Nervous Illness* (Cambridge, MA: Harvard University Press, 2008).

Nixon, Mark. *Samuel Beckett's German Diaries 1936–1937* (London: Continuum, 2011).

Nordau, Max. *Degeneration*, translated by George L. Mosse (Lincoln and London: University of Nebraska Press, 1993).

Piette, Adam. 'Beckett, Early Neuropsychology and Memory Loss: Beckett's Reading of Claparède, Janet and Korsakoff', *Samuel Beckett Today/ Aujourd'hui*, 2 (1993): 41–8.

Sass, Louis. *Madness and Modernism: Insanity in the Light of Modern Art, Literature and Thought* (Cambridge, MA: Harvard University Press, 1992).

Sheehan, Paul. 'Beckett's Ghost Dramas: Monitoring a Phenomenology of Sleep', in *Beckett and Phenomenology*, edited by Ulrika Maude and Matthew Feldman (London: Continuum, 2009), 158–76.

Showalter, Elaine. *The Female Malady: Women, Madness and English Culture, 1830–1980* (London: Virago, 1987).

Weller, Shane. *Beckett, Literature, and the Ethics of Alterity* (Basingstoke: Palgrave Macmillan, 2006).

Zilliacus, Clas. *Beckett and Broadcasting: A Study of the Works of Samuel Beckett for and in Radio and Television* (Åbo: ÅboAkademi, 1976).

8

Samuel Beckett, Video Artist

Mark Nixon
University of Reading

Samuel Beckett has often been described as a multimedia artist, embracing new technology and experimenting creatively in radio, television and film.[1] In the last 15 years, critical scrutiny of Beckett's work in these media has intensified. Moreover, a lot of criticism is currently exploring the way in which Beckett has influenced contemporary media artists working in a variety of fields. One such field is video art: already in 2000 the former director of the Pompidou Centre in Paris, Werner Spies, stated that Beckett stands 'unübersehbar am Beginn der Videokunst (unmistakably at the beginning of video art)'.[2] Indeed, Beckett's influence on video art has been well documented, as studies of Beckett's relationship with artists such as Bruce Nauman and Stan Douglas, to name but these, attest. What is perhaps less well-known is that Beckett himself played with the idea of working with video technology, in a piece entitled 'Film Vidéo-Cassette projet'. This ultimately abandoned play is extremely revealing, as it shows how Beckett revisited long-held thematic concerns, yet at the same time was seeking formal innovation within his work.[3]

In a letter dated 7 January 1973, Beckett told George Reavey that he was, once again, struggling to write; he had not finished anything he had begun, and had not begun anything he could not finish. Indeed, having finished *Not I* in June, and the short piece *Still* in July 1972, the remainder of the year was marked by what Beckett called, in that same letter to Reavey, 'speechlessness'. During this period the new play *Not I*, which was premièred in New York in September under the direction of Alan Schneider, was uppermost in his thoughts. In October he told Ruby Cohn that he was going to attend rehearsals of the play in London in December, anxious to 'find out if *NOT I* is theatre in spite of all'.[4] However, what Beckett neglected to tell any of his correspondents was that he had in fact begun a new piece, even though it ultimately remained 'unfinishable'. Notes towards this creative project, entitled 'Film Vidéo-Cassette projet' and inscribed 'Nov[ember] 1972 Paris' are found in a small notebook held at the Beckett International Foundation's Archive at the University of Reading, the cover marked 'FRAGMENTS PROSE DEBUT 68' (UoR MS 2928). The first 12 pages of this notebook contain, as its title indicates, several prose fragments related to the text *Endroit clos*, the fifth of the *Foirades* (*Fizzles*). These drafts are followed, on the last four pages of the notebook, by two pages of text (in French) and two pages of diagrams relating to the 'Film Vidéo-Cassette projet'. It is difficult to ascertain whether Beckett made further notes on this project as many pages have been removed from the notebook. However, and despite the fact that the existing notes contain only very few corrections, the exploratory nature of the material suggests that these notes are indeed a first draft, or rather a first record of a creative idea, committed to paper without any clear sense of where it would lead.

Beckett's 'Film Vidéo-Cassette projet' has so far received little critical attention, which is perhaps not surprising considering its embryonic nature. It is briefly discussed in the catalogue of the 'Samuel Beckett / Bruce Nauman' exhibition as well as Ruby Cohn's *A Beckett Canon*, where it is given the title 'F1 and F2'; however, the most comprehensive description remains the one in the *Catalogue of the Beckett Manuscript Collection at the University of Reading*.[5] All point to the fact that parts of the manuscript notes are hard to decipher, but agree on the basic premise established by Beckett. The plan is based on two films, 'Film I' and 'Film II', each of which depict the same bare room, containing a door, a window, two chairs and a television set. In 'Film I' we see a woman F1 sitting on a chair waiting for someone who does not arrive. 'Film II' shows a woman F2 going through a routine of preparations before sitting down to watch a video recording of 'Film I'.

Although it is unclear whether this project was intended for film or television, the fragment is important for the way in which it revisits and develops Beckett's previous work in these media, and for the way in which it anticipates the later TV plays, in particular *Ghost Trio*. That Beckett was thinking of writing something for TV in the rather large span of time intervening between *Film* (written 1963, filmed 1964) and *Eh Joe* (written 1965) on the one hand and *Ghost Trio* (written 1975) on the other is evident from a letter he wrote to Jack McGowran on 7 January 1968, in which he mentions that he is trying to come up with a new TV piece for the actor.

What is most striking about Beckett's sketch is his envisaged creative use of the video medium. In 1972 video recording was still a relatively new (and expensive) technology, although the professional sector and television networks had been using it since the mid-1960s. Its creative potential was only gradually discovered when Sony introduced the mobile but unwieldy PortaPak system in 1967, and avant-garde artists such as Nam June Paik (already in 1963) and Bruce Nauman (from 1968 onward) began to experiment with the possibilities of the medium. Yet despite being increasingly used by performance and conceptual artists, in 1972 video art was on the whole still a fringe activity.

Beckett's reference to the video *cassette* format in his outline suggests that he was very much aware of the technical advances being made at the time. Replacing open reels and cartridges, cassettes for video recorders had only recently been made available when Sony launched its U-matic system in September 1971.[6] Beckett first came into contact with the video format in 1966, when he travelled to Stuttgart to direct the television production of *He, Joe* at the Süddeutscher Rundfunk. Moreover, Beckett in the late 1960s and early 1970s was in touch with a variety of people working at the BBC, who may also have spoken to him about this increasingly important technology. Thus, for example, in the same month (November 1972) in which he jotted down the notes on his video cassette project, the BBC broadcast *Krapp's Last Tape* with Patrick Magee.

Beckett was surely quick to recognize that video offered him a similar range of possibilities as the tape recorder had done when he wrote *Krapp's Last Tape* 14 years earlier. Video recording not only allowed the flow of narrative time to be manipulated in an auditory sense but also introduced the additional visual dimension with which Beckett had experimented in *Film* and *Eh Joe*. Indeed, in many ways the 'Film Vidéo-Cassette projet' revisits several thematic and formal concerns addressed by these pieces. Beckett's letter to McGowran of 1968, in which he mentioned the possibilities of a new TV play, shows that he was explicitly thinking about 'the old idea of a man waiting in a room seen first at normal remove then investigated in detail'.[7] The 'old idea' – both in its emphasis on the solitary man in a room and the investigative camera moving ever closer – is of course the one explored in *Eh Joe*, and then later again in *Ghost Trio*. Beckett developed this scenario, with the additional element of waiting mentioned in his remark to McGowran, in the video project of 1972.

The first film of the fragment thus shows the woman F1 who waits in vain. It is not made clear who or what she is waiting for, although at a later point in the draft Beckett indicates that it must be a person. At various stages in this first film, F1's hopes are raised by noises that seemingly announce the longed-for arrival of the other person. Thus Beckett asks himself at one point how the waiting is to be interrupted, and runs through a series of possible 'interventions', listing a note under the door, a knock on the door or the window.

Having shown that F1 waits in vain, 'Film I' then ends with a close up of the female figure; her face is described as being happy and turned to sounds coming from the stairs. The first film thus ends at precisely the point when the woman's waiting finally appears to be at an end, when the tension induced by the absence of the other is on the brink of being released in happy reunion. The outcome of this little drama is never stated, although Beckett's opening note that F1 waits 'in vain' suggests that the footsteps on the stairs represent yet another false hope.

The similarities between this scenario and the one presented in *Ghost Trio* are obvious. In the latter play the 'Tryst', to use the original title, invokes the presence of Beethoven's music which is absent in the video piece. But the notion of waiting remains the same, even if the little boy in *Ghost Trio* gives the expectant figure at least some kind of relief by imparting the news that the time has not yet come. Moreover, as in *Ghost Trio* (and for that matter, *Eh Joe*), the video project describes a room that is bare apart from some essential furniture – 'the familiar chamber', as the Voice in *Ghost Trio* calls it.[8] In both the sketch of the room as well as the accompanying notes Beckett thought about including one ornamental object, either a small statue or a stuffed bird. Both bring to mind similar objects used in *Film*, although their potential gaze is here (as elsewhere) not viewed as a threat. In the video project, Beckett specifies that only those elements in the room are to be shown that are necessary to determine the nature of the action, such as a door, a window and a chair. In *Ghost Trio*, this act of identification is made explicit by the Voice at the beginning of the play, in that each element of the room is introduced singly to the viewer. These activities resemble what the influential film theorist Erwin Panofsky called the 'Dynamisierung des Raumes'.[9] Beckett himself, when he directed *Waiting for Godot* in Berlin in 1975, stated that he was concerned with staging the play's 'dynamics', which concentrated on movement and spatial arrangements.[10]

'Film II' shows the same room as the first film, and similarly posits simplicity to identify the essential features it contains. It does so by making F2 go through a series of preparations: she locks the door, pulls the blinds and turns on the video recorder. She presumably does this in some haste, as she is described as sitting down as soon as possible after preparing the room. Similar to Krapp's instalment of the tape recorder at the beginning of *Krapp's Last Tape*, or Joe's preparation of the room in *Eh Joe*, F2's routine focuses the viewer's attention on the television screen and the video recording she is about to watch, that is to say, 'Film I'. Thus Beckett summarizes 'Film II' as showing figure F2 watching Film I on video.

By leaving the room unchanged and having F2 watch a recording of F1, the temporal chronology of the two films is established. This is underlined by the very first note in the manuscript draft, which declares that F2 is an older version of F1. It is implied that F1 was left waiting at the end of the first film, and that F2 incessantly returns to the scene depicted in 'Film I', as if the visual memory contained a decisive moment in time that cast a shadow over all that followed after. Beckett thus emphasizes the aspect of memory underlying the second film by placing objects of memory on one of the chairs, such as a book. As such it could be brought into relation with Krapp's return to the scene with the girl in the punt, which also marks a decisive moment in his biography in which, perhaps, the rift between something resembling happiness and something inducing loneliness opens up. Indeed, 'Film I' offers the possibility of happiness and even love, which is indicated by F1's expectant, happy face when hearing footsteps on the stairs. This is further underlined by the fact that the scene in 'Film I' takes place in summer, and F1 is, perhaps in expectance of a romantic encounter, dressed in a light morning gown made of silk. In contrast, 'Film II' is set in winter, and F2 is wearing a dark woollen gown. The light/dark dichotomy established by the clothing furthers the sense that the time depicted in 'Film I' still retained some notion of hope and happiness. Although not quite as threatening as the room in *Film*, which in an early draft is described as being 'the trap', a feeling of isolation is achieved in the second film when F2 locks the door and closes the windows and shutters. F1 in contrast is still connected to the outside world, as Beckett specifies that the door and the window are open, and the shutter not fully closed.

Throughout the draft notes, Beckett is at pains to establish optical relations. He thus specifies that the close-up gives the same perspective as the normal view, and later, recalling the gradual intrusion of the camera in *Eh Joe*, draws attention to the systematic nature of the close-up shots. Moreover, the function and features of the observer-camera in the Video-Cassette project bears a resemblance to Beckett's specific instructions in an early draft of *Ghost Trio*:

> Camera: Once set for shot it should not explore, simply look. It stops + stares. Its mobility is confined to stealthy or lightning (cut shots) advance or withdrawal to positions established in views of the most telling stills.[11]

This 'staring vision', as he calls it at another point in the *Ghost Trio* manuscript, differs from the personified camera advocated in Beckett's suggestions for the TV version of *Krapp's Last Tape*, in which the 'camera listens and its activity is affected by words spoken'.[12]

Beckett's use of camera, and its function as an observing eye, is of course based on an interest in the theoretical nature of vision and (self)perception which has been well documented, not least in discussions of his use of Berkeley's *esse est percipi* (CDW 323). Already in the 1930s, Beckett had studied the practical uses of perspective in the visual arts, as his reading notes and numerous entries in the 'German Diaries' of 1936/1937 indicate. For example, after a visit to the studio of the Hamburg painter Karl Kluth, Beckett noted in his diary that his work posited the contrast between the natural and the human, and described his landscapes as 'Berkleyan'.[13] Interesting here is the introduction of the Berkleyan landscape: Beckett had read Berkeley extensively in the early 1930s – as he did periodically throughout his life – but he had returned to the *Principles and Dialogues* in January 1936, re-reading the sections in which the philosopher denied that perception was an act of will. Beckett's re-reading of Berkeley in early 1936 appears to have been triggered by his encounter with Geulincx at the time in Trinity College, Dublin, as notes in Beckett's library and a letter to MacGreevy indicate. In this letter (dated 5 March 1936) he justifies reading Geulincx by pointing to the 'saturation in the conviction that the *sub specie aeternitatis* [from the perspective of eternity] vision is the only excuse for remaining alive. He [ie Geulincx] does not put out his eyes on that account, as Heraclitus did & Rimbaud began to, or like the terrified Berkeley repudiate them'.[14] If Beckett felt that there was a fundamental difference between Geulincx's and Berkeley's theories of perception, it is the latter who, on the whole, guides Beckett's approach to the visual arts in Germany. Berkeley's empirical, subjective view of how individuals perceive, is, for example, evident in Beckett's description of an exhibition of Max Klinger's work: 'Throughout concepts projected on to canvas (i.e. on to the world), the optical experience *post rem*, a hideous inversion of the visual process, the eye waiving its privilege'.[15] In contrast he praised Vermeer's Lesendes Mädchen (Girl Reading), for establishing precisely such a direct optical experience. He surmised that it had probably been painted in a mirror, and drew attention to the fact that Vermeer always stressed the way his figures used their eyes in order to establish an optical relationship with the viewer.[16]

The emphasis on optical relations, and indeed their possible multiplication, also appears in the 1972 'Film Vidéo-Cassette projet', in what is undoubtedly the key moment in the fragment. In 'Film II', F2 stops the video of 'Film I' near its end, at the close-up of F1. Thus 'Film II' shows a close-up of F2 looking at the close-up of F1, whose gaze is turned towards the noise on the stairs. In Beckett's description of this 'confrontation', the close-up of F2 watching F1 finally leads to a juxtaposition of the reflection between the two in the mirror. Through the succession of images F1 and F2 become both one and different, same and other, an effect which is finally made clear by the introduction of the mirror, in which the two close-ups of the figures are brought together. In the subsequent diagrams and notes Beckett lists various 'confrontations' between the gazes of F1 and F2 evident in the close-ups. Although it is not quite clear, it appears as if he envisaged the possibility that F1 could stare back at F2, 'out of the tape' as it were. Beckett also sketches a variety of gazes and optical relationships achieved by the use of the mirror, whereby the reflected images projected by the camera are distinguished as being either static or mobile according to whether the video recording is frozen or running. Towards the end of the notes, Beckett plays with the possibility of introducing a figure F3, who would watch F2 watching F1 with three close-ups juxtaposed at the end.

Effectively, the video project envisages something similar to *Film*, where the camera 'performs a function whereby each beholder sees himself' (*CDW* 323) except that in the later piece the self in question is a past self. As in *Film*, then, Beckett's 'Film Vidéo-Cassette projet' moves from an interplay between perceiver and perceived to self-perception. In the script to *Film*, this is called the 'inescapability of self-perception' (*CDW* 323). In Beckett's video project, this is described in the second film through the facial expressions of F2 as she stares at the image of F1. These change with every subsequent 'confrontation': at first they are tragic, but then gradually a small smile appears. Beckett thus invests faces with clear expressions that allow interpretation – this differs from the generally expressionless faces used in his other TV pieces. In *Eh Joe*, for example, Joe's face is '[p]ractically motionless throughout . . . impassive except in so far as it reflects mounting tension of *listening*' (*CDW* 362. Beckett's emphasis).

Whereas in the first close-up F2's face is described as being unsettled, perhaps even shocked, the smile in the second confrontation is somewhat ambiguous. It could either be the site of happy remembrance or the expression of wry acceptance. As such it resembles the slight smile Beckett envisaged at the end of *Eh Joe*, as stated in a letter dated 7 April 1966 to Alan Schneider: 'I asked in London and Stuttgart for a smile at the end (oh not a real smile)'.[17] Furthermore, a similarly wry smile occurs at the end of the 1977 Süddeutscher Rundfunk production of *Geistertrio* as well as the BBC production of *Ghost Trio* of the same year.

The smile of F2 in the 'Film Vidéo-Cassette projet' may also be read in the light of a quotation which Beckett notes at the bottom of the second page of his manuscript notes:

Car je suis tant navrée en toutes parts
que plus en moi une nouvelle plaie
pour m'empirer ne pourrait trouver place.

These lines form the last stanza of 'Sonnet III', written by the sixteenth-century poet Louise Labé.[18] Already in *Dream of Fair to Middling Women* the Polar Bear (modelled on Beckett's university tutor Rudmose-Brown) had declared Labé to be 'a great poet, perhaps one of the greatest of all time, of physical passion, of passion purely and exclusively physical'.[19] 'Sonnet III' opens with an address of complaint, 'Oh futile hopes, oh long desirings', expressions of sorrow which are exacerbated by the 'pitiless glances from the stars above'.[20] Grieving over lost love, or love unrequited, the speaker in the third stanza adopts an attitude of resignation, but also resilience: 'Too bad! Let Eros [...] be spiteful and renew his curse!' Beckett's 'Film Vidéo-Cassette projet' may thus have found its creative spark in Labé's poem. Read in this light, the ritual of perception and self-perception enacted by F2 in her confrontation of the site of absence staged in 'Film I' results in a smile that acknowledges that 'there's no place left to wound me worse'.

Notes

1. This essay is a revised and expanded version of my 'Beckett's Film Vidéo-Cassette projet', published in *Journal of Beckett Studies* 18.1–2 (2009): 32–43.
2. Michael Glasmeier, Christine Hoffman, Sabine Folie, Gaby Hartel and Gerald Matt, *Samuel Beckett / Bruce Naumann* (Vienna: Kunsthalle Wien, 2000), 34.
3. Beckett never returned to working with video. He was however aware of it during his work on productions, especially of his TV plays in Stuttgart. In advance of recording *Nacht und Träume* in 1982, for example, he thought of introducing slow motion using video (letter to Barbara Bray, 23 August 1982). On 12 July 1982, Beckett told Bettina Jonic that he had no access to a 'video tape machine'.
4. Samuel Beckett, letter to Ruby Cohn, 18 October 1972; quoted in Patrizia Fusella, 'Samuel Beckett's *Pas Moi/Not I*: pas traduction, not creation', *Textus* 15.1 (2002), 125.
5. Glasmeier et al., *Samuel Beckett / Bruce Naumann*, 134; Ruby Cohn, *A Beckett Canon* (Ann Arbor: The University of Michigan Press, 2001), 321; Mary Bryden, Julian Garforth and Peter Mills (eds). *Beckett at Reading: Catalogue of the Beckett Manuscript Collection at the University of Reading* (Reading: Whiteknights Press and Beckett International Foundation, 1998), 132.
6. Video recorders only established themselves on the mass market in the mid-1970s when more accessible videotape formats were introduced – Sony's Betamax in 1975 and shortly thereafter JVC's VHS.
7. Samuel Beckett, letter to Jack McGowran, 7 January 1968; quoted in James Knowlson, *Damned To Fame: The Life of Samuel Beckett* (London: Bloomsbury, 1996), 555.
8. Samuel Beckett, *The Complete Dramatic Works* (London: Faber, 1990), 408. Subsequent references are made parenthetically as *CDW*.
9. Quoted in Gaby Hartel and Michael Glasmeier (eds). *The Eye of Prey. Becketts Film-, Fernseh- und Videoarbeiten* (Frankfurt am Main: Suhrkamp, 2011), 21.
10. See letters to Barbara Bray, 6 and 9 September 1974.

11   Samuel Beckett, UoR MS 1519/1, 3r; quoted in James Knowlson, 'Ghost Trio. Geister Trio', in *Beckett at 80. Beckett in Context*, edited by Enoch Brater (New York: Oxford University Press, 1986), 207.
12   Clas Zilliacus, *Beckett and Broadcasting: A Study of the Works of Samuel Beckett for and in Radio and Television* (Åbo: Åbo Akademi, 1976), 203.
13   Beckett, 'German Diaries', 25 November 1936.
14   Samuel Beckett, *The Letters of Samuel Beckett. Volume 1: 1929–1940*, edited by Martha Dow Fehsenfeld, Lois More Overbeck, George Craig and Dan Gunn (Cambridge: Cambridge University Press, 2011), 319.
15   Beckett, 'German Diaries', 28 January 1937; quoted in Erik Tonning, *Beckett's Abstract Drama* (Bern: Peter Lang, 2007), 25.
16   Beckett, 'German Diaries', 5 February 1937.
17   Maurice Harmon (ed). *No Author Better Served: The Correspondence of Samuel Beckett and Alan Schneider* (Cambridge, MA: Harvard University Press, 1998), 202.
18   Beckett's surviving library contains a copy of *Élégies et Sonnets de Louize Labé, Lionnoize* (1958), which was given to him on his birthday in 1959. Beckett recommended Labé to Anne Atik; see *How It Was: A Memoir of Samuel Beckett* (London: Faber, 2001), 49.
19   Samuel Beckett, *Dream of Fair to Middling Women* (Dublin: Black Cat Press, 1992), 164.
20   Louise Labé, *Œuvres poétiques* (Paris: Gallimard, 1983), 111; my translation.

Works cited

Atik, Anne Atik, *How It Was: A Memoir of Samuel Beckett* (London: Faber, 2001).
Beckett, Samuel. *The Complete Dramatic Works* (London: Faber, 1990).
—. *Dream of Fair to Middling Women* (Dublin: Black Cat Press, 1992).
—. *The Letters of Samuel Beckett. Volume 1: 1929–1940*, edited by Martha Dow Fehsenfeld, Lois More Overbeck, George Craig, Dan Gunn (Cambridge: Cambridge University Press, 2009).

—. 'German Diaries' [6 notebooks], Beckett International Foundation, The University of Reading.

—. [manuscript] 'Film Vidéo-Cassette projet', Beckett International Foundation, The University of Reading, UoR MS 2928.

—. [manuscript] *Ghost Trio*, Beckett International Foundation, The University of Reading, UoR MS 1519/1.

—. Letters to Barbara Bray, Trinity College Dublin, TCD MS10948/1.

—. Letters to Ruby Cohn, Beckett International Foundation, The University of Reading.

—. Letters to Jack McGowran, Harry Ransom Humanities Research Center, The University of Texas at Austin.

—. Letters to George Reavey, Harry Ransom Humanities Research Center, The University of Texas at Austin.

Bignell, Jonathan, *Beckett on Screen. The Television Plays* (Manchester: Manchester University Press, 2009).

Brater, Enoch (ed.). *Beckett at 80 / Beckett in Context* (New York: Oxford University Press, 1986).

Bryden, Mary, Julian Garforth and Peter Mills (eds). *Beckett at Reading: Catalogue of the Beckett Manuscript Collection at the University of Reading* (Reading: Whiteknights Press and Beckett International Foundation, 1998).

Cohn, Ruby. *A Beckett Canon* (Ann Arbor: The University of Michigan Press, 2001).

Fusella, Patrizia. 'Samuel Beckett's *Pas Moi/Not I*: pas traduction, not creation', *Textus* 15.1 (2002): 121–44.

Glasmeier, Michael, Christine Hoffman, Sabine Folie, Gaby Hartel and Gerald Matt (eds). *Samuel Beckett / Bruce Naumann* (Vienna: Kunsthalle Wien, 2000).

Gossens, Peter. *We Do it to have Fun Together. Samuel Beckett beim SDR in Stuttgart* (Marbach: Deutsche Schillergesellschaft, 2000).

Harmon, Maurice (ed.). *No Author Better Served: The Correspondence of Samuel Beckett and Alan Schneider* (Cambridge, MA: Harvard University Press, 1998).

Hartel, Gaby. 'Von Caligari bis Rondinone. Becketts Stummfilmrezeption als Anreger neuester Videokunst', in *Samuel Beckett und die*

Medien: Neue Perspektiven auf einen Medienkuenstler des 20. Jahrhunderts, edited by Peter Seibert (Bielefeld: transcript, 2008), 189-209.

—. '"Better [...], simpler and at the same time more extreme". Samuel Beckett's Television Work in West Germany's *Kulturbetrieb*', in *The International Reception of Samuel Beckett*, edited by Mark Nixon and Matthew Feldman (London: Continuum, 2009) 73-82.

Hartel, Gaby and Michael Glasmeier (eds). *The Eye of Prey. Becketts Film-, Fernseh- und Videoarbeiten* (Frankfurt am Main: Suhrkamp, 2011).

Herren, Graley. *Samuel Beckett's Plays on Film and Television* (New York: Palgrave Macmillan, 2007).

Knowlson, James. 'Ghost Trio. Geister Trio', in *Beckett at 80. Beckett in Context*, edited by Enoch Brater (New York: Oxford University Press, 1986), 193-207.

—. *Damned To Fame: The Life of Samuel Beckett* (London: Bloomsbury, 1996).

Labé, Louise. *Œuvres poétiques* (Paris: Gallimard, 1983).

Lemke, Inga. 'Fernsehtheater – Videoperformance: Samuel Beckett und die Videokunst', in *Samuel Beckett und die Medien: Neue Perspektiven auf einen Medienkuenstler des 20. Jahrhunderts*, edited by Peter Seibert (Bielefeld: transcript, 2008), 157-87.

Maude, Ulrika and David Pattie (eds). 'Beckett on TV', *Journal of Beckett Studies* 18.1/2 (2009).

Tonning, Erik. *Beckett's Abstract Drama; Works for Stage and Screen 1962-1985* (Bern: Peter Lang, 2007).

Zilliacus, Clas. *Beckett and Broadcasting: A Study of the Works of Samuel Beckett for and in Radio and Television* (Åbo: Åbo Akademi, 1976).

9

Sounds Worthy of the Name: Tone and Historical Feeling in Beckett's Drama

Iain Bailey
University of Manchester

It's things like tone and timing that can't be dealt with outside the theatre, but perhaps I am wrong in thinking they are of peculiar difficulty and importance here. Anyway don't let my nervousness make you nervous.[1]

(*Beckett to Alan Schneider, 1961*)

It is not easy to say what kind of a thing tone is, still less to describe its fluctuations: a property or a practice, an 'assemblage' of 'sonic mobilities' or 'diverse gestures of the voice',[2] perhaps a variety of 'imponderable evidence'.[3] In drama, tone certainly involves a discipline, as the above note from Beckett to Schneider suggests. In this letter (which concerns the 1961 New York production of *Happy Days*), Beckett is articulating a reluctance to travel and assist with rehearsals in person, and writes: 'We can't do much by letter, but we can do a certain amount'.[4] Tone appears to be one of those things that cannot be done in writing. This apparent fact does not, however, prevent Beckett's written texts – the prose as well as the drama – from displaying a persistent fascination with tone and intonation.

Though they never speak, there is a kind of voice to the silent figures who populate the flattened cylinder of Beckett's prose text *Le Dépeupleur* (1970), translated into English as *The Lost Ones* (1972). As they roam around, the various bodies 'brush together with a rustle of dry leaves', coming together sometimes for a 'kiss [that] makes an indescribable sound'.[5] Dryness affects the sounds as it does the air and the skin, and it is perhaps little surprise that this quality also translates, as in Ruby Cohn's reading of *The Lost Ones*, to the perception of a 'dry narrative tone' in the story.[6] Little resounds: the floor and walls are made of 'solid rubber or suchlike' so that even when struck hard 'the sound is scarcely heard'. Tones are deadened by the material of the cylinder, the heat and the quality of the air. They seem to be sustained only among what Beckett's text calls 'the only sounds worthy of the name [. . .] the thud of bodies striking against one another or of one against itself as when in a sudden fury it beats its breast'. By contrast, the figures' feet make no apparent sound as they walk. The main difference between these silent steps and the 'thud' that can be considered as a sound 'worthy of the name' seems to be their respective capacity to resonate. Rustles do not register; similarly, the muting effect of the rubber walls and floors deadens percussive intonation. *The Lost Ones* stills or negates almost all sounds, but it allows nonetheless for a latent tone in the 'thud' of bodies coming together, or in the 'sudden fury' of a flagellant. The text glosses its discovery, briefly: 'Thus flesh and bone subsist' (*Texts* 101).

This essay will begin to explore the functions and the difficulties of tone in Beckett's dramatic work, examining the ways in which this elusive, fundamental property emerges in the relationship between published text, 'grey canon' and performance. Evidently, tone in the theatre differs materially from tone in written texts like *The Lost Ones*. It is also something distinct from sound and noise, with its own particular exigencies for the performance of voice in the theatre. It may, in fact, seem inappropriate to speak of tone in the same breath as the mere 'thud' of bodies: tone, one might argue, is both more specific and more difficult to fix upon in either performance or an analytical reading. Nevertheless, as is very often the case in Beckett's work, there are intersections between the different genres that cause them to impinge on one another. The situation established in *The Lost Ones* can help contextualize a reading of tone in the drama, partly in the way it makes an image out of the space's flat acoustics, and partly by the uneasy separation it describes between rudiments of sound and a thorough silence.

Same tone: Flatness and negation

Tone, we will see, operates in the same sphere as voice, an idea or a phenomenon in Beckett's work that has received much critical commentary and has, indeed, been put forward as his 'most profound literary creation'.[7] In a certain sense tone is simply a subcategory of voice, as it appears when Beckett imagines the 'voice [that] comes to one in the dark' in the late novel *Company*:

> Another trait the flat tone. No life. Same flat tone at all times. For its affirmations. For its negations. For its interrogations. For its exclamations. For its imperations. Same flat tone. You were once. You were never. Were you ever? Oh never to have been! Be again. Same flat tone.[8]

In the expository early paragraphs of *Company*, other explicit 'traits' of the voice are proposed: 'its long silences', 'its repetitiousness'. This assignation of 'trait' replaces (first) 'characteristic' and then 'peculiarity' in the first manuscript draft, begun in May 1977.[9] But the 'flat tone' itself is carried over from 'The Voice (Verbatim)', an unpublished text drafted earlier in the same year that is relatively well documented in Beckett studies because of the transcription Charles Krance includes in his variorum edition of *Company*.[10] In the manuscript of 'The Voice', a reflection on tone breaks into the flow of prose (which the text itself seems to be imagining as a flow):

> Then dies as it flows back to faint full. How through age and long disuse estranged from words and things. The effect of all this on

discourse generally. Then before it forgets the flat tone manifest to all with ears to hear. Always the same flat tone. For its interrogations. For its affirmations.[11]

The curious act of remembrance performed in the text, as though recollecting an everyday task to be discharged, is mirrored on the facing verso sheet in a list that seems to describe the requisite traits of the voice: 'Harping./Old./Breathless./Faint.' and last of all, 'Same flat tone'. On the previous verso is a similar list of the different types of proposition (interrogation, affirmation, imperation) which ends, at the bottom of the page, with 'Same flat tone'.[12] The repetitiousness of these insistences on 'same flat tone' is reproduced in *Company*, where the phrase tolls through the paragraph quoted above. The particular trait implied by both epithets is one of non-differentiation: sameness for each of the different kinds of proposition, and flatness so that the contours never vary.

From a certain point of view, this vision of neutrality and a lack of differentiation is the apogee of Beckett's aspiration for voice in his writing. Tone has been presupposed in numerous existing accounts of voice in Beckett, and where it is dealt with explicitly this tendency to flatten has been registered. Jean-Pierre Martin's discussion of 'VOIX' in the *Dictionnaire Beckett* remarks on the 'dead voices' of the dramaticules, 'toneless and impersonal, close to the rustle or the murmur', and links these characteristics to a 'process of dwindling' in which the voice begins to 'announce its disappearance'.[13] We see in this account the way that tone can be registered as a trait of the voice which follows the same trajectory of reduction that is seen again and again – and for some very good reasons – in commentaries on Beckett's work, and on the voice in particular. This general assessment of tone follows the logic of *Company* by describing it in terms of a negation of difference. According to a reading along these lines, 'Same flat tone' would be a kind of settlement, the end (or at least the beginning of a last chapter) in that story of reduction which has become a commonplace in commentary on Beckett's theatre. There are good reasons for tone to be situated in a narrative of this kind; but besides corresponding to a too limited idea of negation, it also skates over an enduring difficulty for analyses of Beckett's works in which the phenomenon of tone is immersed: the curious place for emotions, feeling, even sentimentality in a writer often received as austerely cerebral or remorselessly anti-sentimental.

Nevertheless, much of the rhetoric around the drama – in its assertions at least – upholds the sense of an inclination towards unadulterated flatness. Much of that rhetoric is ascribable to Beckett himself. Directions in the play texts, for example, go in the direction implied by *Play* (1963), whose opening instructions specify that the voices should be 'toneless'.[14] This 'notorious prescription', as Xerxes Mehta calls it, is followed by directions in *Come and Go* (1967) for 'colourless' (*CDW* 357) voices, and in *Eh Joe* (1967) for a voice that should be 'remote, little colour' (*CDW* 361).[15] These directions also correspond to the dulling and stilling of voices that takes place in the author's prose texts of the late 1960s. The rustles and thuds and otherwise toneless sounds of what takes place in *Le Dépeupleur*'s cylinder are of a piece with the quiet that falls in Beckett's writing around the laboured composition of that work (begun in 1965 and not completed – following a long hiatus – until 1970) (*Texts* xv). *Imagination Dead Imagine* begins with signs of vocalization: direct address and a little exhalation of disgust ('No trace anywhere of life, you say, pah' (*Texts* 87)). But the scene it imagines in a sealed rotunda tends towards 'absolute stillness' and the only sound it describes is a single 'murmur', (*Texts* 89) towards the end of the text. *Ping* follows with its own 'murmurs' in an otherwise silent space, though the narration here has none of the signs of vocalization threaded through the earlier story. As in *The Lost Ones*, sounds in *Ping* barely register, though they sustain at the same time a quavering possibility of live flesh and bone

('Murmur only just almost never one second perhaps not alone' (*Texts* 123)). The disjunction in this story is between an apparently absolute silence ('all white heart breath no sound'), recurrent murmurs, and a tone that sounds throughout the text – namely, the 'ping' of the title (*Texts* 123–5). A similar disjunction takes place in *Lessness*: the 'endless' space described in the story is marked by 'no sound no stir', and the assertion of 'no sound' is repeated again and again; but the nameless male figure 'will curse God again as in the blessed days' (*Texts* 129). *Lessness* describes a disjunction between absolute silence and a clamour in the imagination where sound – and in this case also a particular quality of sound – is an issue: 'Never but silence such that in imagination this wild laughter these cries' (*Texts* 132).

Writing about language, materiality and the audible in the context of a discussion about Beckett's negotiations with 'nothing', Laura Salisbury identifies in Beckett's 1937 letter to Axel Kaun the image of a 'paradoxical "silence" that nevertheless whispers', which would be produced in a language that aims 'to render audible within words the condition of noise in which something *and* nothing seep into one another'.[16] In these 'closed space' texts, a similarly paradoxical silence is apparent, one that 'murmurs' or, as in *Lessness*, renders audible the seeping of a laugh, a cry, a scream into the otherwise negatively constructed ('no sound . . . never but') quiet. Beckett's drama of this period is invested with similar images and difficulties, both in the texts themselves and in production. At this practical level we might consider again the direction for 'toneless' voices in *Play*. Does this imply an absolute negation? If that were the case, there would be no question of intonation at all on the stage; it is difficult to see how a voice without any tone whatever might be played, unless as a hiss (if tone is held to imply a vibration of the vocal chords) or as absolute silence (if even a hiss can be understood as a kind of tone). In this sense, it is easy to see why Mehta refers to the direction as an interpretative challenge, and equally apparent why the questions he would ask of this lessness are questions of quantity: 'How toneless? The same in each of the play's eight segments? [...] Increasingly toneless?'[17] Beckett's direction calls for tone to be understood quantitatively, separating it off from specifically qualitative terms and especially from the descriptive language of feelings. And yet the interpretation and the translation required to make this into a practice, turning it into a vocal discipline, is by no means straightforwardly quantitative.

Right tone: Matter and emotion in the theatre

The practical immediacy of tone in the theatre, its specifically *felt* qualities, and its peculiar challenges when staging Beckett's works, are attested to quite often in the gathered correspondence, interviews and anecdotes that have emerged to surround the author's dramatic oeuvre. Many of these document actors and directors directly engaged with Beckett, whose involvement with the theatre has been widely discussed. What is remarkable about the way tone appears in some of these accounts is how it becomes a focal point for the transference of authority and interest involved in producing the plays. The correspondence between Beckett and Alan Schneider is threaded through with references of this kind. 'I have been trying to achieve what you would call "the right tone"', Schneider writes to Beckett on 5 January 1958 concerning *Endgame*, 'but, of course, this is not always knowable or achievable. But coming'.[18] In a later exchange about *Happy Days*, Beckett responds to a question from Schneider on the same matter: 'What tone? This of course is *the* problem. I can find no better word for it than "mild"'.[19] If there is a 'right tone' with the author behind it (as Schneider's quasi-citation implies), there are clear impediments to achieving 'it'; and in Beckett's reply to the question of tone he is clear that 'it' is a problem not to be solved at the level of description. He goes on in the letter to speak of 'monotony [. . .]

tranquillity & transparency', such that the performance should rely on 'speech rhythms and speech-gesture complexes, eyes, switching on and off of smile, etc., to do the work'.[20] On the one hand, tone should not be *doing the work*; on the other, it is '*the* problem'.

For Schneider, this recurring problem presents itself in terms of 'what you would call "the right tone"': in other words, an appeal to authority that has to be realized deictically in the absence of the author. In the letters, he continues to be concerned with tone in this way. Writing to Beckett on 24 November 1976 concerning a production of *That Time*, he observes that the actor Donald Davis 'I'm sure, has a voice tone quite different from Pat [Magee]'s; but we did listen to Pat's MALONE tape just to hear what you originally liked when you wrote KRAPP for him'.[21] In this everyday, informative and somewhat anxious letter, Schneider speaks easily of tone as a belonging of the individual actor; he frets a little about difference, 'but' (as if in reassurance) describes their efforts to flatten that difference by seeking out the taped voice of Magee. What he is after in that recording is a matching affect: an impression of what the author *liked* in Magee's voice.[22] No longer is the 'right tone' quite so much a matter of following descriptive instruction, but of attempting to accommodate and mirror a particular kind of feeling. The same language is reproduced in the transcript of Schneider's directions during his 1981 *Rockaby*, starring Billie Whitelaw:

> The same old thing, 'No color', but there is color. What he means is, it's not hammed up . . . When he reads it, he reads it with color. You know damn well. He did it with that 'whom else'. He's searching for that 'whom else' all his life.

And then again, shortly after:

> The weakness was there, Billie. The weakness was there. That was the right tone. She's not dragging . . . it's a sigh.[23]

The tone needs both no colour and, at the same time, colour, which for Schneider is bound up with a specific, personal longing. The colour that Schneider wants to keep is thus affective and authorial, and embodied in a discrete unit of text: those two words, 'whom else'. But tone is also there, subsisting, in the general tonelessness: *The weakness was there. That was the right tone.* Importantly, the 'right tone' is recognized only a posteriori, and deictically: '*That* was the right tone'. If tone seems to be aligned with emotion, it is arrived at nonetheless through practice. The feeling that Schneider locates in the text and ascribes to the author he finally recognizes in the voice of Whitelaw. Tone's affective dimension turns out to be proximal and involve transference, translation and interpretation between bodies, rather than being the simple 'issue' of an individual subject.

In her book *Ugly Feelings* (2005), Sianne Ngai makes a thorough case for the recuperation of tone as an analytical category in the consideration of literary emotion. Surveying a series of attempts to taxonomize tone since I. A. Richards and the New Critics, Ngai observes a general avoidance in literary critical writing of the ways in which tone is invoked and used in the context of feelings in everyday usage. More pointedly, she articulates a suspicion that 'the motivation for this avoidance comes from the perceived threat of a "soft" impressionism which has always haunted feeling's role in any analytic endeavour'.[24] For Ngai, by contrast, tone seems a very appropriate category for registering 'compressed assessments of complex "situations", for indicating the *total* web of relations sought after' when critics describe works as, for example, 'paranoid', 'euphoric', or 'melancholic'.[25] The idea that tone is a compressed assessment of complex relations means that its ambit is flexible: the tone of the work is one thing; the tone of a particular chapter, another; it is equally possible to speak of the tone or 'affective bearing' of a whole class of works. An expansion and contraction of contexts is intrinsic to the structural opposition between the 'compressed assessment' and the 'hyper-relational' aspects of tone that Ngai describes, and is reflected in a division along the lines of critical practice. Tone:

> actually seems unpropitious for a purely formalist literary criticism – and this for the same reasons it seems so ideally suited for the analysis of ideology, which, as the materially embodied representation of an *imaginary relationship* to a holistic complex of real conditions, clearly shares tone's virtual, diffused, but also immanent character.[26]

The practical utility Ngai accords to tone emphasizes that it is social and experiential, as well as affective. It is understood in this way as a felt response to a zeitgeist: a way of registering historical consciousness that reins in the dizzying 'gehenna of links' into which social existence can be discomposed.[27] On these terms, tone pulls against the particular kind of political historicism that seeks to read Beckett in context, as Andrew Gibson puts it, 'by isolating particular and localized features of its unfolding horror'.[28] Put another way, and adapting Beckett's own formula, tone might be regarded as a useful aspirin for those critics suffering headaches among the overtones.[29] Gibson writes that 'If Beckett's works cannot simply be "matched up" with historical contexts [...] they are streaked by historical turmoils and the emotions provoked by them'.[30] This specifically affective way of thinking about Beckett's works' relationship to history also entails a specifically historical way of thinking about their relationship to affect, departing from an idea of the emotions which focuses squarely on the individual subject as their source and horizon.

Wild tone: Distress and *All That Fall*

Beckett seems to have been unsympathetic to the latter kind of view. In his 1961 interview with Tom Driver for *Columbia University Forum* he embarks on an anecdote about 'an English intellectual – so-called', who hastens his departure from a party by asking why he always writes about distress, and whether it is the product of an unhappy childhood. Beckett explains that his childhood was very happy, leaves and gets into a taxi:

> On the glass partition between me and the driver were three signs: one asked for help for the blind, another help for orphans, and the third for relief for the war refugees. One does not have to look for distress. It is screaming at you even in the taxis of London.[31]

Distress, as Beckett interprets it for Driver, is in circulation. He brushes off the intellectual's idea of his works' emotion deriving from a personal wound, and conceives of distress as a feeling that is there in 'signs', is not hidden but is put about (on glass partitions, in taxis), comes in the form of appeals and explicitly addresses *you* in a voice that amounts to a *scream*. None of what he says here claims to identify with this extant distress, but only to perceive it in a particular way, closer to sympathy than to egoism. The scream of the voices on the signs in the taxi seem to herniate a silence, and in this sense recall the line from *Lessness*: 'Never but silence such that in imagination this wild laughter these cries' (*Texts* 132). That line also provides a very specific recollection within the context of Beckett's oeuvre: if the 'cries' have something of the 'screams' about them, the 'wild laughter' exactly reproduces a crucial stage direction from the radio play *All That Fall*. A little climax in the play comes when the Bible verse from which the title is taken (Ps 145.14) is quoted in full by Maddy Rooney to her husband Dan, upon which the pair of them are silent for a moment, then '*join in wild laughter*' (*CDW* 198).

In a review of the then rather surprising 2008 stage production of the play by final year students at *RADA*, Sean Lawlor observes how, at the arrival of the train carrying Dan Rooney, 'dense smoke engulfed the stage' (bringing into play the 'dark' which Beckett thought so essential to *All That Fall*) and in it 'Mrs Rooney's desperate cries could be heard'.[32] This tonal desperation runs against other minor affects Lawlor finds conveyed by the actors: 'a residue of irritation', or 'a thread of tenderness and affection'.[33] Lawlor's review emphasizes the contingencies of tone and the affective dimensions of the play that issue from it in performance. It is little surprise that *All That Fall* has tended to invite certain kinds of affective reading, ranging from the generic and existential, through the personal and authorial, to the social and ideological. The desperation that Lawlor hears in Mrs Rooney's voice is felt by Enoch Brater to suffuse the play in an 'agonizing despair that none of Maddy's voices will be able to mask', provoked by the fact that there will be 'finally, no "helping hand"'.[34] Sinéad Mooney registers a 'horror of being looked at, an anguish at perception' in Mrs Rooney that is both generic (being tied to the Gothic) and national-political (an Irish Gothic and a 'spectacle of conspicuous, unintegrated Protestantism').[35] In his biography, James Knowlson reads the play as a bruising surge of Beckett's own feelings provoked by the protracted death, two years earlier, of his brother Frank.[36] The play's evident engagement with religion, not least in its title and in the gale of cutting laughter at the Bible verse, correspond on this reading to Beckett's own agitated feelings about a religion which failed self-confidently in the face of suffering.[37] Whether it is framed as a universalized, typically human 'despair', a personal anguished outrage or an affiliated Anglo-Irish response to historical trauma, the play is one that seems to put emotion on display. But the question we are left with is exactly how *All That Fall* makes feeling materialize: what takes it from being a meditation on distress and makes it so much nervier, less cool and more affecting? Correspondingly, we might ask whether it is productive to think of the play's affective force being prompted by a particular trauma; if so, which; and conversely whether it is inappropriate to consider the play's displays of emotion according to a logic of cause and effect.

The *wildness* of the laughter is one of several moments in the play where a tone of sorts is specified in the script and made to do work in performance. The wildness demanded is indeed a compressed assessment of a complex situation that implies a response to distress; it is also a description (like the 'mild' of Beckett's letter to Schneider) that has to be translated into performance. But the tone and affective force of this moment are not fully accounted for by the instruction or the quality it describes. Just as Beckett calls tone '*the* problem' in his letter to Schneider, but also suggests that other aspects of the drama should 'do the work', the affective work here is being done by a combination of elements. The wildness and the distress that the play manifests, as will be apparent to anyone who has listened to a recording of the BBC production directed by Donald McWhinnie, are also a matter of rhythm in the piece.[38] Between Maddy's recitation of the Bible verse and the laughter that follows intervenes a spell of silence; immediately after cutting off the laugh, the pair '*move on*', as they do throughout the play, with '*wind and rain, dragging feet, etc.*' (*CDW* 198). Up to this point only silence has intervened between each of these movements, so the wild laughter comes out of nothing and breaks both the intensified metrical order of the Bible verse, and the general order of '*dragging feet, etc.*' These are two separate contexts, however, for the distress that takes form in the play. By apparently rising to the provocation of the Bible verse, the laughter skirts around a different kind of distress that seems to be implicit in this wildness which ruptures the play's general sense of strain. Far from communicating itself as really 'wild', the laughter can be received as active and purposive: an attack, first of all in the musical sense as a rupture of the silence, but also in the ideological sense. It leaves the play open to the charge of a crass atheism, or what Donald Davie scathingly calls 'a fascination with blasphemy that most non-Irish readers will find childish and trivial' in his review of the first BBC production.[39] Although Davie's patrician disapproval, with its brazen national caricature (the Irish as rebellious children, yet to sublimate religiosity) may be quickly pulled apart, the sense of Dan and Maddy's '*wild laughter*' as a direct response to the message of the

Psalm, which the play certainly solicits, does risk masking its more various manifestations of distress.

All That Fall is not magnanimously humanitarian. It does not display an unqualified sympathy for all those war refugees' voices, nor does it present distress as a fixed value, nor does it purport to offer an especially appropriate response to distress (whatever that might be). But the work does present a sympathetic and social concern for distress, partly in the gruesomeness of its failure to be propitiated, but much more movingly, I think, in a complex and variable tone whose diversions into blunt aggression are only naggingly central to the play. Distress in *All That Fall* is not primarily resident in the moment of rupture. This is the importance of the play's pulse, and can be seen again in the very last lines:

> **Jerry** It was a little child fell out of the carriage, Ma'am. [*Pause.*] On to the line, Ma'am. [*Pause.*] Under the wheels, Ma'am.
> [*Silence.* Jerry *runs off. His steps die away. Tempest of wind and rain. It abates. They move on. Dragging steps, etc. They halt. Tempest of wind and rain.*]. (CDW 199)

Here as before they move on, and the '*dragging steps, etc.*' take place one last time. The sound of wind and rain intensifies to a tempest, but the importance of this tonal shift is less the pathetic fallacy it looks like, and more the fact that it abates, they move on, '*dragging steps etc.*', they halt, and that it rises again. It is not the irruption itself that matters, nor the old metaphor of tempest, but the rushing movements between intensity and abeyance that accompany the repetitious gesture of steps and halts.

'ATOMS!' History and the holistic tone

Lawlor's review of the *RADA* production suggests that its most pressing effects were in its 'recurrent irritability' as well as the 'violent changes of mood'.[40] *All That Fall*'s gruesome and affective rendering of distress, one might say, materializes through these movements: steady, recurrent, straining, irritable and also violently changeable. To read the play in this way appears to map very neatly onto a non-atomistic conception of affect which characterizes Ngai's 'holistic' idea of tone, and which is also characteristic of Raymond Williams's 'structures of feeling': an idea of social being, or 'meanings and values as they are actively lived and felt', that can be imagined as 'in solution', or 'in a living and inter-relating continuity'.[41] More recently, Sara Ahmed has written of affect in terms of economy, where feelings are passed about in a shifting passage between bodies: rather than 'resid[ing] in a subject or figure', these '*involve* subjects and objects' in a processive manner.[42] In fact, contemporary discourses concerning affect and the emotions are widely marked by a critical vocabulary dedicated to intensities and forces, passages between, circulation and economy, all of them characterized above all by movement, and often a certain suspicion of atomism.

One might say that the vision of distress Beckett puts forward in his conversation with Driver takes up a similarly holistic and mobile view of feeling, and that the distress played out in *All That Fall* follows suit. But it would be rash to think that atoms do not matter for the play's dealings with emotion, and not only on the basis of Maddy's frenzy at the mention of the word: 'oh to be in atoms, in atoms! [*Frenziedly.*] ATOMS! [*Silence. Cooing.*]' (*CDW* 177). Certainly, it would be tendentious to suggest that there is not a discretely religious element to the play's complex tone. The '*wild laughter*' sticks to the language of the Bible and involves this particular text, its particular expression of impotent sentiment, in the play's injured feelings. Similarly, the specific historical traumas discussed by Seán Kennedy linger and provoke in the ideological context which *All That Fall* registers among its distressed characters.[43] The psychoanalytic case mentioned by Maddy of a little girl who had 'never really been born' (*CDW* 196), and its historical connection with the lecture by Carl Jung which Beckett attended on 2 October 1935, is also elemental in the play's swarming affects: Mrs Rooney weeps at the remembrance, as Mr Rooney later weeps upon hearing Schubert's 'Death and the Maiden' (*CDW* 197) or as Miss Fitt responds hysterically to the lyrics of her hymn (*CDW* 184).[44] Taken altogether, *All That Fall*'s affective bearing cannot be extricated from this array of particulars that thread through, surround and occasionally pierce it. These include anger at the impostures of certain forms of Christian cultural practice, sensitivity to the fretfulness of a particular community in its twilight, and also a feeling for the individual pains of loneliness, issuelessness, and lost loved ones.

A performance of *All That Fall* features a strikingly varied set of vocal tone that are especially marked when compared to the 'toneless' or 'colourless' voices of some of the later plays. It would be possible to read this alongside the conventional account of Beckett's work progressively abstracting itself from particularities and to treat *All That Fall*'s particular manifestation of distress, therefore, as a late gasp of socially and historically invested affects. The counterpoint to this view is perhaps to be found, at least partially, in understanding how even the neutral, flat or negated tone of the later drama entails forms of social production, as we began to see earlier via the correspondence with Schneider. As a final example, I quote from a 1984 conversation between Billie Whitelaw and Mel Gussow:

BW	When he says, 'Take all the emotion out of it. No colour, no colour', I think what he means is 'no acting'.
MG	But *Not I* is filled with emotion. It's a frenzy.
BW	He kept on saying, 'Flat, no emotion, no colour, flat', and I would say, 'Yes, yes'. I think what we finally got back to is something not acted; it just happens. With *Not I* what happened for me was a terrible inner scream, like falling backward into hell. It was the scream I never made when my son was desperately ill.[45]

Whitelaw is moved to recall Beckett's insistent direction for 'no colour', and a 'flat' delivery. In her recollection these qualities are also of a piece with 'no emotion'. But this comes in the form of a persistent injunction, as Whitelaw tells it, rather than as a property inherent to the work. Moreover, neither Gussow nor Whitelaw is able to receive the text on these terms; nor will Whitelaw quite assent to the idea that 'no colour' and 'no emotion' mean exactly what they say: the negation of these dramatic traits has to be translated (for practical reasons, or in order to understand) into 'no acting', and then 'no acting' has to be acted. Alongside these practical and acoustic considerations, performing *Not I* leaves the actor situating emotion between sound and silence (internalized or 'never made'), flatness and a scream, and between a metaphysical analogy and personal memory. Reading these remarks alongside the deadened soundscape of *The Lost Ones* and the insistence on a flat tone in *Company*, or in contrast to the hugely varied directions of voice and emotion in *All That Fall*, is not so much to say that they demonstrate an aesthetic trajectory – which would recapitulate the common claim that Beckett's work progressively negates and reduces aspects of speech in service of a raw, oddly unsentimental affectivity – as to indicate the contingencies and contradictions that come up both in Beckett's writing and in the discourses surrounding it where matters of tone and of the emotions are concerned. Crucially, the contingencies and contradictions do not reach their limit in the phenomenon of tone, nor the articulation of personal emotional experience: they are integral to the complicated structure of feeling attached to Beckett's work for both Gussow and Whitelaw (the critic responding to the work and the actor tasked with performing it).

The risk, talking of tone, is not so much of a critical impressionism (though it can edge towards that), but of a 'compressed' assessment that completely occludes the relations which, on this reading, compose it. A study of tone, then, needs to be able to account for those relations. On the other hand, if we take seriously Ngai's sense that tone is 'hyper-relational', or follow it in Williams to an expression of social experience 'in solution', analysing discrete relations would never account for the tone, however many were gathered up. Tone, in this sense, is not a compression of a finite set of determinate correspondences. The challenge however is not to occlude such correspondences: lean too heavily on the 'compressed assessment' and its own internal logic of relations, analogs, combinations, elisions and contiguities disappears; focus on determinate relations and you risk missing the active character of feelings in social experience. To tread between these two positions is by no means a new critical problem: it is one of Williams's main concerns throughout *Marxism and Literature*, for example. But it is a challenge that a consideration of tone in Beckett's work brings back very sharply.

Tone, then, stands in an important but difficult relation with negation and with nothing, both of which have received renewed attention in Beckett scholarship of late. This return to nothing has gone hand in hand with the increasing visibility of substantial quantities of archival material, together with a corresponding increase in explications of Beckett's work which make use of it; and at the same time, an increasing attention to different ways of historicizing Beckett as a writer in the world, whose texts are situated or worldly despite the ways in which they strive to appear otherwise. To propose a reading of tone in the light of these tendencies might seem nostalgic at best, since the term has so often been associated with aesthetic immanence, rather than social production, and with the privileged intuition of the critic, rather than the rigorously descriptive eye of the scholar. But the various ways in which tone comes to matter in Beckett's work, determinately and materially as well as in the language of abstraction, suggest that there may be some 'peculiar difficulty and importance' to them.[46] Tone serves as a holistic material counterpoint to the rhetoric of negation in Beckett's drama, inviting with it a consideration of these works' emotional life and its involvement in an exceptionally complex but often powerfully, even distressingly compressed set of historical circumstances.

Notes

1. Maurice Harmon (ed.). *No Author Better Served: The Correspondence of Samuel Beckett & Alan Schneider* (Cambridge, MA: Harvard University Press, 1998), 90.
2. Brian Rotman, 'Gesture and the "I" Fold', *Parallax* 15.4 (2009), 73.
3. Ludwig Wittgenstein, *Philosophical Investigations*, translated by G. E. M. Anscombe. 2nd edn (Oxford: Blackwell, 1997).
4. Harmon, 90.
5. Samuel Beckett, *Texts for Nothing and Other Shorter Prose* (London: Faber, 2010), 101. Subsequent references are made parenthetically as *Texts*.
6. Ruby Cohn, *A Beckett Canon* (Ann Arbor: University of Michigan Press, 2001), 313.
7. C. J. Ackerley and S. E. Gontarski (eds). *The Grove Companion to Samuel Beckett* (New York: Grove Press, 2004), 607.
8. Samuel Beckett, *Company/Ill Seen Ill Said/WorstwardHo/Stirrings Still* (London: Faber, 2009), 12.
9. Charles Krance (ed.). *Samuel Beckett's Company/Compagnie and A Piece of Monologue/Solo: A Bilingual Variorum Edition* (New York & London: Garland, 1993), 72.
10. Ibid., 189–94.
11. Ibid., 191.
12. Ibid., 190–1.
13. Jean-Pierre Martin, 'Voix', in *Dictionnaire Beckett*, edited by Marie-Claude Hubert (Paris: Honoré Champion, 2011), 1137. Translations mine: *voix mortes; atones et impersonnelles, proches du bruissement ou du murmure;processus d'amenuisement;annonce sa disparition.*

14 Samuel Beckett, *Complete Dramatic Works* (London: Faber and Faber, 1986), 307. Subsequent references are made parenthetically as *CDW*.
15 Xerxes Mehta, 'Scholars/Artists/Beckett', *Samuel Beckett Today/Aujourd'hui*, 11 (2001), 127.
16 Laura Salisbury, '"Something or nothing": Beckett and the matter of language', in *Beckett and Nothing*, edited by Daniela Caselli (Manchester: Manchester University Press, 2010), 232.
17 Mehta, 127.
18 Harmon, 25.
19 Ibid., 95.
20 Ibid., 95.
21 Ibid., 347.
22 Barbara Bray (with whom Beckett worked at the BBC after *All That Fall*) recounts how tapes would circulate among actors, directors and the writer, and describes 'Pat's attempt to produce this particular voice which Sam wanted and which Donald managed to coerce out of him – or curse out of him'. Marek Kędzierski, 'Barbara Bray: In Her Own Words', *Modernism/modernity Samuel Beckett: Out of the Archive*, edited by Peter Fifield, Bryan Radley and Lawrence Rainey, 18.4 (2011), 891.
23 Lois Oppenheim (ed.). *Directing Beckett* (Ann Arbor: University of Michigan Press, 1997), 15–16.
24 Sianne Ngai, *Ugly Feelings* (London: Harvard University Press, 2005), 42.
25 Ibid., 42–3.
26 Ibid., 47.
27 Samuel Beckett, *More Pricks Than Kicks* (London: John Calder, 1993), 63.
28 Andrew Gibson, *Samuel Beckett* (London: Reaktion, 2010), 161.
29 Harmon, 24.
30 Ibid., 22.
31 Tom Driver, 'Beckett by the Madeleine', *Columbia University Forum* 4 (1961), 23. Reprinted in Lawrence Graver and Raymond Federman (eds). *Samuel Beckett: The Critical Heritage* (London: Routledge and Kegan Paul, 1979), 220.

32 Sean Lawlor, 'Review of *All That Fall/Catastrophe*, directed by William Gaskill at *RADA*', *Journal of Beckett Studies*, 18 (2009), 176.
33 Ibid., 175–6.
34 Enoch Brater, *The Drama in the Text* (Oxford: Oxford University Press, 1994), 22.
35 Sinéad Mooney, 'Beckett's Irish Gothic', in *Beckett and Ireland*, edited by Séan Kennedy (Cambridge: Cambridge University Press, 2010), 139.
36 See GraleyHerren's essay for an account of this event, and his argument that *Endgame* rather than *All That Fall* is the primary product of Beckett's distress.
37 James Knowlson, *Damned to Fame: The Life of Samuel Beckett* (London: Bloomsbury, 1997), 429–30.
38 'All That Fall', 13 February 1957 edition of *BBC Third Programme* (BBC).
39 Donald Davie, 'Kinds of Comedy', *Spectrum*, 2 (1958): 25–31. Reprinted in Graver and Federman, 157.
40 Lawlor, 176.
41 Raymond Williams, *Marxism and Literature* (Oxford: Oxford University Press, 1977), 132–4.
42 Sara Ahmed, 'Affective Economies', *Social Text*, 22.2 (2004), 119.
43 Séan Kennedy, '"A Lingering Dissolution": *All That Fall* and Protestant Fears of Engulfment in the Irish Free State', *Assaph*, 17–18 (2003), 247–61.
44 Shane Weller, *A Taste for the Negative: Beckett and Nihilism* (Oxford: Legenda, 2005), 134–5.
45 Mel Gussow, *Conversations With and About Beckett* (New York: Grove, 1996), 85.
46 Harmon, 90.

Works cited

Ackerley, C. J. and S. E. Gontarski (eds). *The Grove Companion to Samuel Beckett* (New York: Grove Press, 2004).

Ahmed, Sara. 'Affective Economies', *Social Text*, 22.2 (2004): 117–39.

Beckett, Samuel. *Complete Dramatic Works* (London: Faber and Faber, 1986).
—. *More Pricks Than Kicks* (London: John Calder, 1993).
—. *Company/Ill Seen Ill Said/WorstwardHo/Stirrings Still* (London: Faber, 2009).
—. *Texts for Nothing and Other Shorter Prose* (London: Faber, 2010).
Brater, Enoch. *The Drama in the Text* (Oxford: Oxford University Press, 1994).
Cohn, Ruby. *A Beckett Canon* (Ann Arbor: University of Michigan Press, 2001).
Gibson, Andrew. *Samuel Beckett* (London: Reaktion, 2010).
Graver, Lawrence and Raymond Federman (eds). *Samuel Beckett: The Critical Heritage* (London: Routledge and Kegan Paul, 1979).
Gussow, Mel. *Conversations With and About Beckett* (New York: Grove, 1996).
Harmon, Maurice (ed.). *No Author Better Served: The Correspondence of Samuel Beckett & Alan Schneider* (Cambridge, MA: Harvard University Press, 1998).
Hubert, Marie-Claude (ed.). *Dictionnaire Beckett* (Paris: Honoré Champion, 2011).
Kędzierski, Marek. 'Barbara Bray: In Her Own Words', *Modernism/modernity Samuel Beckett: Out of the Archive*, edited by Peter Fifield, Bryan Radley and Lawrence Rainey, 18.4 (2011), 887–97.
Kennedy, Séan. '"A Lingering Dissolution": *All That Fall* and Protestant Fears of Engulfment in the Irish Free State', Assaph, 17–18 (2003): 247–61.
Knowlson, James. *Damned to Fame: The Life of Samuel Beckett* (London: Bloomsbury, 1997).
Krance, Charles (ed.). *Samuel Beckett's Company/Compagnie and A Piece of Monologue/Solo: A Bilingual Variorum Edition* (New York & London: Garland, 1993).
Lawlor, Sean. 'Review of *All That Fall/Catastrophe*', directed by William Gaskill at *RADA, Journal of Beckett Studies*, 18 (2009), 172–7.
Mehta, Xerxes. 'Scholars/Artists/Beckett', *Samuel Beckett Today/Aujourd'hui*, 11 (2001), 125–31.
Mooney, Sinéad. 'Beckett's Irish Gothic', in *Beckett and Ireland*, edited by Séan Kennedy (Cambridge: Cambridge University Press, 2010), 131–49.

Ngai, Sianne. *Ugly Feelings* (London: Harvard University Press, 2005).

Oppenheim, Lois (ed.). *Directing Beckett* (Ann Arbor: University of Michigan Press, 1997).

Rotman, Brian. 'Gesture and the 'I' Fold', *Parallax*, 15.4 (2009), 68–82.

Salisbury, Laura. '"Something or nothing": Beckett and the matter of language', in *Beckett and Nothing*, edited by Daniela Caselli (Manchester: Manchester University Press, 2010), 213–36.

Weller, Shane. *A Taste for the Negative: Beckett and Nihilism* (Oxford: Legenda, 2005).

Williams, Raymond. *Marxism and Literature* (Oxford: Oxford University Press, 1977).

10

Wyndham Lewis's Pseudocouple: *The Childermass* as a Precursor of *Waiting for Godot*

Yoshiki Tajiri
University of Tokyo

Introduction: The term 'Pseudocouple'

Samuel Beckett used the term 'pseudocouple' in *The Unnamable* to refer to the eponymous heroes of his earlier work *Mercier and Camier*. Toward the beginning of *The Unnamable*, the narrator, who is unsure of everything including his own identity, feels that Malone, or perhaps Molloy, is passing before him. He also believes that 'they are all here, at least from Murphy on'.[1] After evoking the names of the characters in Beckett's earlier works in this manner, the narrator mentions an incident in which two shapes, 'oblong like men', collided with each other, fell and vanished before him. Then he says, 'I naturally thought of the pseudocouple Mercier-Camier' (*Unnamable* 11). Thus the term pseudocouple was originally intended specifically for Mercier and Camier. But it is now commonly used for the many couples that appear in Beckett's work. *The Grove Companion to Samuel Beckett* gives a standard account, defining it as 'halves of a single personality' and linking it to the question of the self and its other that is persistently thematized in Beckett's work.[2] On the other hand, Shane Weller uses the term in a much broader sense when he applies it to the relation between two authors such as Derrida and Beckett. Here it means the general condition in which 'neither identity nor difference, neither unity nor separation, is to be taken for granted'.[3] In this essay, however, I intend to place Beckett's pseudocouples in a wider historical and intertextual context and demonstrate that while a significant characteristic of Beckett's work they are part of a literary tradition of similarly entwined couples.[4] Such a perspective will tease out the literary context in which Beckett created his pseudocouples and thereby highlight some key features of modernism, especially the tendency to mechanize the human. I will start by discussing Wyndham Lewis's 1928 novel *The Childermass*, which features a couple remarkably similar to Mercier and Camier, as well as to their successors Vladimir and Estragon.

The Childermass and *Waiting for Godot*

The Childermass is a novel that is now little read, despite its credentials as a modernist text of considerable stature. A summary will therefore be helpful. The protagonists of the novel are two old school friends Pullman and Satterthwaite (Satters) who, after being killed in the First World War, happen to meet near the River Styx in the underworld. Like Dante and Virgil, they wander in this eerie modern Inferno, described by Lewis almost in the style of science fiction: the objects around them, for instance, appear, disappear or move as if in a film. The two men themselves go through strange temporal and spatial distortions and at one point stray into an eighteenth-century England. Pullman, having come to this world a little earlier, plays the role of a guide or nurse for younger Satters who is constantly dismayed by his fate. Pullman can be calm because he blindly believes the words of the Bailiff governing this world, whereas Satters seems to see through the latter's tricks. Eventually they reach a large auditorium where they find the Bailiff judging applicants seeking to enter Heaven. The second half of the novel is largely devoted to rather tedious descriptions of the Bailiff's peculiar philosophical debates with the oppositional power led by Hyperides (who often represents Lewis's own ideas), during which Pullman and Satters are marginalized as mere spectators.

Pullman and Satters bear a striking resemblance to Beckett's couples, and indeed, as will be seen later, Fredric Jameson refers to them as a 'pseudocouple'. Three common features in particular stand out. First, the aimlessness of Pullman and Satters' existence. When they start their journey, Pullman says to Satters, 'Come along; it's best to keep moving here'.[5] Pullman is here thinking of guiding Satters to 'their eyrie their coign of vantage', but the priority is movement itself: 'action is everything; to keep moving is the idea, this is [Pullman's] law of existence' (*Childermass* 16). And toyed with by uncanny temporal and spatial phenomena, they wander helplessly in the first half of the novel. At the very end of *The Childermass*, Pullman says to Satters, 'Step out. Pick your feet up. If you must go nowhere, step out' (*Childermass* 401), thus acknowledging the sheer pointlessness of their journey, and in terms which evoke Beckett's work.

The second point of contact between Lewis's and Beckett's pseudocouples is that Pullman and Satters find it difficult to separate from one another, just as Beckett's pseudocouples do. Satters says, 'It is so jolly to have someone to talk to. [. . .] Oh do let's not part Pully! Will you promise?' (*Childermass* 33-4). For his part, Pullman remains rather indifferent to Satters' request that they stay together, prefiguring the beginning of Act I of *Waiting for Godot*, where Vladimir excitedly says, 'Together again at last! We'll have to celebrate this', to which Estragon replies irritably, 'Not Now, not now'.[6] At one point, while Pullman and Satters are discussing the shifting reality around them, 'The dialogue prevents [Pullman] from leaving' (*CDW* 43).

This is reminiscent of the sequence in *Endgame* where Clov, reluctant to stay, asks:

Clov   What is there to keep me here?
Hamm   The dialogue (*CDW* 120–1).

Even when they quarrel Pullman says to Satters, 'I apologize, I lost my temper. But we need not part' (*Childermass* 144). Satters is in turn obliged to accept him.

A third similarity between the authors' pseudocouples is their uncertainty about the reality that they inhabit. In one sense it is apt that Pullman and Satters struggle to make sense of the reality around them: they are, after all, ghosts in the world of the dead. But the ever-sceptical Satters continues to ask Pullman about the reality of their surroundings as they appear, vanish or move. For example, when they see the peons disappear soon after their encounter at the beginning of the novel, Satters asks, 'Are we very different [i.e. from the peons]? I believe we only think we're so different' (*Childermass* 43), but Pullman evades this question. Knowing that their surroundings are simulacra, Pullman coolly accepts the fact, saying, 'Had I been managing this show [. . .] I shouldn't have placed the city there' (*Childermass* 45). When Satters asks aggressively, 'why do I see things that are not there? It must mean something or is it nothing or it's silly to notice as you say?' (*Childermass* 83). Pullman encourages him to believe the Bailiff's idea that they are mirages. Satters goes as far as to question the reality of Pullman himself: 'Is that really you I am talking to am I really – with – *you*?' to which Pullman says with a laugh, 'you suspect *me* too? Do I seem real? How do I strike you?' (*Childermass* 86). Although their attitudes to their surroundings are different – Satters questioning, Pullman accepting – they are both confronted with the absurdity of being placed in a strangely uncertain and elusive world. In like manner, in *Godot* too, the two tramps do not have a secure sense of their existence, as is suggested by Estragon's following remark: 'We always find something, eh Didi, to give us the impression we exist?' (*CDW* 64). The following dialogue from *The Childermass* recalls *Godot* in that it suggests the futility of attempting to quit the situation in which the characters find themselves:

> '[. . .] To absolutely pass out absolutely, I [Satters] have meant to but what is it prevents us, I'm sure it does what is it?'
> 'What?'
> 'Oh I don't know!' (*Childermass* 82–3)

In *Godot* it is usually Estragon who complains childishly about his situation: 'Nothing happens, nobody comes, nobody goes, it's awful!' (*CDW* 41) or 'But I can't go on like this!' (*CDW* 63). In this sense he corresponds to Satters. On the other hand, Vladimir seems to have a firmer grasp of their situation, as is shown by his frequently reminding Estragon of their need to wait for Godot, just as Pullman can guide his partner with his knowledge of their world. Such correspondences arise because both of these couples are modelled on the familiar comic pair of the fool and the straight man: Estragon and Satters are close to the fool while Vladimir and Pullman resemble the straight man. Like all figures in this role, Vladimir's superiority is only relative; he is just as frail as his partner. His slightly better memory, for example, leaves him no more able to understand his situation than the deeply forgetful Estragon. For his part, Pullman derives his authority mainly from his belief in the Bailiff's (obviously deceptive) words.

Pointing out passages in *The Childermass* that he considers Beckettian, Dennis Brown succinctly concludes:

> If there is no single precedent for Lucky here, the Bailiff is a convincing prototype of Pozzo, while Satters and Pullman are dead ringers for Estragon and Vladimir – infantile and dependently conjoined in frictional male companionship, in a wholly *Absurde* universe. So Joyce's greatest disciple finally became his own man-of-words by the

ultimate betrayal – choosing the precedent of Lewis, the rival, to find his own way.[7]

Brown gives an accurate description of Pullman and Satters' resemblance to Vladimir and Estragon, which would be discernible to many readers of *The Childermass*. On the other hand, the link between the Bailiff and Pozzo seems more difficult to maintain not only because there is no equivalent of Lucky but also because the scenes of his confrontation with oppositional forces contain so many arcane philosophical debates that they appear far more than a pastime for the two men. A different picture emerges, however, if we pay attention to the ending of the novel. After the lengthy passage featuring the Bailiff concludes, we are left with a one-page dialogue between Pullman and Satters that ends the entire novel. That dialogue contains the following exchange:

> SATTERS: 'Can't we go, Pully?'
> PULLMAN: 'Don't you want to find out which of the two is real?'
> SATTERS: 'I couldn't care less, Pully! Could you? What does it matter which isn't real! I was never real. Am I?'
> PULLMAN: 'I suppose you *were*. In the way that a toadstool is.'
> (*Childermass* 401)

Here Satters asserts his wish to leave, just like Estragon, who says repeatedly 'I'm going' or 'Let's go'. Pullman tries to draw Satters' attention to the immediately preceding debate between the Bailiff and one of his opponents, Polemon, about which of them is real. But it simply induces Satters to reassert his usual sense of unreality. And as we saw earlier, this dialogue ends in a *Godot*-like tone, dwelling on futility of departure. Pullman and Satters must face each other again just like Vladimir and Estragon after Pozzo and Lucky leave them and the distraction of their company is over. In other words, the Bailiff's agon with his opponents, although taking up half of the novel and containing many sub-debates, is in the end nothing more than a distraction from the problem of existing that Pullman and Satters must face.

Brown's final sentence about Beckett betraying Joyce by siding with Lewis needs qualification because it is clear that Beckett had no such intention. As is well known, Lewis was acidly critical of the *transition* circle including Joyce and Gertrude Stein (whose styles he in fact parodies in *The Childermass*)[8]. For his part, though Beckett depended on Lewis's publisher Charles Prentice at Chatto and Windus, who published his *Proust* and *More Pricks Than Kicks*,[9] he was of course closer to Joyce and *transition*. Indeed, in July 1930 Beckett wrote to Thomas McGreevy that Nancy Cunard had lent him a copy of Lewis's 1930 novel *The Apes of God* and commented, 'Apes of God is truly pitiful. If that is satire a child's petulance is satire'.[10] In February 1938 he reported, again to McGreevy, that he had read Lewis's autobiography *Blasting and Bombardiering* '4 pages at a time, with considerable disgust'.[11] It is uncertain whether Beckett read *The Childermass*, but he was undoubtedly so hostile to Lewis that Brown's claim that he chose him as a precedent does not convince. The question, then, is why pseudocouples emerged in the two different authors' works; what elements in modernism induced them to adopt the same literary device? In order to address this question, it will be useful to turn to Fredric Jameson's view of the pseudocouple.

Jameson on the Pseudocouple

In *Fables of Aggression: Wyndham Lewis, the Modernist as Fascist* (1979), Fredric Jameson gives a seminal formulation of the pseudocouple. He argues that in Lewis's novels, *The Childermass* in particular, the characters are not autonomous subjects as in the traditional novels but reduced to poles of an agonistic relation; now the characters themselves are less important than the relation between them. After analysing the relation between Pullman and Satters in *The Childermass*, Jameson names such twin characters the 'pseudo-couple' [*sic*] and places it in a broad historical context:

> [T]his is a very different relational category from the conventional pairing of lovers or partners, of siblings or rivals; we need a different word to convey the symbiotic 'unity' of this new 'collective' subject, both reduplicated and divided all at once. It is therefore useful to borrow Samuel Beckett's term for similar character relationships in his own work, and to designate as the *pseudo-couple* all those peculiar and as yet imperfectly studied pairs in literary history which reach well beyond the twin 'heroes' of *The Childermass* and the familiar Beckett teams of Vladimir and Estragon, Hamm and Clov, Mercier and Camier, through Flaubert's Bouvard and Pécuchet (and the less articulated pseudo-couple of Frédéric and Deslauriers in *L'Education sentimentale*) all the way back to Faust and Mephistopheles, and beyond them, to *Don Quixote*.[12]

Jameson adds that the pseudocouple is masculine. Referring to the idea that the nineteenth-century novel often featured bachelors deviating from matrimonial or familial bondage, he goes on to argue that the male pseudocouple emerged halfway between the subject's 'construction in bourgeois individualism and its disintegration in late capitalism'.[13] In other words, the individual strength of traditional bachelor characters diminished and a pair of males who relied on each other became necessary 'as a kind of compensation formation'.[14] They are not independent subjects but they have not yielded to schizophrenic disintegration either. Jameson also argues that the pseudocouple could also be described as 'a structural device for preserving narrative',[15] appearing in a transitional stage after conventional plot-making had come to the point of exhaustion with Flaubert but before narrative had become completely schizophrenic. In the light of this, it seems significant that *Waiting for Godot* was written immediately before *The Unnamable*, the unmistakably schizophrenic text.

It is worth noting here that Jameson mentions *Bouvard and Pécuchet* as a precursor of Beckett's pseudocouples. From the very beginning of Flaubert's novel, the two eponymous characters are presented as mechanically symmetrical. The following is the description of how they met at the beginning:

> Two men appeared.
> One came from the Bastille, the other from the Jardin des Plantes. The taller of the two, in a linen costume, walked with his hat pushed back, waistcoat undone and cravat in hand. The smaller one, whose body was enveloped in a brown frock-coat, had a peaked cap on his bent head.
> When they came to the middle of the boulevard they both sat down at the same moment on the same seat.
> Each took off his hat to mop his brow and put it beside him; and the smaller man noticed, written inside his neighbour's hat, *Bouvard*; while the latter easily made out the word *Pécuchet*, in the cap belonging to the individual in the frock-coat.[16]

The repetitive descriptions of their symmetrical movements ('One [...], the other [...]', 'The taller [...]. The smaller one [...]', 'the smaller man [...]; while the latter') and simultaneous movements ('both sat down at the same moment on the same seat', 'Each took off his hat to mop his brow and put it beside him') make the two men seem like cartoon figures or puppets. The fact that they find each other's name through written signs is in keeping with their profession, namely copying. And indeed, they are destined to copy everything around them after trying in vain to master various disciplines of human knowledge one after another. As such, instead of a conventional plot there are only comical yet empty repetitions. In other words, repetition is their mode of being. Little more than an embodiment of this principle, they have no real personalities. They are nothing but a 'structural device' through which the emptiness of human knowledge could be exposed. External and superficial differences between the two are enough to make this device function.[17] In this sense, they seem to be a direct precursor to *The Childermass, Mercier and Camier* and *Waiting for Godot*, where a pair of flat male characters resides in a world without any possibility of a conventional plot. *Bouvard and Pécuchet* brought the pseudocouple to the centre stage for the first time in the history of the Western novel.

The two copyists in Flaubert's novel are both mechanical and comical; or better, mechanical and *therefore* comical if we remember Bergson's thesis in *Laughter* (1899), namely that laughter arises as a corrective when life loses its elasticity in becoming mechanical. On the use of repetition in contemporary light comedies Bergson contends that, 'One of the best-known examples consists in bringing a group of characters, act after act, into the most varied surroundings, so as to reproduce, under ever fresh circumstances, one and the same series of incidents or accidents more or less symmetrically identical.'[18] This is indeed a common feature of traditional comedies from Shakespeare's *The Comedy of Errors* to Oscar Wilde's *The Importance of Being Earnest*, and by extension applicable to Flaubert's two copyists' repeated failures as well. But in a sense, the 'device' of the pseudocouple is itself a product of the symmetrical patterning of human life that induces laughter. It is a more recent derivative of the historically common pair of clowns or comedians, and characterized with more overtly artificial symmetry and flatness.

In the twentieth century, the mechanization and technologization of life advanced on a scale unimaginable in Flaubert's age, and society was increasingly filled with mechanical reproductions. In the process, the intrinsic link between the comic and the mechanical began to be foregrounded in a new manner. Michael North recently discussed the phenomenon under the rubric of 'machine-age comedy', represented by film comedians such as Buster Keaton and Charlie Chaplin. Discussing Chaplin in *Machine-Age Comedy*, North argues that 'the machine age seems to have brought, along with all its other dislocations, a new motive for laughter and perhaps a new form of comedy'.[19] He also says that in this age, 'mechanically reproduced comedy became the dominant form, affecting even the ancient humour of jokes and pratfalls. The effect of that change can be seen throughout the art and literature of the twentieth century'.[20] How can we consider the pseudocouple in Lewis and Beckett in this context? In the next section, I shall discuss *The Childermass* in relation to Lewis's concern with the mechanical and the comic.

Wyndham Lewis on the mechanical and the comic

The pseudocouple emerges from the nexus of the mechanical and the comic. In the age of modernism the nexus was theorized by Bergson and embodied by Chaplin. Both of these figures were key to Wyndham Lewis in the formation of his own ideas on laughter and the mechanization of the human. Let us first turn to a typical passage of *The Childermass* where Pullman and Satters are presented in symmetrical patterning reminiscent of the above-quoted passage of *Bouvard and Pécuchet*. Soon after they meet near the River Styx towards the beginning of the novel, we read the following description:

> Both pairs of eyes withdrawn into the respective shells, faces towards the ground, with one movement they now wheel and begin walking in step away from the quay slowly, Satters with a long-legged slouch, Pullman with a slowing-down of his light-limbed machine, hugging, high-shouldered, his stick. Their feet sink into the exuviae and migrating sand, dust and gypsum, of the riverside, kicking, first one and then the other, a stone or fragment of jetsam of the camp or flood, Pullman outwards towards the shore, Satters inland campwards. Their minds continue to work in silent rhythm, according to the system of habit set in motion by their meeting. (*Childermass* 11)

First, we note that the two wanderers' postures and actions are described with detachment as if they were material objects or machines. Even their minds 'continue to work in silent rhythm' like machines. It may be useful to note Anthony Paraskeva's observation that the descriptions of Pullman and Satters in this novel recall Lewis's characterization of Chaplin in his critical essays.[21] Second, there are symmetrical descriptions of the two figures ('Satters with [...], Pullman with [...]', 'Pullman outwards [...], Satters inland campwards') that enhance the impression of their mechanical character. We find many examples of such symmetrically arranged descriptions in *Bouvard and Pécuchet* and *Mercier and Camier*. The faintly comic effect evoked by Pullman and Satters moving like two stiff robots ('with one movement they now wheel and begin walking in step') stems from the mechanization of the human that Bergson discussed. Indeed, the pseudocouple in general can be regarded as created by reducing human relations to their mechanical minimum. And the pseudocouple of Pullman and Satters here seems to be a product of the wholesale mechanization of the human represented in this novel.

In *The Childermass* the mechanization in question is almost synonymous with the effect of film on human beings. As we noted, the reality of this after-world is shaky and illusionary as if it were a film. Indeed, the connection is made explicit at several points. One of the peons who appear and disappear 'is fainter than any of the rest, he is thin and shabby mustard yellow, in colouring a flat daguerreotype or one of the personnel of a pre-war film' (*Childermass* 23–4). A little later, the city that the two men see suddenly recedes: 'The whole city like a film-scene slides away perceptibly several inches to the rear, as their eyes are fixed upon it' (*Childermass* 32). Pullman and Satters' world is made up of simulacra, preventing them from attaining an accurate sense of reality. In the auditorium, spectators are bewitched by a mirage or 'phantom picture' and some wonder if 'it's not a cinematograph' (*Childermass* 176). The Bailiff, who seems to be employing this trick to control people, says, 'They always do that film business when the Phoenix comes. It's quite pretty, but as archaeology it's all nonsense I'm afraid. I hope you enjoyed it?' (*Childermass* 181). The Bailiff is thus consciously making use of cinematographic effects to deceive the masses. As Paul Tiessen argues, this feature reflects Lewis's idea, expressed in *Time and Western Man* (1927), that film hypnotizes people and deprives them of critical faculty, thereby contributing to the standardization and mechanization of the human in modern society. In Lewis's view, Chaplin's films that entertain the masses with his often mechanical antics represent the deplorable tendency. At one point in *The Childermass*, a big mask of Chaplin replaces the Bailiff as if to indicate their similarity in deceiving the masses (*Childermass* 230–1).

In addition, Satters is described as a 'Keystone giant' who is knocked down by Pullman. 'Keystone' is the name of the American company that produced Chaplin's early films in the 1910s. As Anthony Paraskeva points out, there is an allusion to 'similar square-ups between Chaplin and the Keystone cops'.[22] If we remember that their physical action itself is often Chaplinesque, it is clear that Pullman and Satters are created with a criticism of Chaplin in mind. It seems that if Chaplin's performance accords with Bergson's idea that mechanical action generates comic effects, Lewis conceived of a different kind of conjunction between the comic and the mechanical.

Although Lewis was influenced by Bergson when young, he persistently criticized him as representing what he considered the lamentable 'time-philosophy'. But he also objected to Bergson's theory of laughter. In his essay 'The Meaning of the Wild Body' (1927), Lewis argued:

> The root of the Comic is to be sought in the sensations resulting from the observations of a *thing* behaving like a person. But from that point of view all men are necessarily comic: for they are all *things*, or physical bodies, behaving as *persons*.[23]

This view, which neatly reverses Bergson's theory ('a *thing* behaving like a person', and not the opposite, is funny), suggests that Lewis in principle regards human beings as material objects. If we adopt such a view, human bodies and activities will be completely defamiliarized and reveal their grotesque aspects. In *Men without Art* (1934), Lewis argues that if we can laugh at a shell-shocked man, we can laugh at anybody because all human beings are no more than defective machines. He writes:

> It is unnecessary to enumerate the tragic handicaps that our human conditions involve – the glaring mechanical imperfections, the nervous tics, the prodigality of objectless movement – the, to other creatures, offensive smells, disagreeable moistures – the involuntary grimace, the lurch, roll, trot or stagger which we call our *walk* – it is only a matter of degree between us and the victim of locomotor-ataxy or St. Vitus's dance....[24]

These actions – indeed Lewis includes practically every human action in this category – are susceptible to his satirical laughter. Lewis criticized the wholesale mechanization and standardization of society in his essays. That is why he began to see Chaplin as the symbol of the dehumanizing tendency of the modern times. On the other hand, his art begins from the premise that human beings are always already material objects or imperfect machines. In his art laughter does not work to restore the proper elasticity of human life as Bergson argues. It becomes stiff, hollow and hysterical just like the grotesque frozen grins Lewis often portrayed in his paintings.[25]

Pullman and Satters are created from Lewis's impulse to satirize the mechanized nature of human beings in modern society filled with simulacra. The pseudocouple, in being flat, mechanical and repetitive, is a suitable literary figure for that purpose.[26] However, compared with Bouvard and Pécuchet, Mercier and Camier and Vladimir and Estragon, Lewis's two wanderers seem rather grim and joyless.

Even in the above-quoted long passage where they start to walk together like two robots, we may feel that comic effect is somehow subdued by the coldly detached observation of their actions. Lewis's scorchingly satirical gaze at the mechanical quality of human beings undermines the potential comic effect of the pseudocouple. While the pseudocouple is created by mechanically reducing human relations to the minimum, in Lewis's case the reduction is so relentless that only the husk of laughter seems able to remain.

The machine-age comedy of Beckett

Scholars have long noticed a variety of mechanizations of the human in Beckett's works from Watt's walking to the geometrical patterning of the dancers' movements in *Quad*. Beckett's use of technologies in his later career has also been extensively discussed. As we noted earlier, the pseudocouple can be regarded as forming part of a wider concern with mechanization of the human. While the two tramps in *Godot* are not necessarily acting as mechanically as Chaplin, they are created by formally patterning and reducing human relations. Pozzo and Lucky are a pseudocouple created in the same way but with an explicit power relation. *Godot* consists of the combination of these two minimal human relations as if the two pseudocouples summed up all human relations. What is notable is the impulse to reduce the complexity of human relations to the minimal units. It is part of the tendency to mathematically regulate human action, most salient in *Quad* or *What Where*.

The same impulse seems to underlie Beckett's fondness for the Russian pair of clowns Bim and Bom.[27] They were authorized clowns under Stalin's regime and allowed to criticize the government openly. They first occur in the short story 'Yellow', in *More Pricks than Kicks*, as Belacqua's comical allies, along with Grock (the Swiss clown who also appears in *Dream of Fair to Middling Women*) and Democritus. They reappear in *Murphy* as the names of the twin nurses of the mental asylum where Murphy works. Much later they will recur as Pim and Bom in *How It Is* and in the series of Bom, Bim, Bem and Bam in *What Where*. But more significantly, the first published edition of *En attendant Godot* mentioned them. It contained the following dialogue:

Estragon	On se croirait au spectacle.
Vladimir	Au music-hall.
Estragon	Avec Bim.
Vladimir	Et Bom.
Estragon	Les comiques staliniens.[28]

This dialogue occurs in the middle of Act I when, after some exchanges with Pozzo and Lucky, they ironically compare their own situation to a music-hall or a circus.[29] Therefore Bim and Bom here appear to refer to Pozzo and Lucky; Pozzo and Lucky are giving a poor show like that of Bim and Bom to Vladimir and Estragon. Alternatively, Vladimir and Estragon may be likening themselves to Bim and Bom; their situation is like a show and in it they are playing fools like Bim and Bom. Their introduction into *Godot* in this manner suggests that Bim and Bom are one of the origins of Beckett's pseudocouples.[30] Moreover, their names are reductive and repetitive – the defining characteristics of the pseudocouple. In Beckett's fascination with Bim and Bom, we can see how one of the traditional pairs of clowns and comedians was refined and abstracted into the more mechanical pseudocouple.

But how can we consider *Godot* and its pseudocouples in relation to the machine-age comedy dominated by film? It is well known that from early on Beckett was interested in film comedies; those of Chaplin, Keaton, Laurel and Hardy and the Marx Brothers in particular. While *Film*, which famously featured Buster Keaton, is his only work in that medium, Beckett's stage dramas including *Godot* bear the marks of his interest in film comedies. Ruby Cohn enumerates the Chaplinesque gestures of the two tramps in *Godot* such as 'their difficulties with the trousers', 'their imitation of the tree', 'their hat-juggling routine' and their vulnerability and status as victims of society.[31] Another instance is Lucky's 'thinking', which sounds like an uncontrollable broken phonograph that can be switched off only by removing Lucky's hat. In the Marx Brothers' *Duck Soup* there is a similar comical scene in which a phonograph suddenly starts playing at a high volume and agitates Harpo, who, having sneaked into a mansion as a spy, needs to keep absolutely quiet. Lucky's 'thinking' is a very clear example of the Bergsonian mechanization of the human generating laughter. It may be possible, however, to consider the relation between *Godot* and film at a more general level.

At the beginning of *Mercier and Camier*, the two old travelling companions fail to meet at the appointed place several times, before finally encountering each other. Every time one arrives, the other has gone for a stroll to pass the time while waiting. This is a slowed-down version of a routine seen in slapstick comedies and its comic effect no doubt arises from the mechanical repetition of failed attempts. Beckett later employed a more authentically paced routine in *Film*, where Buster Keaton has to go out of and come back to the room again and again to put out a dog and a cat by turns. While he puts one out, the other always comes back in. At the beginning of the script of *Film*, Beckett states, 'Climate of film comic and unreal. O should invite laughter throughout by his way of moving' (*CDW* 323). *Film* as a whole is not particularly funny but Buster Keaton reveals his comic skill in the scene where he has to deal with two animals by turns repetitively. According to Michael North, this scene is paying homage to the tradition in which such a repetitive routine was linked to the discontinuous nature of the medium of film itself:

> [. . .] Keaton's back-and-forth with the animals is just as much a figure for cinema as the staring eye that begins and ends this work.

If the eye suggests the unwinking lens, repetitive byplay suggests the string of nearly identical still images that combine somehow to make the illusion of movement. Jerky, repetitive movements and circular routines, especially in the silent era, have traditionally been taken to suggest the discontinuous, flickery nature of film. In Beckett's film, the repetitive routine is virtually an homage to this tradition.[32]

The repetitive routine is a quintessential product of the machine-age comedy. Significantly, North immediately adds, 'But it is also, of course, a kind of homage to Beckett's own work, in which such routines play an important role'.[33] It could be said, then, that those routine repetitions in actions and speeches in *Godot* are at a general level also affected by film, or 'inevitably influenced and shaped by this most powerful form of mechanical reproduction'.[34] The pseudocouple itself adds to its significance in this context because by doubling the repetition, the two partners foreground the repetitive routines. The pseudocouple has assumed in the age of mechanical reproduction a new role as an appropriate vehicle for the filmic repetition.

After *Godot*, however, this quality unique to the machine-age comedy seems to weaken in Beckett's pseudocouples. Paradoxically, in *How It Is*, Beckett's own Bim and Bom do not operate like a pseudocouple. In the third part of *How It Is*, the narrator thinks that he forms a couple with Bom and Pim alternately, he tormenting Pim and in turn tormented by Bom. But this basic formulation is soon unsettled by the narrator's idea that there may be an infinite number of such couples or that there may be nobody else but himself. Here the descriptions of the pseudocouples are too much mired in chaos and uncertainty to generate the Bergsonian laughter. Similarly, although *What Where* regains brisk mechanical repetition by neatly patterning the relation between Bom, Bim, Bem and Bam, its vision is far darker, making each the torturer of his predecessor. Only Bam remains as if he were the very last human being.

We often laugh heartily while seeing *Waiting for Godot*, especially because it directly incorporates many traditional comic routines. But, as a contrast, Beckett's second major play *Endgame* subdues the vaudevillian element, while still featuring pseudocouples. Even when we have a potentially comical scene, laughter tends to die down in the face of the grim reality of Hamm and Clov's or Nagg and Nell's painful state of existence. Nell's following remark might be representative of this play's overall tone:

> Nothing is funnier than unhappiness, I grant you that. [...] Yes, yes, it's the most comical thing in the world. And we laugh, we laugh, with a will, in the beginning. But it's always the same thing. Yes, it's like the funny story we have heard too often, we still find it funny, but we don't laugh any more. (*CDW* 101)

This 'willed' laughter is strained, arising after the possibilities of genuine laughter are extinguished. After *Godot*, Beckett's pseudocouples seem to deviate from their original nexus of the mechanical and the comic still discernible in *Godot*. In other words, the Bergsonian laughter is reduced and hollowed out as in the case of Lewis, although the element of social satire is markedly weak in Beckett's mechanical reduction of the human.

Conclusion

In his 1999 book *Late Modernism: Politics, Fiction, and the Arts Between the World Wars*, Tyrus Miller argues that in late modernism, represented by Beckett, Wyndham Lewis and Djuna Barnes, the authorial subject is reduced to an 'anthropological minimum' which is barely preserved by 'self-reflexive laughter'.[35] The term 'anthropological minimum' is appropriate for the pseudocouple because this literary device precisely embodies a relentless reduction of human relations to their minimal components. Following Bergson, we might say that it has a comic effect because of the mechanization of human beings, and as we have seen, it became a useful device for the 'machine-age comedy' of the twentieth century. Lewis and Beckett adopted the pseudocouple independently because both were concerned with the new kind of conjuncture of the mechanical and the comic, particularly in relation to film. But in both Lewis and Beckett, the simple Bergsonian laughter tends to be undermined and then replaced by more constrained laughter. In Lewis's case, only stiff, hollow laughter is possible under his excessively satirical gaze at the intrinsically mechanical quality of human beings. And there seems to remain only a residue of laughter in Beckett's works with pseudocouples where the abyss of existential uncertainty opens up and engulfs those reduced figures like Bim and Bom. Despite this difference, the device of the pseudocouple was necessary for both in order to explore the realm of the minimized humanness lying beyond the Bergsonian laughter.

Notes

1 Samuel Beckett, *The Unnamable* (New York: Grove Press, 1958), 6. Subsequent references are made parenthetically in the text as *Unnamable*.
2 *The Grove Companion to Samuel Beckett: A Reader's Guide to His Works, Life, and Thought*, edited by C. J. Ackerley and S. E. Gontarski (New York: Grove Press, 2004), 463–5.
3 Shane Weller, *A Taste for the Negative: Beckett and Nihilism* (London: Legenda, 2005), 182.
4 For a different discussion of this topic, see Yoshiki Tajiri, 'Transforming the Pseudo-Couple: Beckett in Kenzaburo Oe's *Good-Bye, My Book!*' in *Beckett's Literary Legacies*, edited by Matthew Feldman and Mark Nixon (Newcastle-upon-Tyne: Cambridge Scholars Publishing, 2007), 78–94.

5 Wyndham Lewis, *The Childermass* (London: John Calder, 2000), 16. Subsequent references are made parenthetically in the text as *Childermass*.

6 Samuel Beckett, *The Complete Dramatic Works* (London: Faber and Faber, 1990), 11. Subsequent references to plays in this volume are made parenthetically in the text as *CDW*.

7 Dennis Brown, *Intertextual Dynamics within the Literary Group – Joyce, Lewis, Pound and Eliot: The Men of 1914* (Basingstoke: Macmillan, 1990), 118.

8 As in the following example: 'Satters day-dreams and stares and steins [...]. Pully has been most terribly helpful and kind there's no use excusing himself Pully has been most terribly helpful and kind – most terribly helpful and he's been kind. He's been most terribly kind and helpful, there are two things, he's been most kind he's been terribly helpful, he's kind he can't help being – he's terribly' (*Childermass* 50).

9 Beckett might have been invited to Prentice's lodgings where, according to Richard Aldington, there was 'a chaos of books, boxes of cigars, wines and pictures by Wyndham Lewis' (qtd in James Knowlson, *Damned to Fame: The Life of Samuel Beckett* (London: Bloomsbury, 1996), 115).

10 Samuel Beckett, *The Letters of Samuel Beckett. Volume 1: 1929–1940*, edited by Martha Dow Fehsenfeld and Lois More Overbeck (Cambridge: Cambridge University Press, 2009), 25, 32.

11 Quoted in Knowlson, *Damned to Fame*, 295.

12 Fredric Jameson, *Fables of Aggression: Wyndham Lewis, The Modernist as Fascist* (Berkeley: University of California Press, 1979), 58.

13 Ibid., 59.

14 Ibid.

15 Ibid.

16 Gustave Flaubert, *Bouvard and Pécuchet*, translated by A. J. Krailsheimer (Harmondsworth: Penguin, 1976), 21. Beckett liked the opening of this novel. See his letters to Barbara Bray dated 29 and 30 June 1965 (IE TCD MS 10948/1/338 and 339). I am grateful to Professor John Pilling and Professor Daniel Gunn for informing me of these letters.

17 In contrast, Faust and Mephistopheles and Don Quixote and Sancho Panza seem to have a solid enough individual character, *pace* Jameson.

18 Henri Bergson, 'Laughter' in *Comedy*, edited by Wylie Sypher (Baltimore: Johns Hopkins University Press, 1980), 119.
19 Michael North, *Machine-Age Comedy* (New York: Oxford University Press, 2009), 5.
20 Ibid., 18.
21 For details, see Anthony Paraskeva, 'Wyndham Lewis *VS* Charlie Chaplin' *Forum for Modern Language* 43.3 (2007), 224–6.
22 Ibid., 226.
23 Wyndham Lewis, *The Wild Body* (Harmondsworth: Penguin, 2004), 158.
24 Wyndham Lewis, *Men without Art*, edited by Seamus Cooney (Santa Rosa: Black Sparrow Press, 1987), 93.
25 Typical examples include *A Reading of Ovid (Tyros)* (1921) and *Mr Wyndham Lewis as a Tyro* (c 1920–1).
26 For a revealing argument that Lewis's conception of the self is dual and repetitive by nature, see North 125–6. This directly leads to the creation of the pseudocouple Pullman and Satters, though North does not discuss *The Childermass*.
27 For an interesting discussion of the possibility that Beckett might have read Wyndham Lewis's article on Bim and Bom, see Tyrus Miller, *Late Modernism: Politics, Fiction, and the Arts Between the World Wars* (Berkeley: University of California Press, 1999), 190–5.
28 Samuel Beckett, *En attendant Godot*, la première édition (Paris: Minuit, 1952), 56.
29 In the subsequent French editions and in the English editions, the reference to Bim and Bom is excised. In addition, Estragon's and Vladimir's speeches are exchanged and slight changes are introduced to the sequence in question. See *En attendant Godot* (1988) 47–8, *CDW* 34–5.
30 In one of the drafts of the later play *Fin de partie*, X mentions Bom as an old woman who demanded a drop of water, and F says it is Bim instead of Bom (Gontarski 39).
31 Ruby Cohn, *Samuel Beckett: The Comic Gamut* (New Brunswick: Rutgers University Press, 1962), 211.
32 North, 162.

33 Ibid.
34 Ibid.
35 Miller, *Late Modernism*, 63.

Works cited

Ackerley, C. J. and S. E. Gontarski (eds). *The Grove Companion to Samuel Beckett: A Reader's Guide to His Works, Life, and Thought* (New York: Grove Press, 2004).

Beckett, Samuel. *En attendant Godot*, la première édition (Paris: Minuit, 1952).

—. *The Unnamable* (New York: Grove Press, 1958).

—. *En attendant Godot* (Paris: Minuit, 1988).

—. *The Complete Dramatic Works* (London: Faber and Faber, 1990).

—. *The Letters of Samuel Beckett. Volume 1: 1929–1940*, edited by Martha Dow Fehsenfeld and Lois More Overbeck (Cambridge: Cambridge University Press, 2009).

Bergson, Henri. 'Laughter' in *Comedy*, edited by Wylie Sypher (Baltimore: Johns Hopkins University Press, 1980), 61–190.

Brown, Dennis. *Intertextual Dynamics within the Literary Group – Joyce, Lewis, Pound and Eliot: The Men of 1914* (Basingstoke: Macmillan, 1990).

Cohn, Ruby. *Samuel Beckett: The Comic Gamut* (New Brunswick: Rutgers University Press, 1962).

Flaubert, Gustave. *Bouvard and Pécuchet*, translated by A. J. Krailsheimer (Harmondsworth: Penguin, 1976).

Gontarski, S. E. *The Intent of Undoing in Samuel Beckett's Dramatic Texts* (Bloomington: Indiana University Press, 1985).

Jameson, Fredric. *Fables of Aggression: Wyndham Lewis, The Modernist as Fascist* (Berkeley: University of California Press, 1979).

Knowlson, James. *Damned to Fame: The Life of Samuel Beckett* (London: Bloomsbury, 1996).

Lewis, Wyndham. *Men without Art*, edited by Seamus Cooney (Santa Rosa: Black Sparrow Press, 1987).

—. *The Childermass* (London: John Calder, 2000).

—. *The Wild Body* (Harmondsworth: Penguin, 2004).

Miller, Tyrus. *Late Modernism: Politics, Fiction, and the Arts Between the World Wars* (Berkeley: University of California Press, 1999).

North, Michael. *Machine-Age Comedy* (New York: Oxford University Press, 2009).

Paraskeva, Anthony. 'Wyndham Lewis VS Charlie Chaplin', *Forum for Modern Language* 43.3 (2007), 223–34.

Tajiri, Yoshiki. 'Transforming the Pseudo-Couple: Beckett in Kenzaburo Oe's *Good-Bye, My Book!*' in *Beckett's Literary Legacies*, edited by Matthew Feldman and Mark Nixon (Newcastle-upon-Tyne: Cambridge Scholars Publishing, 2007), 78–94.

Tiessen, Paul. 'Wyndham Lewis's *The Childermass* (1928): The Slaughter of the Innocents in the Age of Cinema', in *Apocalyptic Visions Past and Present*, edited by JoAnn James and William J. Cloonan (Tallahassee: Florida State University Press, 1988), 25–35.

Weller, Shane. *A Taste for the Negative: Beckett and Nihilism* (London: Legenda, 2005).

Index

Abbott, H. Porter 147–8
Ackerley, C. J. 114
Addyman, David 81n. 11
Adorno, Theodor 2, 50, 54
Agamben, Giorgio 5
Albright, Daniel 159
Andrew (St) 51
Anouilh, Jean 150n. 13
Antonescu, Ion 47
Apollinaire, Guillaume 40
Aragon, Louis 159
Arikha, Avigdor 40
Arrabal, Fernando 47
Augustine (St) 43, 44

Babbitt, Irving 44
Babinski, Joseph 153, 154
Bach, Johann Sebastian 41–2
Badiou, Alain 4
Bair, Deirdre 41, 109
Baker, Phil 164–5, 166, 167
Bally, Charles 28
Barnes, Djuna 233
Barry, Elizabeth 19, 25, 29, 31
Barthes, Roland 10
Baudelaire, Charles 27, 43, 44
BBC (British Broadcasting Corporation) 134, 136, 137, 142, 143, 144–5, 150n. 13, 165, 180, 186, 203
  Third Programme 142, 143, 150n. 13
Beaumarchais, Pierre 28
Beauvoir, Simone de 23
Beckett, Edward 112, 119, 121–2
Beckett, Frank 9, 12, 110–19, 122, 124–5, 202
Beckett, May 41, 43, 110, 111, 112–13, 114, 116, 124

Beckett, Samuel, works of
  All That Fall 14, 118, 134, 145, 161, 200–2, 204–7, 210n. 22
  ... but the clouds ... 165
  'The Calmative' (*Four Novellas*) 13, 158, 168, 169
  The Capital of the Ruins 20, 23, 33
  Closed place / Endroit clos 93, 178, 196
  Collected Poems 9
  Come and Go 4, 195
  Company 14, 43, 193–4, 207
  'Dante...Bruno.Vico..Joyce' 53
  '*Dream* Notebook' 157, 158
  Dream of Fair to middling/Middling Women 12, 12, 58n. 26, 85, 186, 230
  'Echo's Bones' 9, 11
  Eh Joe / He Joe 125, 165, 179–80, 181, 182–3, 185–6, 195
  Eleutheria 11, 40, 162
  Embers 13, 118, 124, 133–5, 137, 144–8
  'The End' (*Four Novellas*) 13, 168, 169
  Endgame / Fin de partie 1, 2–3, 9, 10, 12, 14n. 1, 15n. 10, 39, 50, 51, 103, 111, 112, 114–22, 124, 125–6, 127n. 5, 127n. 10, 128n. 14, 169, 197, 218, 233, 236n. 30
  'The Expelled' (*Four Novellas*) 13, 95, 168, 169
  Film 13, 158, 179, 180, 181, 183, 185, 230–1
  'Film I' 179, 181–2, 184, 186
  'Film 2' 179, 182, 184
  'Film Vidéo-Cassette project' 177–8, 180, 184–6

Index

'First Love' (*Four Novellas*) 13, 168, 169
Fizzles 178
Footfalls 161, 166–7
'German Diaries' 9, 48, 183
Ghost Trio / Geistertrio 165, 166, 179, 180, 181, 183, 186
Happy Days 15n. 10, 161, 191, 197
How It Is 4, 50–3, 55, 56, 103, 230, 232
Ill Seen Ill Said 169
Krapp's Last Tape 13, 118, 170, 180, 182–3, 198
Lessness 42, 196, 201
The Letters of Samuel Beckett (2 vols) 8–10, 21, 23, 24, 28, 29, 41, 64, 65, 66, 75, 76, 77, 80, 100, 110–18, 123–6
The Lost Ones 14, 191–2, 195, 207
Malone Dies 4, 5, 44, 54, 56, 100, 101, 112, 169, 198, 215
Mercier and Camier / Mercier et Camier 19, 20, 25–33, 36n. 32, 49, 50, 75, 169, 215–16, 222, 223, 226, 228, 231
Molloy 4, 5, 10, 13, 50, 100–1, 112, 168–9, 215
More Pricks than Kicks 9, 39, 44, 221, 229
Murphy 12, 44, 89, 90–3, 95, 97–100, 102–3, 162, 215, 230
Nacht und Träume 187n. 3
Nohow On 15n. 8
Not I 161, 177–8, 206–7
'Ooftish' 45–6
'La peinture des van Velde ou le monde et le pantalon' 76, 80
'Philosophy Notes' 9, 65
Play 15n. 10, 137, 161, 169, 195, 196
Proust 81n. 7, 87, 92, 148, 221
Quad (Quad I and *Quad II)* 103, 166, 229
Rockaby 161, 166, 198
Rough for Theatre II 9
'Saint-Lô' 20
Still 141, 177
Texts for Nothing 4, 45, 112
Three Dialogues 64, 65, 77, 103
The Unnamable / L'Innomable 4, 5, 12, 25, 50, 89, 91, 96, 100–3, 110, 112, 169, 215, 223
Waiting for Godot / En attendant Godot 1, 4, 6–7, 12, 33, 63–5, 76–80, 100, 103, 112, 137, 148, 167, 169, 181, 216–20, 222, 224, 229–33, 236n. 29
Watt 27, 29, 41, 93–4, 169, 229
What Is the Word 169
What Where 229, 230, 232
'Yellow' 229–30
Beckett, William (Bill) 113, 114, 116, 124, 159
Benda, Julien 87
Bergson, Henri 14, 65, 67–71, 73–6, 80, 87, 88, 95, 97, 156–7, 224–8, 231–4
Berkeley, George (Bishop) 183–4
Bible 4, 5, 6–7, 39, 116–18, 120, 201–3
Bion, Wilfred 96, 160
Black, Kitty 41
Blake, William 46
Blin, Roger 144
Boccaccio, Giovanni 5
Boehme, Jacob 42
Boissier-Sauvages, Pierre-Augustin 29
Bonaventura (St) 89
Bonnefoy, Yves 66
Brasillach, Robert 21
Brecht, Bertolt 150n. 13
Breton, André 159
Breuer, Josef 154, 162
Brouillet, André 153
Brown, Dennis 219–21
Bryden, Mary 43
Buñuel, Luis 163
Burnet, John 88, 91, 92, 96

Cahiers d'art 66, 82n. 12
Calder, John 53–4, 128
Camus, Albert 150n. 13

Index

Cavell, Stanley 2
Celan, Paul 41
Céline, Louis-Ferdinand 47
Cézanne, Paul 75, 79, 80
Chamfort, Nicolas 28, 49, 53
Chaplin, Charlie 163, 164, 167, 225-31
Charcot, Jean-Martin 153-60, 164, 169
Chateaubriand, François-René de 27
Chaucer, Geoffrey 95
Christ 4-7, 45, 46, 52, 68, 93, 116
Christianity 23, 40, 45, 46, 48, 52, 55, 89, 206
Cioran, E. M. 39-44, 47-9, 51-6, 58n. 23
Clarke, Austin 45
Cocteau, Jean 150n. 13
Coe, Richard N. 63
Coffey, Brian 45
Cohn, Ruby 26, 128n. 13, 178, 192, 231
Columbus, Christopher 44
Combat 21
Connor, Steven 19, 20, 63
Cronin, Anthony 23, 31, 41, 133
Cunard, Nancy 221

Dali, Salvador 163
Dante 5-6, 7, 53, 216
Darley, Arthur 44
Dawkins, Richard 43
Democritus 50, 98, 230
Derrida, Jacques 216
Descartes, René 64, 70, 88, 89, 90, 92, 98, 99, 101, 103
Deschevaux-Dumesnil, Suzanne 41, 118, 123, 128n. 15
Devlin, Denis 54
Didi-Huberman, Georges 153
Dilks, Stephen 10, 16n. 19
Dionysius 86, 89
Donne, John 52
Don Quixote 222, 235n. 17
Douglas, Stan 177

Durcan, Paul 39
Duthuit, Georges 64-9, 71-7, 79-80, 81n. 7, 103

Eckhart (Meister) 89
École Normale Supérieure 21, 163
Editions de Minuit 25, 112
Eliot, T. S. 43-4, 56, 94, 157
Éluard, Paul 159
Empson, William 46, 52, 55
Epstein, Jean 164
Esslin, Martin 135, 145
Euclid 90, 91, 101

Faust 222, 235n. 17
Fauvism 65-79
Feldman, Matthew 160, 161
Fibonacci, Leonardo 94
Fifield, Peter 15n. 8, 128n. 14, 173n. 49
Fish, Stanley 148
Fisk, Robert 21
Flaubert, Gustave 222-5, 228, 235n. 16
Fónagy, Ivan 28, 36n. 39
Foucault, Michael 3, 10
Francis of Assisi (St) 49
Freud, Sigmund 100, 153, 154, 160, 162
Frost, Everett 144
Furlong, George 47-8

Gaulle, Charles de 21, 24, 30
Genet, Jean 32
George (St) 44
Geulincx, Arnold 90, 184
Giacometti, Alberto 40
Gibson, Andrew 20, 80, 200
Girvin, Eric 21
Gontarski, S. E. 66, 109-10, 114, 120-1, 127n. 10, 128n. 14
Gordon, Rae Beth 156, 162
Gunn, Dan 111

Halberstam, Barbara 33
Hamsun, Knut 47
Harvey, Lawrence 109

Havel, Václav 40, 47
Hayden, Henri 40
Hayman, Ronald 133
Henry, James 46
Hensher, Philip 9
Heraclitus 50, 184
Higgins, Aidan 125
Hustvedt, Asti 154

Inge, William Ralph 89
Ingold, Tim 74
Ionesco, Eugene 150n. 13

James, William 153–4
Jameson, Fredric 217, 221–3
Janet, Pierre 96, 154, 159, 172n. 43
Johnson, Samuel 49
Jones, Ernest 160, 161
Joyce, James 1, 39, 43, 46, 95, 219, 221
   Finnegans Wake 1
   'Grace' 39
   Ulysses 1, 92, 123
Julian of Norwich 44
Jung, Carl 12, 96, 100, 102, 206

Kafka, Franz 33
Kant, Immanuel 64, 72, 80, 86, 90
Keaton, Buster 163, 224, 230, 231
Kempis, Thomas à 88
Kennedy, Séan 19, 26, 30, 31–2, 205
Kenner, Hugh 46, 133, 144
Kiberd, Declan 54–5
Kitson, Simon 32
Klinger, Max 184
Kluth, Karl 183
Knowlson, James 19, 20, 41, 65, 115, 122, 123, 126, 128n. 15, 160, 163
Kubrick, Stanley 52

Labé, Louise 186
Labrusse, Rémi 65, 66, 67
Lang, Fritz 163, 166
Lautréamont, Comte de (Isidore-Lucien Ducasse) 43
Lawley, Paul 144

Lawrence, D. H. (David Herbert) 43
Leibniz, Gottfried 12, 64, 87, 90, 97–103
Lemass, Noel 26
Leonardo da Vinci 68
Leo XIII (Pope) 39–40
Les Temps modernes 21
Lewis, Wyndham 216–22, 224–7, 229, 233–4
Libera, Antoni 40
Ligeti, György 52
Lindon, Jérôme 112, 115, 122
Lord Chamberlain, The 39
Lubitsch, Ernst 156

McCarthy, Ethna 124
MacDiarmid, Hugh 52
McGowran, Jack 143, 165, 179, 180
McGreevy / MacGreevy, Thomas 24, 45, 47, 55, 64, 113, 114, 184, 221
McQuaid, John Charles 55
McQueeny, Terence 98
McWhinnie, Donald 133, 143–4, 203
Magee, Patrick 180, 198
Manning Howe, Mary 158
Maritain, Jacques 45
Marx, Karl 3, 54, 208
Marx Brothers, The 230–1
Masson, André 64, 75, 81n. 7
Matisse, Henri 64, 66, 67–9, 73–7, 79, 80
Maupassant, Guy de 156–7, 158
Méliès, Georges 156
Merleau-Ponty, Maurice 64, 65, 71, 72, 76
Micale, Mark S. 153
Michelangelo 86
Mihalovici, Marcel 42
Miller, Tyrus 233, 236n. 27
Milton, John 46
Mitchell, Pamela 9, 110–11, 114–17, 123–5
Molière (Jean-Baptiste Poquelin) 28
Morin, Michel 26
Motherwell, Robert 66
Murnau, F. W. 163

Index

Nauman, Bruce 177, 178, 179
Newton, Isaac 50, 99, 100, 101
Nietzsche, Friedrich 48, 49
Nordau, Max 157-8, 170
North, Michael 224, 231-2, 236n. 26
Nouvelle Revue Française 21

O'Brien, Flann (Myles na gCopaleen) 44
O'Faolain, Sean 55
O'Toole, Adam Duff 46-7

Paik, Nam June 179
Panofsky, Erwin 181
Paraskeva, Anthony 226-7
Patrick (St) 44
Pattie, David 63
Paul (St) 44, 89
Paxton, Robert 20
Pelorson, George, 85
Perloff, Marjorie 133
Pétain, Philippe 24, 32
Petreu, Martha 47
Phillips, Siân 165
Pilling, John 9, 87, 144-5
Pinget, Robert 126
Pius X (Pope) 40
Plato 87
Poincaré, Henri 100
Pound, Ezra 47
Prentice, Charles 9, 221, 235n. 9
Prichard, Matthew Stewart 64, 67, 68, 69
Proust, Marcel 87, 91, 95, 148
Pseudocouple(s) 162, 215-19, 221-30, 232-4, 236n. 26
Pythagoras 88, 92, 93

Queneau, Raymond 28

Racine, Jean 25, 35n. 28
Reavey, George 177-8
Rimbaud, Arthur 27, 36n. 36, 184
Robbe-Grillet, Alain 63, 79

Rochefoucauld, François de la 28
Rosset, Barney 112, 116, 118
Rudmose-Brown, Thomas 186
Rushdie, Salman 55
Ruskin, John 86

St Ruth, Charles Chalmant 33
Salpêtrière Hospital 153, 154, 155, 163, 167
Samuel Beckett Digital Manuscript Project 9, 15n. 7
Sarsfield, Patrick 26, 33
Sartre, Jean-Paul 21, 27
Saussure, Ferdinand de 28, 95
Schneider, Alan 178, 186, 191, 197-9, 203, 206
Schopenhauer, Arthur 12, 64, 80, 87-9, 91, 94, 96, 97, 98, 100, 102
Schuwer, Camille 67, 69
Shainberg, Lawrence 128n. 15
Shakespeare, William 4, 123, 125, 129n. 18, 224
Sheehan, Paul 165-6
Sheridan, Richard Brinsley 29
Shklovski, Viktor 146-7
Sinclair, Peggy 112, 124, 125
Space 2, 63-81, 87, 89, 92, 93, 94, 95, 97, 101-2, 103, 136, 141, 181, 183-4, 196
Sperber, Dan 145-7
Stein, Gertrude, 221, 235n. 8
Sterne, Lawrence 50
Stevens, Brett 103
Stewart, Paul 128n. 16
Stuart, Francis 48
Surrealism 13, 159, 163, 170
Swift, Jonathan 29

Taylor, Jeremy 48-9
Tennyson, Alfred 49
Thompson, Geoffrey 160
Tiessen, Paul 227
Time 136, 182
Toland, John 46

Tonning, Erik 188n. 15
Tourette, Georges Gilles de la 153, 155, 173n. 51
transition / Transition 65, 221
Trinity College Dublin 87, 113, 157, 163, 184

Valera, Éamon de 22–3, 24, 31
Van Velde, Bram and Geer 40
Vermeer, Johannes 184
Virgil 5, 6, 216
Voltaire 99

Wagner, Richard 85, 102
Walshe, Joseph 22
Weller, Shane 41, 162, 215

Whitehead, Kate 150n. 13
Wiene, Robert 156, 163, 166
Wilde, Oscar 224
Wills, Clair 21, 23, 31
Wilson, Deirdre 145–7
Windelband, Wilhelm 12, 99
Woodworth, Robert S. 160, 161, 171n. 25
Woolf, Virginia 95
Worth, Katharine 144, 145
Wright, Colin 33

Yeats, W. B. 54, 56, 125–6

Zarifopol-Johnston, Ilinca 48
Zilliacus, Clas 165